ALL ABOUT
SUCCESS
FOR THE
BLACK WOMAN

ALL ABOUT SUCCESS FOR THE BLACK WOMAN

by Naomi Sims

DOUBLEDAY & COMPANY, INC.
Garden City, New York
1982

Library of Congress Cataloging in Publication Data

Sims, Naomi, 1949–
   All about success for the Black woman.

   Includes index.
   1. Afro-American women. 2. Success. I. Title.
E185.86.S58   158'.1'0896073
ISBN 0-385-17041-6   AACR2
Library of Congress Catalog Card Number 82–45229

Contents

Acknowledgments

❦❦❦❦❦ For the material in this book I have leaned very heavily on firsthand accounts of the feelings, experiences, and aspirations of American Black women from all walks of life. Most are mentioned by name, and to them all I extend my warmest thanks. Without hesitation or restraint they answered probing questions and gave unstintingly of their valuable time.

Other information that I have used was supplied by a large number of professionals, Black and white, female and male, to whom I am indebted. In particular I would like to mention Dr. Jerre Levy, Dr. Harriet Lerner, Professor Warren Bennis, Dr. George Serban, and Dr. S. P. Hersh.

For providing me with valuable source material I owe a special debt of gratitude to a very fine journalist, Mr. Sey Chessler, editor in chief of *Redbook*. Most importantly I would like to thank Susan Taylor, editor in chief of *Essence*. Apart from giving me the benefit of her personal insights, she continues to be, as a dedicated professional Black woman who has never compromised her personal values, an inspiration to us all.

Special thanks indeed must go to my husband, Michael Findlay for his constant support and encouragement, and to the dear friends who provided me with a peaceful place to write, Shirine and Peter Gill.

N.S.

Introduction

✤✤✤✤✤ True or false: Black women in America have made tremendous social and economic progress in the past two decades and are finding meaningful and profitable positions in business, medicine, law, industry, education, entertainment, and the fine arts?

Based on the evidence in the mass media, this statement is *true*. Based on the statistics of the U. S. Department of Labor, this statement is *false*. What does your personal life experience tell you?

Every night, through the medium of television, America tells itself that Black women have risen to the top. Black women are presented reading the news. In our society this means they are "in charge of" the news, and by extension the newscaster simulates leadership. Talk shows feature Black women discussing prominent women's issues, and Black women are seen earning large sums of money as dancers and singers. In situation comedies Black women are happy-go-lucky college students, office workers, and all-around breadwinners. In serious dramas Black women are doctors, lawyers, administrators, and well-to-do suburban housewives. In commercial messages we are depicted as being well able to afford fine consumer products or all the good things in life.

The facts do not support this rosy panorama of progress. One out of every two adult Black females is attempting *single-handedly* to support her family on an income well *below* the national average.

Television is the principal distorting mirror in which we examine our lives. What we see is often presented so forcefully that we are constrained to absorb it as the truth. Yet in most cases the images and situations on the screen have little or no relevance to our lives. Even on so-called serious shows, on publicly funded programming, Black women are frequently presented as new achievers, *on the way up*. Some of us *are,* a minority within a minority, but the complete picture is not encouraging.

The gap between myth and reality is very great and very dangerous. White America watches television and, unless we are rioting, sees a preponderance of good-looking, intelligent, upwardly mobile Black women. This provokes complacency in the rich and aggressive jealousy in the poor. We ourselves are led to believe that with an M.B.A., hard work, luck, and affirmative action there is no reason why we should not reach the very pinnacle of the power structure in this country. Of this image, one who has reached such a pinnacle says this:

> *"This seductive portrait would have us navy-suited dynamos bearing briefcases, cutting our executive-suite teeth with high-rolling, hip-switching savvy. We are somehow Lola Falana, Patricia Roberts Harris, and Mary McLeod Bethune rolled into one upscale, uppity, and ubiquitous Black business-woman—Ms. Biz. We buy the myth. We buy a lie. Most Black women sweat out a living. I know I do. The few who reach a higher rung in life than our mothers did do so against overwhelming odds. In general we are outnumbered in high-paying jobs by white women, Black men, and white men—not in that order! If we feel guilty that we are taking jobs from our men, it is because white society wants us to believe that. We buy the myth because reality is cold and unrelenting. Truth is we don't need myths. We need numbers, we need push, and we need help from one another."*

Stirring words indeed from Susan Taylor, editor in chief of *Essence,* a woman who refuses to compromise, a woman who tells it like it is, a woman who uses her power as a leading member of the Black media elite to open our eyes, not to distort them with the blatantly sanitized images of working Black women that flicker from our small screens.

There are well-intentioned Black groups that lobby for increased media exposure of dignified Black personalities so that Black youths can have appropriate role models. I am all for that so long as there is the concomitant exposure of the fact that when it comes to actually achieving the dignity we seek (that of success, for instance), we as Blacks, and Black women in particular, have a much tougher time than anyone else; and that there are other potential paths to success than athletics and music.

The perpetual propaganda that is television creates depression and disappointment in all of us who fail to live up to that artificial mirror image. We must never forget that it is the image which is sorely distorted, not ourselves.

As a group, Black women are the most exploited in society, on every level. The paucity of truth about us in all the media is a symptom, not a cause of our plight. A major problem is that many of us are under the impression that all other Black women are out there, ahead of the game, and that here I am—stuck, alone. If you want to begin to break the bonds that have held all of us back, you must acknowledge that you are *not* alone. Why do you think our median income is still below the poverty level, even though we have been working harder and longer than white women? We are all in the same boat. Why do you think our unemployment rate is *twice* the national average? Vast numbers of us are kept out of well-paying jobs. Don't kid yourself that every other Black woman is grabbing a slice of the pie. You are not the only one angry, powerless, and frustrated. One of the themes that I will echo again and again in this book is *solidarity,* the strength of numbers. On the face of it, we have a great potential for success—but what is stopping us? Together we can knock down the hurdles, push past the barricades, and hurl open the gates. Some of our obstacles are part of the fabric of the society in which we live, a society which we will have to change; some of our obstacles are self-imposed, and these are the first and the easiest for us to eradicate. I will demonstrate how. It is not done by magic. Mostly it means hard work (which we have never been afraid of) and the ability to focus that hard-work energy as if it were real solid fuel for our ambitions.

I have a young friend. She is seventeen, bright, attractive, and hard-working. She has an amazing talent for getting along with young children, almost a special gift. Her school grades are good, and there is every indication that she could have a very successful career in pediatrics, a field that is not only growing but virtually recession-proof. When I asked her what she wanted to be, she said that her ambition in life was to become an actress. Acting is a fine profession. It requires training and a great deal of personal sacrifice, and the earlier one starts the better. But my young friend only *thinks* about becoming an actress. She does not audition, take lessons, train, or try out for amateur productions. If she really wants to be an actress, she will soon find herself competing with thousands of young women who at age seventeen spend half their waking hours actively preparing for their career.

This is a prime example of the triumph of myth over reality. She has been raised on a steady diet of television and fan magazines. Her home life is so broken and impoverished that she insists she will never marry and have children. For her, dreaming of becoming a famous actress (or a "star") is the only way that she can devise to overcome the poor hand she was dealt as a child. To that extent I would say that her ambition is really and truly blind. As we will see in the chapters ahead, ambition alone, no matter how strong, is impotent unless it can be applied *realistically.*

Black women have a perfect right to be leery of any advice that translates as "be realistic." My aim with this book is to get you to the top of your personal mountain—not simply to help you figure out how to pay this month's bills—so it is important that we both understand what I mean by being realistic. I do not mean "settle for less"; I do not mean "play it safe"; I do not mean "play by white America's rules."

When I was fifteen, I knew that I wanted a career in the beauty business. I wanted to be a fashion model, and I wanted to make cosmetics for Black women. I knew what I wanted even though I did not know *how* to achieve it. My teachers told me that I was not *being realistic* because:

a) I was Black.

b) I had no money.

According to my teachers, fashion models were white (that has never been strictly true, although until I emerged few Black models achieved great success), and in order to go into business one had to be born with money (America would still be an agricultural paradise if that were true). What did my teachers want me to become? A teacher, no less. Why? Because:

a) I had good grades.

b) I was polite.

Masquerading as *being realistic,* the advice given me served to perpetuate role distinctions and reactionary stereotypes. "Nice" young Black women become underpaid schoolteachers, not cosmetic tycoons. As a schoolteacher I may not have been particularly successful because by temperament I tend to be impatient and inflexible. I could certainly have worked hard, earned my diplomas, and done the job—but both I and my pupils would have been unfulfilled, and you would have had fewer beauty products and books!

My teachers erred by confusing popular notions of the world with how it actually is (reality). We believe hundreds of things about ourselves and others that have no factual foundations. Some of these things are harmless—for instance, that spinach contains more iron than other green vegetables (it does not). That myth may give spinach growers an unfair edge over the competition, but it is hardly a destructive myth. On the other hand, the proposition:

"In order to be President of the United States, you must be a white male"

is believed by almost everyone in this country. We all know that it is not *strictly* true and that legally any one of us may be elected to the White House, but come on, let's *be realistic,* it is not going to happen for a long time, is it?

Wrong! There is nothing inherent in the duties of a President that automatically disqualifies a Black female. The office of President requires a person with the mental abilities and political know-how of a Patricia Roberts Harris or a Gloria Toote, both of whom have achieved leadership positions on a par with those previously held by successful presidential aspirants.

The fact that previous Presidents have been selected from among one narrow section of the population increases the probability that future ones may also come from that section, but it is totally *unrealistic* to suppose that such will always be the case. After all, if countries that are as male-chauvinistic as Great Britain, India, and Israel can elect female heads of state, then we stand a very good chance of seeing a Black woman elected President soon.

Had my teachers informed me that I should not try to become a fashion model because:

"Fashion models must be under five feet in height"

or that I could not make beauty products for Black women because:

"Black women do not allow themselves to wear beauty products," and if these statements were found to be empirically correct, then my teachers would have been what I consider realistic.

Most occupations have no physical requirements; even fashion models do not usually have to be particularly tall anymore. If you stand five-ten and weigh two hundred pounds, I would say your ambition to become a jockey could be doomed to failure—but not because you were a woman and not because you were Black. The point I am trying to make is:

There is nothing you cannot do!

Consider my ambition to make beauty products for Black women. It was very realistic because the need existed. The fact that I was a Black woman myself more than compensated for my lack of money and business experience. Both are acquirable, just like any skill. I also knew, at the age of fifteen, that most Black women were forced to buy cosmetics designed by companies that were owned and operated by white men and that what they knew (*realistically*) about our needs and our skin could be printed on the head of a pin.

On the other hand, consider part of the saga of one of America's legendary heroes: Mr. Henry Ford, Jr. He had all the money he needed. He had manufacturing and marketing and design skill galore. He had the American public eating automobiles out of his hand. Yet he created a product so unwanted that the name of it has become synonymous with ludicrous failure: the Edsel. Mr. Ford, in that venture, was very *unrealistic*.

If you want to be a success, you must be able to superimpose two pictures, one on top of the other, and bring both into sharp, clear focus. The first is a picture of ourself, an objective rendering of what we have the skills to do. The second picture, the one that must fit over the first, is a picture of the state to which we aspire. The more concise the second picture, the easier it is to make the superimposition accurately. Thus, if you simply aspire to be "rich and famous," it is virtually impossible to merge all the meanings of those words into one picture. If, on the other hand, you say:

"I want to own my own hair salon" or
"I want to be head of General Motors"

then you can begin to pinpoint what is going to be required of you *realistically* and subtract it from what you already have. The parts of the picture that are missing tell you what needs to be done, what you need to acquire: marketing skills, capital, an M.B.A. degree. Whatever it is that you need must be thrown into high relief.

One of the hardest things to figure out, strangely enough, is what success means to the individual. The younger you are, the easier it is to define. Most teenagers aspire to occupations that would seem to gratify the need for recognition and luxury. Such occupations (particularly in the fields of entertainment and sport) are the most competitive and subject the individual to much exposure in hostile situations (known as paying one's "dues"), and they are occupations that in the end often deprive the individual of privacy, peace of mind, and the opportunity to enjoy the benefits of family life *whether or not* the career is ultimately a success. For this reason it is important to know all about your goal, not just the silver lining, and to assess the minuses as well as daydream about the pluses.

My overwhelming reason for writing this book is that in the last ten years, as I traveled across the country speaking and making personal appearances, I met hundreds of Black women in a very great variety of jobs, from unskilled labor to the major professions of medicine and law. The majority of them were intelligent and hard working, yet in one way or another they all told me that they were being exploited

—overworked, underpaid, and not appreciated. No amount of television spectaculars or Broadway shows is going to change that; it is up to *us*.

We must ignore what is preached for and about us by the white media and the white government and the white business system and the white colleges and the white liberals. Each of us has to retrieve our personal destiny from the demoralizing grip of society and direct it *up*. We must:

1. Know what we want.
2. Find out what it takes to get it.
3. Get what it takes.
4. Take what we want!

Not for nothing have we spent over two centuries in this country working harder, from sunrise to beyond sunset, than any men, Black or white, and certainly much harder than any white women. Work is not a stranger to us. In the last ten years we have been pouring out of universities with skills that should put us way out ahead in the job market. But we are still in chains! We are still unable to focus our energies and drive to the top. We are still allowing white America to impose on us a psychology that insists we be satisfied with any occupation that pays one cent above the minimum wage and for which we can dress decently.

I do not care if you are in college, have a job, or are out of a job, or are simply not rising fast enough—I know that you agree with me about one thing at least: you *want more!* Not just a better salary, but more respect from your colleagues, more chances for promotion, more opportunities to prove what you can accomplish. I say that you *deserve more*. Follow the principles in this book, and you *will get more*.

I am called a success, but I feel that my work has only just begun. I have worked extremely hard toward achieving a very personal sense of success, not simply the limited affluence that a number of us are permitted to enjoy. I have a long way to go. What I have achieved so far did not happen overnight, and it was not because of that lucky Big Break so favored by novelists. It took skills I had, skills I learned, and skills that I pulled out of the thin air. It took hard work, heartache, years of risk, and sacrifice. It took gambling with "I can" against all who said, over and over again, "You can't possibly." It took planning, strategy, study, grooming, and the very forceful personality we *all* share. It took all of the things I have set down in this book. For you.

N.S.
South Kortright, New York

1

What Is Success?

"Success, to me, is accomplishing what you set out to achieve. It means setting goals and heading for those goals with all deliberate speed. It's feeling self-satisfied about doing a job well, like when you make a table and the parts fit."

Mary Campbell
Executive Director, Studio Museum in Harlem

One woman's success is another woman's poison. Or failure. Our age, upbringing, and life experience condition each of us to consider success in a slightly different light. To an orphan, success may mean raising a brood of happy children. To the youngest of six children, success may mean moving a thousand miles from home to a new job and an independent life.

There are two types of success possible for every Black woman, and the distinction is vital. First there is *public success*. I am not talking about "fame," but about your success as perceived by others—your immediate family, friends, or total strangers. This type of success requires tangible manifestations: awards, an increase in material goods, impressive job titles, the ability to tell others what to do. Judging by the media, this is the type of success most valued by our society. Such a bias dates from the times of our (white male) Founding Fathers, whose religious beliefs, as embodied in the Protestant Work Ethic, decreed that one's standing in the eyes of God was reflected in one's material condition on earth. Thus a person who was able to accumulate wealth was by definition favored by God and "saved," whereas the poor were "damned." It is a neat but specious rationalization for, among other things, slavery.

White feminists often preach that the female potential for public success has always been limited by a tradition that relegated the role of the American woman to that of finding a worthwhile husband and managing his household. Our tradition has not been quite so cut and dried, to say the least. For generations of Black women, success was spelled S-U-R-V-I-V-A-L! Often there were many children, no husband, a backbreaking twelve-hour work day, six days a week, and a social life that consisted of Sunday church.

With that in mind, it is fascinating to review one version of how we measure our own public success in *The Ebony Success Library, Volume II: Famous Blacks Give Secrets of Success* (Edited by Charles Sanders and *Ebony* staff, Chicago: Johnson Publishing Company, 1973). Of seventy-two profiles, only fifteen are of women. Of those, more than half (eight) are featured on account of their direct involvement with the federal government—the same federal government, of course, that perpetuates itself by virtue of many votes from, among others, Black women. These Black women include three congresswomen, a judge, an ambassador, and a state administrator. The seven remaining "successful" Black women are in occupations that involve a great degree of public exposure and in which the quality of the success is usually defined by the quantity of public acceptance—i.e., fame, as opposed to merit, a harder commodity to measure. These include two singers (one popular, one operatic), an actress, a stand-up comic, a painter, a poet, and a fashion model (yes, yours truly).

The Black males featured in the same volume are drawn from a much wider spectrum of occupations. Along with the mandatory politicians, entertainers, and sports heroes, we and our children learn about Black male journalists, historians, structural engineers, a college president, labor union officials, a corporate executive, a rear admiral, a stock exchange director, a cosmetics manufacturer, a publisher, a research chemist, a penologist, a psychiatrist, several clergymen, a mortgage banker, and a host of other high achievers who merit the stirring corporate titles of president, vice president or, succinctly, businessman. There are no male poets or fashion models, although Black men have distinguished themselves in both fields, and there is not one Black female included who is a success in banking, labor, education, medicine, or to take in one fell swoop that leviathan of employers: private business. That is how we see ourselves, and it is *not accurate*. Without Black women there would be no education, banking, labor, medicine, or private industry in this country—our work underpins the way those sectors operate, from the bottom to the top. We keep things running, especially in the virtually invisible middle-management positions. We are there in *fact*, but not there as defined by public success.

There are few opportunities for us to be perceived as successful outside a tiny group of activities that accounts for less than half of one per cent of all our jobs! This means that even when we achieve the positions for which our men are applauded, we are ignored. This does not mean that we should cease to strive for public success, but we must recognize the limitations of how everyone else views our potential for success. Think of your husband's idea of how you could be really successful: make a lot of money but do not distinguish yourself at work; find the time to cook, clean, and look after the children, *and* still have the energy to be amorous! Let us define *private success*.

Where do *you* want to go? How far and how fast? Never be afraid to admit that you want to go a short distance slowly if that is your temperament, any more than someone else should be afraid to admit that he or she wants the earth and the moon and the stars, preferably before lunchtime tomorrow! If you are over eighteen, you probably realize (and if you do not, it is about time you did) that you cannot have *everything*. Most successful people I know have a dash of cynicism, a gritty understanding with Fate that gives to the Devil his (or her) due.

This means that success is expensive. Decide what you want to achieve in very *specific* terms; that is the overriding issue. If success to *you* means job security, then you had better not play office politics because instead of a promotion you might wind up with a pink slip. If success to *you* means nothing less than owning your own business, then be prepared to sacrifice vacation time, family, and friends. Now, if you are saying to yourself:

"No, she is wrong, I know this woman (at least I know someone who knows her) who really does have it all—a great job, a high salary, a fine family; bakes her own bread, and still has time for yoga lessons—why can't I be like her?"

If you are thinking that (and still believe in Santa Claus), I still insist you are dead wrong. That woman has some inherent problems that are simply not in evidence, and time will bring them out. My point is: success is a state of being, not a single incident. Being elected to public office is not success; it is a symptom of success. Success consists of staying in office and performing well in office. Success is a condition, not an event. The kind of success that you yearn for must be compatible with all the other events in your life.

My favorite definition of success is: to accomplish what you set out to achieve. Easy to say. Also easy to do if you set your sights at ground level. This is a game too many of us play:

"I know I'm overqualified for this job, but I need time for my child, and my husband doesn't really want me to work."

So you take an easy job that is beneath you. For a while the extra money justifies the tedium or the indignities; then it pales, and you realize just how much *more* you could be doing, given the chance. Soon you are blaming your boss, your husband, your child, and your dog for holding you back. In fact, you should have set your goals much higher, but after time out to marry and have a child, you were afraid that you would *fail*.

Failure. Let's not talk about it. Let's move quickly ahead and compare dictionary definitions of success. But wait a minute. Success does not exist without failure as its corollary. You cannot succeed unless you are prepared to fail. Not only do you have to know what your goals are, you must know what the downside holds. If you fear failure, just stay where you are, unemployed or in a rut. It is just as well. If nobody were afraid of failure, everyone would be a boss—and then who would there be left to do the work?

Seriously, examine the consequences of your goals in the light of what it will cost if you fail. The more conventional your goal, the less expensive the failure. If you enter the Civil Service determined to become a superintendent of schools and you have the qualifications and are prepared to work hard, what is the worst that can happen if you fail? You end up as an assistant superintendent of schools. Maybe you can live with that, maybe not. But if your goal is to star in a Broadway musical, and you train and audition every day for five years, living on sardines and love, what is the worst thing that can happen if you fail? You stay in the chorus line until you are old enough to be a theater usher!

I have always felt that one great advantage of being both Black and a woman was that I started off with nothing to lose. As we grow up, we acquire—and rightly so—responsibility, caution, and an unwillingness to give up what has been earned. Roberta Long decided when she was eighteen that she wanted to be a nurse, and after three years training and two years in the intensive care unit of a major Cincinnati hospital, she became restless with her career. This is what she told me:

> *"I can't decide what to do. I don't mind this job, but my new boyfriend is a computer programmer, and if I retrain, he says I can earn much more working for his company."*

I tried to find out what it really was that Roberta wanted. Did she want to get away from day after day with the sick and dying, or did she want to marry her boyfriend, or did she want a meaningful career in the computer industry? A little bit of each, as it turned out. I made her assess the situation on paper and write out what she would lose and what she would gain by:

a) Making the move.

b) Remaining a nurse.

It turned out that her nursing credentials would support her later if the computer job did not work out and that the added skills she would have learned might even help her get a better nursing job if she decided to go back. Proximity to the boyfriend was just a bonus, not an objective. It turned out that Roberta preferred to be a relatively mediocre computer operator, privately successful, than a successful nurse, while miserable deep inside.

It is impossible to separate your life into compartments and pretend that one does not interfere with the others. To me, success means achieving a set goal but *also,* as we shall see in Chapter 9, being able to integrate it with all the facets of your life, such as recreation, marriage, and child rearing.

For the purpose of this book I generally avoid defining success in its broadest possible terms—"Life, Liberty, and the Pursuit of Happiness," noble words from long dead white Americans—but I concentrate on the more mundane and crasser aspects of success that are incorporated in the notion of *gainful employment.* That is my target and, I hope, yours. Black women who do not need to work are few and far between. Black women who are out of work or in soul-destroying jobs define success as a working day that is measurably more rewarding than their present circumstances. In most cases (not all, as we shall see), jobs that produce high financial rewards also produce the emotional satisfaction of tangible accomplishment. Such is a legal decision rendered, a product sold, a life saved, a corporate profit earned. These are things about which you can say, "Without me, that would not have happened." These types of jobs, creative and decision-making, usually require higher education and multiple skills.

The very basic problem for the Black woman today is that she is not used to defining herself solely in terms of job success. We are competing in the job market with men who are quite comfortable with a one-dimensional image, one that is determined solely by their occupation. If that were not bad enough, we increasingly find ourselves behind white women in the line that forms when an employer is compelled to hire minorities.

A man, Black or white, who is named vice president in charge of corporate sales, is considered by family, friends, enemies, and strangers, to be a success. He *feels* successful, and this helps him to *act* successful, whether or not he deserves the promotion. Let us be charitable and say that he did earn his new position. In time it makes demands on him; he has to travel more and sees less of his family. He makes new friends among the senior-management staff and abandons his old buddies. Eventually his marriage breaks up, and he starts to drink heavily. But he does a wonderful job in corporate sales, and he is still very much a vice president, participating in the company's profit-sharing plan. Is he a success? You bet he is! He is a success to himself, to his colleagues, and to his old (jealous) friends. He is only not a success, perhaps, in the eyes of his ex-wife and the children he rarely sees any more. However, he rationalizes that they will understand things better when they are older, and he is probably right. He will tell them how hard he worked to become a success.

Now consider what would happen to you in the same position. For fifteen years you have worked for General Profits, Inc. Starting as a secretary, you moved through accounting to district sales. You took night classes for a business degree and still managed to give your family a hot dinner every night. Your husband is a teacher and helped to raise your nine- and eleven-year-old children. In time you are assistant corporate sales manager and, one day, it is your turn. The company announces that you are its new vice president in charge of corporate sales. You deserve it. Then what happens? A number of people in the office make it very clear that the *only* reason you got the job was because you were a Black woman and the company needed to brush up its image, not to improve sales. All the men that report to you resent having you as a boss. It is a man's job, they think, and somewhere a child is going hungry because you have stolen its father's wages. You find it difficult to perform in this atmosphere, but there are compensating factors, and you throw yourself into your work, traveling a lot and spending less time with your family. Your children, of course, feel completely abandoned because Mom never spent a Sunday away from home in her life, and your husband, ostensibly proud of you, feels emasculated and starts sleeping on the living room sofa.

At that point do you go humbly to your boss and ask to be demoted in order to save your marriage ("we always knew she did not have what it takes"), or do you stick with your job, lose your marriage, and suffer being called a vicious, aggressive, masculine, disloyal schemer only interested in one thing: power.

Just remember, when a man wants to better himself, he is part of a noble tide of aspiration, a divine life force formed at the dawn of history when as a newt he slithered out of the primal ooze; he is following his God-given, U.S.-approved Destiny. When a Black woman wants to better herself, she is simply power-hungry.

No one ever handed us a job on a plate, and anything any of us have we *earned*, and it cost us in every possible currency, emotional and financial, and it cost us twice as much, at least, as it cost any white male.

We do not seek success purely for reasons of ideology or self-fulfillment (like so many of our white sisters, rebelling against housewifery) but because, let's face it, we have to support ourselves and our families; we have to S-U-R-V-I-V-E! For reasons that deserve (and have been given) volumes to themselves, our heritage is one that decrees the Black woman is both mom and chief breadwinner. We have no choice, you might say, but to succeed.

Black women, more than Black men or white women, have been holding down steady jobs (i.e., have been exploited) for generations. As field hands, domestic servants, or factory workers, our mothers and their mothers' mothers helped to build the wealth of this nation. When it comes to job competition, we should be able to run way ahead of the pack because:

a) We know how to work hard.

b) We are not afraid of a struggle.

But in this day and age we can do much more than merely survive. We can qualify for and attain major positions in every field. And I mean many of us, not just a judge here and an editor there. White America considers that a handful of prominently placed Black women in high positions provides it with some kind of immunity from equal consideration of the qualifications of *all* Black women:

> *You can't say we're not hiring you because you are Black. After all, our head of personnel is a Black woman.*

Considered on its merits, such a statement (and it is uttered, in one form or another, a thousand times a day) is utterly absurd and would be laughed at in any introductory logic class. It would be more *realistic* to suppose that if the head of personnel is a Black woman, that is all the more reason for hiring another Black woman.

You cannot picture yourself as a success until you have a firm idea of what success means to you personally. A well-known Black female psychologist conducted a series of group sessions in order to find out how Black women define success. The majority of her respondents emphasized two factors as being much more important than income:

a) Personal growth.

b) Respect from co-workers.

What they did not want was to be treated like a machine in a soul-destroying environment and no matter at how many dollars per hour.

This is a very far cry from the Big Car, Big House, Fur Coat image of success that still seems to dominate the male ambition. Why? Are we more in touch with our needs, more concerned about our inner selves, and not so easily seduced by myths of power and prosperity? Or is the emphasis on growth and respect a typical rationalization by second-class citizens who know they have not a snowball's chance in hell of ever coming close to *real* success, true-blue top-banana success? Which is it? A little bit of both, perhaps. Sometimes I am afraid that we ought not to lose our sense of values by careening toward the brass ring, and at other times I am inclined to feel that a certain kind of sanctimoniousness about avoiding Mammon is simply part of the age-old dogma that has kept us down on the farm.

A flesh-and-blood example of this complex issue: I have a close friend who is in a very high position with a major corporation. I asked her if she felt successful. Yes and no, she told me. She is frustrated because even though she is making the same correct, creative decisions as her white male peers she finds that her decisions are always questioned, and that when she asserts herself it is always categorized as aggression. She told me that she will not really feel successful until she is treated by her colleagues and superiors in a way that is equal to the manner in which they treat white males. There is a Black woman performing well, at the top of her profession, earning a great deal of money, and *still* fighting for equality. What does that mean? It means that we should strive for all the worldly goods and power we deserve (a lot) *and* continue to demand respect *and* be able to experience personal growth and fulfillment on an emotional level. After all, that is all men want.

One of the most hackneyed definitions of success is that often given in interviews by Black female entertainers:

"I'm just very lucky to be paid so much for doing what I enjoy doing the most!"

When that is said truthfully (how often I wonder), it is said by a woman who has been driven since early childhood by a compulsion to perform or create, a compulsion that rules her life and would demand that she do it day in and day out all her life even if she failed to win any acclaim, even if she were judged to be a failure. Even so, "luck" has nothing to do with it!

When it comes to defining success, you are home free when you *know,* beyond any shadow of a doubt, that there is something you must do to the exclusion of everything else. This is the difference between an occupation and a vocation. It would be all right to be a doctor, but what you *have to* do is a high-wire act in a circus. That is a vocation only if you have run away from home three times before the age of seventeen. A young girl who dreams of *being* Diana Ross does nothing about it except to buy records. She might become a successful disk jockey. But the young girl who is determined to be *like* Diana Ross joins a choir across town, spends her babysitting money on singing lessons, and tries to get Berry Gordy's home telephone number—that girl has a vocation. Yet even she has to realize that in order to turn her vocation into a successful career, she must go about it in *the right way.*

The two types of success, public and private, are not mutually exclusive. It is reasonable to expect both personal satisfaction and the outward manifestation of achievement. Men are less likely than women to talk about the emotional rewards of a particular occupation, but they are not driven by a desire for wealth alone and many are truly dedicated, "married" to their jobs. For them, the promise of success is an end in itself.

In recent years neurophysiologists, many of them women, have begun to probe a highly controversial area with startling results. What they may soon prove is that there is a definite biological difference between the structure of the female and the male brain. This translates into functional differences that are inherent, not learned. For instance, the male brain seems to be laterally differentiated and highly structured, whereas the female brain is more symmetrically organized and less tightly structured. Some researchers believe that this indicates women have the potential for certain skills to a greater degree of refinement than the male. And vice versa. But this does not break down into a scientific apologia for the traditional gender roles, although it might give a solid biophysiological explanation for such traits (often found risible by men) as female intuition.

What concerns us about this—and what is relevant to the question of success—is that women outdistance men in certain aptitudes that are important in the work world. Men tend to be good at perceiving concepts that are narrowly focused. They can plug away at a problem for days, usually using the same old methods. Women, on the other hand, are far more sensitive to context, much better able to see all *around* a problem. Women are also superior in verbal skills: reading, grammar, and general fluency.

The "narrow focus" of males may partially explain their potential for satisfaction with success as an end and not a means. I believe that as we drive ourselves to the top, we should pause every once in a while to question the context of our success. We must know what it is *for*.

A lot of people reach the top to find that the struggle to stay there is not half as exhilarating as the trip. Many find that the nature of the responsibilities of being at the top allows no time or peace of mind with which to enjoy the material benefits.

When you choose your goal, it is vital that you consider whether it is an end in itself or the means to a better life. The mere fact that you achieve a position widely regarded as important does not mean that you will be "better off."

In the chapters ahead, I will help you to create a Five Key Plan for success. Always remember that success is not a concept, it is a *fact*. For you that fact has to be outlined as clearly as possible. Knowing the nature of your goal is imperative. Try to get as much firsthand knowledge of that goal as you can. If you want to go into banking, pinpoint a specialized job—loan officer, for instance—and discover what it entails from nine to five each day, not just what it pays. A lot of us are chosen by our jobs. We arrive in the job market with our credits (college degrees and skills), and we are happy to take the first job that comes along. We work hard and take the promotions as they appear, gratefully. So long as we seem to be moving, everything is fine. Is that really the case? Or are we pawns in the company's strategy, passive and manipulatable? We may be acquiring skills in one particular job that are much more valuable in another. Periodic self-evaluation is part of becoming successful, even if things *seem* to be going our way. When "luck" intrudes and your affairs fall into place, be warned! Unless you carefully position your affairs yourself, you are not in charge.

Never forget that you are always worth more. We have been so conditioned to be thankful for work, any kind of work, that not one of us is yet capable of exploiting our situations as much as they exploit us.

So far we have decided that success consists of isolating a specific goal and achieving it. We know that ideally success should involve both "public" recognition and personal satisfaction. There is no magic formula that can be applied to each of our lives that will instantly transform a humdrum job into a successful career. But there are *five key ingredients* to every success story, and every single key can be yours:

> First Key: The Goal
> Second Key: The Work
> Third Key: The Credits
> Fourth Key: The Personal Skills
> Fifth Key: The Strategy

FIRST KEY AND SECOND KEY: THE GOAL AND THE WORK

Most of us have been brought up to believe that success comes to those that work hard. Does it? Most Black women work exceedingly hard, but are all of us successful? Why is it more likely that a white male who works hard will get what he wants? Simply because the work world is geared one hundred per cent to the white male's innate identification with the first four keys. He hardly has to think about *strategy* or *personal skills*. Ninety-nine per cent of all work *goals* have been male-dominated, and our educational system is predisposed toward providing him, above all others, with the appropriate *credits*.

Imagine that workers are birds. We can all flap our wings as hard as possible, but some of us get off the ground and some do not. Why? Some of us know how to fly. The rest have to learn how to fly. Those that do not bother to learn how to fly, in the world of work, remain on the ground, drones, all their lives. One important distinction: we do not have to learn how to fly like white males, or Black males, or even like white females. We have to learn how to fly, and soar, as Black women—in *our way*.

I am not minimizing the importance of hard work, but it is utterly wasted if it is not part of the Five Key Plan. The nation's offices are full of dedicated Black women who work hard and who work well, but for the benefit of the system much more than for themselves. These workers, and perhaps you are one of them, have attained the second key, *the work;* but they have not isolated *the goal,* have not developed their *personal skills,* and so work blindly, without *the strategy.* You need five out of five keys, not two out of five or even four out of five.

The Five Key Plan will triple the effectiveness of your work. It will be more productive; it will do much more than earn a better living; it will shoot you up to where you want to be. Only you can decide on your goal, make it crystal-clear, and see yourself at a particular desk in a particular office doing specific things. Secondly, make up your mind that nothing will interfere with your work; you can expect nothing unless you are firm about this. I can teach you how to get the credits, the personal skill, and the strategy, but I cannot do your work! I am assuming that at the very least you are competent in your field, are probably capable of much more than you are doing.

༤༤༤༤༤

2

The Credits

Earning a doctorate is the best way for women who are interested in biology to explore new fields of research, develop experimental skills, and eventually to work in a private research institute, where the most exciting biological work is being done. I'm something of a perfectionist. I won't settle for less than intellectual satisfaction and the chance to do something worthwhile, not only for myself but for society as well.

Dr. Yvonne Jones-Brown
Genetic Researcher, University of California at Berkeley

At first glance this seems like a very simple issue. If you want to be a lawyer, for instance, you have to have an undergraduate degree, a graduate degree, pass the bar examination, and present your credits to a prospective employer. It's not that simple, even if you are a white male. It matters where you went to school, whether your father or mother is a lawyer, what you did during your sophomore vacation, who you clerked for, and so forth. A friend of mine graduated at the top of her class from Harvard Law School, and fifty students she had beaten won jobs with major New York law firms—she did not even get a single offer!

No matter what endeavor you undertake there comes a point, sooner rather than later, when you are required to present your credits. This is a factual representation of your past experience, your education, and your qualifications for the job. The higher you aspire, the more demanding the credits and the more professional should be your presentation. In most cases you must be able to summarize your credits on paper in the form of a résumé.

Whether you are starting from scratch or looking for a new job, you must tailor your credits to your specific goal. There are three categories of credits:

a) Formal education.

b) Work experience.

c) Achievements.

In most cases you will have no trouble finding out what your goal requires in terms of formal education. There is absolutely *no point* in trying to bypass these requirements. In special circumstances work experience of the right kind is more important to an employer than formal education, but remember that your competition may have both. Stress both and do whatever needs to be done in order to pass the test, get the diploma, and maximize its worth by being able to truthfully represent that you graduated *cum laude*. Obtain the maximum credits, not the minimum.

As a Black woman, last hired and first fired (but we are going to change that!), your credits have to *glow* where others' must merely illuminate because in most cases you will have, in the eyes of the company, agency, or institution you approach, two debits:

1. You are Black.

2. You are a woman.

Even if you are turning your back on the petty world of the organization and striking out into business for yourself, you will eventually be asked to produce your credits—if not by your bank or investors, then at least by your customers!

So, formal education is a must. Sixty per cent of all Black college graduates are women, so as a group we are more highly qualified than Black men and should be on a par with white women. If you are sure of your goal but do not know what qualifications it requires, check the table in the Appendix and if necessary write away for information. Visit your library and look up the various government publications that I mention in the Appendix, such as *Occupational Outlook for College Graduates,* published by the United States Bureau of Labor Statistics. This gives you the precise credits needed for a wide variety of jobs, estimates the state of the job market, and analyzes salary expectations.

Trade journals are also a great source of information. In the "Employment Opportunities" section, they will tell you what credits are needed for specialized careers and will also give you an inside look at aspects of your goal that may not be known to your career counselor or found in promotional literature.

Every time I contemplate a new business venture, I get hold of all the trade papers relating to that particular commodity, and I do not make a move until I have absorbed the literature. Find out what new job categories are on the horizon in your chosen field, and emphasize the skills that are going to be required. Keep *ahead* of your profession or industry.

If you have chosen your goal and know what requirements you need but have not yet enrolled in an educational institution, bear in mind that a "snob system" exists in the job recruitment industry and that it applies across the board, in all the professions, business, government, and even the arts. This system accords preferential treatment to graduates of the "right" schools, those institutions that have previously provided the business with workers who turned out to be highly skilled and motivated. This bias operates on every level, and it is not so obvious as automatically favoring any graduate from an East Coast "Ivy League" college. If you have your eyes on a job with a local company that is rooted in your community, then your best bet might be a degree from the state college where that company does most of its recruiting. If you turn up with a degree from Vassar or Sarah Lawrence, it is quite likely that the head of Personnel will think you are too good for them. On the other hand, a Master of Business Administration (M.B.A.) degree from one of the top fourteen business schools* virtually guarantees you a high-paying position in accounting, finance, management, or advertising. In fact some major corporations only recruit at those colleges.

Check the Appendix thoroughly for education-financing opportunities. You may be eligible for loans, scholarships, or fellowships as part of minority-funding programs. Most college students do not think about the specifics of their future job until they are about to graduate. There are many reasons why this is foolish, not the least of which is that by doing so they decrease their chances for financial aid. If you can articulate your goal at an early stage in your academic career, you will impress the scholarship committee, the entrance board, and finally the corporate recruiter. You do not have to take second-best when it comes to higher education. One of the reasons that scholarships for minority students are decreasing is that in the last ten years the dropout rate was very high, and those responsible for the subsidies felt that the investment was not being returned. A young Black woman who knows where she wants to be five years hence and can accurately define her formal credits is likely to be favored if she shows determination.

Some colleges work so closely with industry that students are able to gain valuable on-the-job experience as interns (and not only in medicine and law) while they work toward a degree. This brings you to the

---

* Stanford, Harvard, Univ. of Chicago, M.I.T., Wharton, Carnegie-Mellon, Northwestern, U.C.L.A., Tuck, Univ. of Michigan, Columbia, Berkeley, Cornell, and Univ. of Indiana.

attention of your potential employer at a very early stage and gives you a big advantage over the sidewalk pounder.

I urge you to fulfill all the requirements in formal education that your goal demands because the very first item on your résumé, under your name, is going to be your degree. If you only have a high school diploma, that goes at the bottom! But be selective in college; do not waste time and energy on courses that are incidental to your goals.

In most situations there are several applicants for every job, and they have about equal qualifications in formal education. The employer is going to look for that person who has something *extra*. If you are still in college or have yet to enroll, try to gear your extracurricular activities to your chosen field. There are plenty of on-campus opportunities for getting experience in management and administration. Most occupations place a premium on the ability to organize and the ability to make decisions. Neither of these skills are *necessarily* evidenced by any type of degree. If you can approach an employment situation with proof of your *performance* in these areas (not just theoretical knowledge), you will stand head and shoulders above the other applicants.

For instance, at college you helped to run the Afro-American Culture Week. Now, a couple of years later, you are applying for a job with a computer company. Is there a connection? Of course. You kept schedules, organized meetings, collected and disbursed funds, dealt with a variety of last-minute problems, and proved to yourself and others that you clearly had management skills.

When it comes to collating your credits, this type of activity is work experience. If your college days are behind you or if you do not need a degree for your goal, you should still periodically re-evaluate your work experience so that it is not just a list of job titles. Let us say you have spent five years in a secretarial position in a small advertising agency and you want to become a television producer. You know that you will have to work your way up from production assistant, but how do you get *that* job?

First, you evaluate your previous and current work experience in the light of what is going to be required in your new job. Forget about all the letters you typed and the coffee you made. Remember that the filing system was nonexistent before you arrived. Make a list of your accomplishments:

1. Created records system.

2. Scheduled production meetings.

3. Supervised creative personnel.

If you work in a small office, your overall responsibility is probably wider than you think, so stretch your imagination and cover all the territory. Never invent, because your new employer may call your former one for verification. If that is likely to happen, it is a good idea to show your new résumé to your old employers so that they know how you are presenting yourself. If you have been doing a moderately good job, they are likely to back all your claims.

A job title *per se* means little to a prospective employer unless you are in a highly technical field such as engineering, physics, or scientific research. A vice president in one company can be one step up from the doorman and in another, the person who is really in charge of the whole show. Never describe yourself as a secretary, clerk, or receptionist. Think in terms of your activities. How many people do you supervise? Work with? Do you report to a company officer? More than one? Have you ever traveled for the company? Organized interdepartmental activities? Recreations? What suggestions of yours have become company policy? Do you deal directly with clients? Salespeople? The public?

There is a peculiar psychological dynamic that hinders Black women from being able to express full self-appreciation of their work efforts. You may *know* that you put in a hard day's work but may insist that it was just routine, nothing special, nothing to write home about. Well, yes, the man from General Sponge *did* come an hour early for his meeting with Mr. Winkle. It *is* a good thing you knew about the order and that you checked the specifications yourself and that the man did not need to see Mr. Winkle after all but just left a new, larger order. But that was all.

All! If you were a white male trainee and handled the same "routine" situation, you would be making darn sure that the department head knew you spent the whole day doing Winkle's job, and would it not be a good idea if you became acting sales director when Winkle went into the hospital for that operation?

I have a personal theory, founded on intuition, my own experience, and conversations with many of you, that crucial facets of complex operations in business, government, and industry are routinely handled by hundreds of thousands of Black women sitting at front-office desks. We make important decisions, cover up for incompetent superiors, and take control of delicate situations. For this we are rewarded with clerical or supervisory salaries. For the same type of work (performed in an inside office, with two windows), a man demands and gets twice the salary and a three-martini lunch. All part of the double standard. Management silently acknowledges that both the white man and the Black woman *can* do the work, but the bias is that the white man *should* be doing it, *ought* to do it, *looks better* doing it (to other white men), and since you and I are quite content to sit here behind this typewriter the system is not going to change.

Change it! If you are going to be doing Winkle's job while he is away, then demand his salary and his office. Or quit! Go to the company next door and tell them exactly how you have been working *with* (never "for") Mr. Winkle for five years and that you want to move on and up, and it is just possible that you will bring the General Sponge account with you.

In her book *Skills for Success*, Dr. Adele M. Scheele divides working people into two distinct categories. There are the *sustainers,* who work hard and wait for recognition that rarely comes, and the *achievers,* who also work hard but who *demand* recognition. Eighty per cent of the Black women in the U.S. work force are *sustainers* (my figures), and I want *all of us* to become *achievers.* One of the worst aspects of *waiting* for recognition is that it develops a bitterness toward co-workers that may not be justified by their attitudes. If you make a good case for yourself and are repeatedly turned down, then you have a reason to be discouraged; but that should motivate you to move on elsewhere. If you never make a case for yourself, you will be passed over again and again, especially if you are doing more than a good job —you are too valuable where you are, and there you will stay!

Before I became a businesswoman, I learned a lot about work and its rewards when I was a fashion model. Most people believe that all you need is the credits (looks), and money and fame beat a path to your door. Not one bit true. The Five Key Plan holds true for *every type of occupation.* If I had been a sustainer, I would still be working as an illustrator's model earning the minimum wage! I built my credits carefully, on my own, with hard work and contacts from my school, the Fashion Institute of Technology. Soon I had appeared in a major print-ad campaign for detergent and on the cover of the New York *Times Fashion Supplement.* Still, I could not get hired by a modeling agency because I was Black; no agency was convinced there would be enough work for me.

At that point I could have turned back, in defeat, and given up the dream. But I knew I could do it—I had the credits! So I took the bull by the horns and spent three frantic days mailing my recent cover to the head of every major advertising agency in New York, with a printed card. Within two weeks I had more work than I could handle in a year, and I was immediately signed by a top agency that could not afford to be *without* me!

When you work on your list of credits, you must be an achiever. Achievements set the seal on your formal education and work experience. When composing your résumé, first list all the activities you engage in which are *not* directly related to your work, and we are going to translate as many of these as possible into tangible achievements. If there is one fine quality that stands out as a unique part of our growth as a force in America, it is our concern for the communities in which we live. Starting with church groups a hundred years ago, Black women have gathered together time and time again, all over the nation, to create sustaining organizations. Black women are the backbone of volunteer efforts on every front: fighting disease and poverty, building churches and hospitals, raising scholarship funds.

As part of our individual record and as an indication of the type of women we are, this information is just as important to your credits, as an aspect of your achievements, as is, for instance, a male's involvement with the Little League or the United Jewish Appeal. Men do not shrink from cramming their résumés full of such "incidental" material, and neither should we. Put down all the community activities in which you have participated.

Now we are going to selectively pool your credits and weave them into a résumé. Most people think that writing a résumé is routine, but as someone who receives hundreds every year let me tell you that I judge a job applicant first by how the résumé *looks,* by how it is *written;* and both of these factors influence my comprehension of the actual *facts* it contains. The most qualified person in the world can make themselves appear dull and inadequate with a poorly written résumé, and quite a few applicants with marginal credits make it on the basis of creatively written résumés.

Adhere to the standard form. Your résumé should be neatly typed on heavy bond and should be concise and clear. Study my example very carefully. Unless you are moving from the middle of the ladder to the very top, one page should suffice. It should not take more than a couple of minutes to read, and it must make an instantly good impression. This is hard currency, and it is well worth taking the time to do it properly. Before you design the actual page, list your academic record, your current experience and achievements as well as travel experience, language proficiency, and willingness to travel. You are not obliged by law to indicate your height, weight, or marital status, and I would suggest that you do so only if such information will have a positive bearing on your ability to do the job. For instance, if you have researched your goal thoroughly, you might have found out that for a position as district sales manager the company is looking for someone who is married and has strong community ties. On the other hand, if your goal is a job that involves a lot of traveling or relocation, then you might want to mention that you are *not* married.

Check your use of job and position titles so that "Chairwoman of Budget Committee" becomes "Chaired Budget Committee." Pare away the excess fat and make your points as succinctly as possible. If you were the administrative secretary for a community fund-raising drive, drop the word "secretary" and say, "Organized Senior Citizens Week netting $15,000."

Emphasize experience *doing,* since that gives your reader a firm grasp of your abilities and aptitudes. Do not mention false starts, jobs

ZITA R. HARRINGTON

4520 Crescent Avenue
Mayville, MA 02116

502-555-6765 office
502-555-0982 home

Birth: May 13th 1951
Health: Excellent

EDUCATION

Graduate School of Business Administration
Boston College, Boston, Massachusetts
Master of Business Administration (June 1980)
Major: Marketing

Adelphi University, Garden City, New York
Bachelor of Business Administration, May 1976
(Magna Cum Laude)
Major: Marketing

CAREER GOAL

A management position in a corporation that
utilizes my marketing experience and problem-
solving skills.

EXPERIENCE

Rogers & Company, Boston, Massachusetts
Sectional Supervisor—Operations Department
1980 to present

Administration and supervision of three support
service units, staff of 20. Responsible for data
input and $24 million of insurance premiums.
Duties include workflow supervision, operation
of IBM 3790, zero-base and expense budgeting,
goal-planning, intensive interdepartmental and
external communication.
Personnel duties include supervision, staffing,
salary administration and performance
appraisals.

Bigelow's Department Store, Garden City,
New York
Managing Salesperson (1976 to 1978)

Responsibilities included supervision of 15
salespeople, sales report evaluation, stock
accountability, markdowns, transfers, RTV's.

ACHIEVEMENTS

Developed fund-raising program for Greater
Boston Nursing Home program, netting $22,000,
1979

Chaired building fund, Mayville Medical Clinic
netting $4,500, 1978

that lasted two weeks, training programs that you dropped out of, or undergraduate work that did not produce a degree.

If you have your eye on two or three jobs, even in the same field, you may want to compose *more than one* résumé. Perhaps the size of the companies or the commodities they handle may vary. One may be a government agency, the other private industry. In each case there may be strengths you want to emphasize in one job application that could be minimized in another. Orient each résumé to a specific job.

Give the dates, month, and year during which you were involved in your achievement activities, and always include the names of the organizations to which you belong.

It is traditional to list your work experience in the sequence of "last job first," but if that does not exactly suit your aspirations, juggle these items judiciously. However, if you do that, be prepared to explain in an interview why you put your current job at the bottom! Use verb phrases in job descriptions and indicate the size of the projects with which you have been involved. Delete all words that indicate smallness or a lack of importance.

Your final layout should present your name in upper case, top and center, with your address, single-spaced, to the left. Your date of birth and health, single-spaced, should be to the right. It is an asset if you can provide both a home telephone number and a daytime work telephone number.

If you have a degree, your education becomes the first entry, followed by your career goal. This should not be more than three lines in length, which is one reason why you might want to make separate résumés for different applications. If you can describe your goal in terms that you know from your research fits the nature of the company to which you are applying, you accomplish a number of things at once:

1. You demonstrate that you know how the company is organized and what it does.

2. You force a comparison between your credentials and those of the current individual holding the job.

3. You pave the way for a specific, not general, discussion about the job.

Depending upon your overall strategy (see Chapter 4), it may not be appropriate to specify your *ultimate* career goal, especially if you are primarily interested in positioning yourself for an assault on the job of the person who will be interviewing you. Your stated career goal should always be reasonable, a step up from what you have been doing. Yes, of course you are ambitious and aim to climb as high as possible—it is perfectly all right to admit that much—but if the battle has just begun, stop short of naming your final target.

After your career goal comes the longest section of your résumé, your experience. Because some of your volunteer efforts may be as valuable in this regard as your paid jobs, I prefer not to put "Work Experience," which is the commonly used term. State the years worked, the name of the companies or organizations, and a pithy account of your duties.

The final items on your résumé should be your language abilities, memberships, and references. If you read and write a foreign language, you are literate in it; if you speak it, you are fluent.

References can be a tricky item. It is better to omit a reference than to provide the name of someone who for any reason at all is likely to give you less than a glowing homily. Never give as a reference someone who has not been informed. A sure bet is to give as a reference someone in your current or previous job who is not necessarily in a superior position but who has a title and can speak authoritatively on your behalf.

Now that you have your résumé, hold on to it. I do not believe in mass mailings. In one study it was discovered that employers made one substantial job offer for every 1,470 blind résumés received! My purpose in making you prepare the résumé *now,* is twofold. First, so that you can alert yourself to your own abilities, see yourself in a new, positive light, and learn to groom yourself, at least on paper. Secondly, so that you will be in a position to produce a good résumé at a moment's notice and so that you will have a tool when you enter the job market or make your move. If you can articulate your credits on paper, they will stick in your mind. I believe a résumé is most effective when left by a job applicant after an interview or read immediately prior to an interview already granted. Do not worry; I will tell you how to get that all-important interview!

Even if you are perfectly happy with your present job and simply want to move faster *within* your organization, it is not a waste of time to write or rewrite your résumé at this point. It will give you a fresh look at the services you are performing and increase your sense of self-worth. A well-known career planner told me that the day to start a job hunt is the day after you land a new job! The average worker looks for a job every three years. Be prepared. The fact that you are always in a position to look for a new job (because your credits are in order) will dramatically and positively affect your attitude toward your current position and will provide you with the security to take the risks you will have to take if you want to succeed.

A middle-management employee, Sarah Rutledge, was laid off during a severe recessionary period by a Chicago manufacturing company, and she diligently prepared a résumé based on the plan I have given you, analyzing her actual work experience rather than just listing job titles. She mentioned her skills both at work and outside. She was still on good terms with her ex-boss, and she asked him to look over her new résumé for verification and feedback. He was staggered to discover the range of Sarah's abilities, and within two months the company had opened a new plant and she wound up with a better job from the very company that had fired her!

The moral of Sarah Rutledge's story is that it is always a good time to review your credits. It is utterly foolish to imagine:

> *"I know what I do and what I'm worth; just give me a chance and I'll prove it"*

because you may never get that chance unless you are able to produce a fluent summary of your abilities *at short notice*. You may not always know when that is going to be, and if you are not prepared at all times you will find yourself in the right situation but at the wrong time. Imagine that you attend a social function and find yourself talking to a woman in a related field whom you recognize as a possible conduit to a much better job. When she asks you how your work is going, what do you say? This:

> *"Pretty good. They're thinking about a new setup for marketing, and we may move into the Humboldt building."*

Or, keeping your new résumé well in mind, this:

> *"I'm researching the structure of a new marketing group, and we're taking over the Humboldt building."*

Strike while the iron is hot. What if you make a good impression but have no résumé? Your new friend tentatively probes your interest in a job that is available in her company:

> *"If you could be interested,"* she says casually, *"send me a résumé in the morning."*

Do you dash home and spend half the night racking your brains, or are you able to slip a neat clean copy in an envelope right away?

According to the laws of the land, our color should be neither a credit nor a debit when seeking employment, and we are certainly no longer obliged to indicate our race on any application. However, since many of us can benefit from affirmative action policies in both the public and the private sector, the question arises as to whether it might be an asset to us if it is known we are Black, in situations that require us to present ourselves solely via the résumé. What then?

In fact, résumé readers are usually good detectives, and the fact that you are Black may be revealed by your memberships, interests, or in some cases by your address. I say stick to the facts that I have outlined. If you do not want to get turned down solely because you are Black, you should not expect to get hired solely for the same reason. If you have done your homework thoroughly (I cannot stress the need for this enough), you will know the nature of the organization at which you are directing your information. The worst thing you can do is eliminate Black references from your résumé in a misguided attempt to get equal consideration. There is no such thing. You are Black. Be proud of it. And make the most of it. It is a credit.

🌴🌴🌴🌴🌴

3

Your Winning
Personality

*"If you do not compete you will be stepped on; I feel one must
compete!"*

Vy Higginson, Publisher and Broadcaster
Professor of Advertising and Promotion
Fashion Institute of Technology, New York City

Personal skills constitute my *fourth key* to Success. You have a multi-
tude of these that you have to develop, train, and expose. Every single
key is important, and this one is often passed over by women who
think it frivolous to concern themselves about their "image." But the
way you work, your *style,* marks you for success (or failure), just as
surely as a sign hanging around your neck. People who act like win-
ners, who project their abilities, who are not afraid of taking risks, are
the people who come out on top. This is true from the chairman of the
board on down.

Black women have what it takes, but it is buried deep in some of
us, almost obliterated by thick blankets of social and cultural conditioning. I am going to tell you how to reach the positive personality
traits that you possess and to stir them up to the surface. If your work
is to receive its just rewards, you have got to develop your personal
skills.

For centuries any kind of work outside the domestic environment
was done by men. Even though Black women traditionally worked a
double shift, running both their own homes and that of their masters/
employers, it was mostly work in a domestic environment. Black
women have been *taking care of* things in a service capacity for centuries, both as genuine mothers and homemakers and as surrogate
mothers and housekeepers for white folks. This heritage has provided
us with excellent decision-making and problem-solving capacities, two

of the most highly prized characteristics of the "outside" work world. The question is: *how do we express our abilities?*

I know many Black women who occupy positions of power. I cannot think of one that I would categorize as tough in the belligerent meaning of the word. Yet every one of them has suffered from being thought of as tough simply because she is able to speak up, firmly and directly, when the situation so requires. Our culture is only very slowly emerging from a cocoon of male/female stereotyping that will be with us for a long time to come. As Black women we have been brought up to be "secretly" strong, to raise the family and work hard, but above all with the expectation that *we must not show it!* Why? Because our men will not like it. White folks will not like it. Do it and do it well, but do it quietly—that has often been our motto. Make it look easy, we say to ourselves, and never complain. Terrible! That attitude has been drummed into so many of us that when we go into the job market we are exploited. We are afraid to make waves. We do not want to be accused of being *like men.* It is bad enough that we steal a job from a man (all jobs outside the home are men's jobs), but for goodness sake, we do not have to act masculine, do we? So what do we do? We go about our business efficiently and quietly, as sustainers, and we go home to be miserable because we are always overlooked when it comes time for rewards and promotions.

Sometimes I think it is just a matter of language. If a man is firm in business, he is respected. If a woman is firm in business, she is tough. If a man dominates a meeting, he is taking charge. If a woman dominates a meeting, she is ruthless. How can we deal with that? If a man asks for a day or two to ponder a decision, he is judicious. If a woman does the same thing, she is indecisive. As Black women, we are called everything under the sun, sometimes to our faces. This will happen more and more as we begin to really make ourselves felt in the working world. Take no notice, remember "sticks and stones." It only matters if you believe what is said.

The fact is that we have already proved our ability to accomplish just as much as any man, more in some instances; but we do not always do it *the same way.* The most important fact to face is that you will not get anywhere unless you are prepared to *advertise* yourself. This can be done in a clumsy, half-hearted, or crude manner or it can be done with flair, wit, and consummate dignity. Eyes may roll when you leave the room, but you will move up the ladder without generating a poisoned atmosphere.

Some career women truly believe that they can win by playing a man's game. They learn to be noisy, abrupt, and to use foul language. Others are convinced that "femininity" is the answer, defined as sex appeal and tears.

Take a look at these words. Are any of them characteristically male or female? Black or white?

Responsible
Firm
Creative
Outspoken

These are the prime characteristics you need. Do you have them? Yes. Can you express them? Probably not. A well-known songwriter told me:

"When you are assertive and become successful, it's hard to keep your femininity."

But I do not agree, unless being feminine means being nonassertive and unsuccessful.

I am a female. I am a Black female. I have *always* been strong and determined; I was a born self-promoter. I have *always* relished every traditionally female attribute, and not once have I ever compromised what I believe to be my femininity. Once you imagine that certain qualities are the prerogative of the male of the species, you are *doomed.*

Walk tall on your high heels, and practice your *natural* skills. Since we are concerned here with *form,* I want to start with the basics. You will never get proper credit for your work unless the form is impressive. Your attitude is expressed in:

1. The way you move.

2. The way you speak.

3. The way you listen.

Our ideal is not to learn how to *act* in a particular way, but to become fully *aware* of all the signals we are sending. If you are aware of the signals, you can control every situation that you encounter. Success is determined by the way you react with others and your ability to present yourself as responsible, firm, creative, and outspoken. This holds true for job interviews, sales pitches, department meetings, asking for a raise, or firing an employee: any and every situation that connects you with another human being in the work environment.

BODY LANGUAGE

Are you a toucher? Or a touchee? Some women like it and some do not. At the office, I do not like hands on my shoulder, around my waist, or grabbing my elbow. Work is not the place for body contact, whether the implication is more or less than affectionate. The implied familiarity is usually *against* us Black women. Getting happy at the Christmas party may be sanctioned, but letting your boss, co-worker, or client break into your body space during a business exchange puts you at a disadvantage. It is better for your career that you get a reputation for being stuck-up or stand-offish than if you allow yourself to be squeezed and grabbed and pummeled as part of some imaginary code or camaraderie.

When should you touch? When you meet people for the first time, you should shake their hand. I notice that many of us have a real problem doing this. Learn how. It is not a masculine gesture; it is a symbolic signal that opens the meeting, registers mutual respect, and finalizes an exchange or transaction. In former times a business agreement "between gentlemen" was binding if sealed by a handshake. There is no reason why business "between gentlewomen" cannot be similarly bound.

Nowadays both men and women are uncertain about whether or not a woman should shake hands. For this reason I always initiate the gesture, and I am impressed by any woman who does so. When you are being introduced or when introducing yourself, move your right arm straight forward, directly and quickly, lowered slightly toward the hand of whoever you are greeting. If they respond smoothly, just give their hand one second's worth of *firm* squeeze and let go. Always make an appropriate statement as you do this:

"It is a pleasure to meet you."
"Please sit down."
"Thank you for coming."

Never shake hands from a seated position. It is an awkward gesture and puts you at a psychological disadvantage. Suppose you are seated at a round table meeting and several new persons are brought into the room. Everyone knows them except you. They come over to greet you. If you bend backward out of your chair, twist your head, and raise your hand, you will be presenting yourself as clumsy, abrupt, and indecisive. Instead, no matter how urgent your meeting, stop. Rise from the table as you would to leave, turn to the newcomers, and reach out your arm. Look them in the eyes, and greet them neatly and swiftly.

When seated, cross your legs at the ankle, not above the knee. Never sit with your hands in your lap at the edge of a chair. This projects extreme insecurity. When seated, listening, fold your arms if you want to reserve judgment or are preparing to be critical. Keep your arms open or flat on your desk, or hold a pen if you want to appear receptive.

If you work at a desk and your chair is adjustable, make it as high as you can with comfort. Chairs near your desk should have seats a fraction lower than your own. This subtle positioning allows you to control situations better, even if you are simply in the typing pool.

In situations that require you to stand, or if you prefer to stand, avoid plunging your hands into your pockets; this indicates that you have something to hide. Keep your *thumbs* out if you have your hands in your pockets; this registers as alert interest. If you stand with your arms folded, you are clearly dissatisfied. One of the most effective postures is arms akimbo; save it for exchanges that require you to appear extremely self-confident.

There are numerous gestures that we acquire which betray our basic attitudes. One woman I know is very shrewd, purposeful, and extremely talented. She concentrates on eye contact, and her body language is precisely what she wants it to be—with one very vital exception. I have noticed that whenever she is in a situation that makes her nervous, she jerks her right foot up, very slightly. What do *you* do when you are nervous?

The most common signs of nervousness are when we play with our hair, touch our neck, or fiddle with beads and earrings. If you find that you need a physical gesture to alleviate or contain your nervousness, the smartest thing to do is to make no bones about it and purchase a set of "worry" beads!

It is not easy to alter a lifetime of habitual physical gestures, but it can be done, in time, with practice. Start now, in front of the mirror at first, until you can see smooth movements that feel comfortable. Then rehearse situations, alone or with a friend. Do not worry about being self-conscious. My ultimate aim is to make you *very* conscious of yourself, so that you can use your gestures to emphasize your abilities.

HOW YOU SPEAK

Your accent is quite unimportant, so long as your English is correct and your tone is clear. You should not attempt to alter your accent in order to avoid racial or regional prejudice. Grammar and diction are the best tools we have for impressing people with our power of speech. You may or may not have been brought up using slang or Black English, but it is not "white" to speak the English language in the way that it is spoken and read by several hundred million women and men of every race and on every continent. You may find that co-workers, Black and white, encourage you to use Black slang expressions whether or not you are familiar or comfortable with them. This is a not-so-subtle put-down, and you would be only pandering to their baser hostilities if you complied, no matter how ostensibly jovial the atmosphere.

There is a great deal of potency to many verbal expressions that are exclusively Black. This potency is lost when they are used repeatedly. Keep them as arrows to be fired very judiciously and only when you are in complete control of yourself. You may want to discourage familiarity, remind someone of who you are, or otherwise make a strong point. But, as in everything, choose what you say and how you say it, and never lapse into street talk out of anger.

Many of my acquaintances think I am a prude about this, but I am absolutely appalled by the casual use of obscene and scatalogical language in the work place. I totally lose respect for women who have to resort to vulgarities in order to express themselves. I do not find it chic, and I do not find it funny. Such language usually rises from the bottom of any organization. It starts in the mail room or with the delivery persons and creeps through the front office into middle management. One word of warning: you will not find it at the top! I have yet to hear the president of a major corporation swear in the course of a business meeting. Those who have climbed that high know how to get along without resorting to profanity. I find it particularly disturbing when Black women swear in public. Cursing is one habit that I undeniably associate with the less majestic aspects of the male of our species.

> Rule 1: Take your time.
> Rule 2: Think!
> Rule 3: Be concise.

If you take five minutes to plan what you are going to say, you will be able to say it in ten minutes rather than half an hour. Time is money, and everyone appreciates ideas, instructions, complaints, excuses, requests, praise, and even criticism that is brief and *to the point*.

This is another matter about which some women imagine it is necessary to "act like a man." No! Men are not by nature any more brief or to the point than women. I have witnessed hours of expensive time wasted by male corporate executives wandering all around (and frequently off) a subject that could have been resolved in one direct exchange. Because men think that only *their* conversation is important, we women have been conditioned to feel that when we converse it is about inconsequentials but that when men converse it affects national security.

Learn to promote yourself by the way that you express your ideas. Don't use this approach:

"Perhaps if we tried switching Bill to Supply, we would increase production—how do you feel?"

Try instead this one:

"I have analyzed the figures, and production will jump six per cent if I move Bill over to Supply. Does that have your approval?"

The direct approach is always likely to be the most appropriate one. Give people an opportunity to say yes and no. If they have qualifying ideas, you do not have to elicit them; they will let you know. My friend Geraldine Stutz, the owner of New York's famous Henri Bendel department store, says:

"I think you can be honest, open, and trusting in business."

In that case, when you speak, speak your mind. Instead of saying "That might work," say "I like it!" And never be afraid of expressing a negative reaction:

"No, it's the wrong approach. I'll tell you why when I have had a chance to examine it closely."

Rather than:

"Well, it really isn't what I had in mind. I don't know; let me think about it."

The first response closes the matter; the second is open-ended and leaves the speaker distracted, worrying about "how-can-I-get-out-of-this," and the listener is encouraged to keep a bad idea alive in the expectation that you will eventually agree.

Your range of tone should be from polite to friendly, not beyond in either direction. Rudeness backfires, and relationships that indicate a mutual desire for more than friendship should be pursued *outside* working hours. It is a very bad idea to get involved with co-workers romantically if it can possibly be avoided. Even deep and sincere personal friendships should be built up over the years; they should not spring up from instant admiration.

Part of being straightforward is your ability to say things like this:

"Excuse me, but I have not finished; please don't interrupt."

This type of communication comes easily to women who are mothers. I am not suggesting that you treat your colleagues and subordinates like infants, but there is a lot to be learned about simple, firm expressions of will when it comes to getting a five-year-old to brush his teeth! Be careful not to adopt a tone that is sarcastic or condescending.

Your best protection is to be calm, polite, and efficient with everyone, on an equal basis. This is especially necessary if you are in daily contact with the same small group of people. Differences become exaggerated, tension rises, and work slows down. Often such a simple thing as the way you speak can prevent this from happening. If you are the most consistent person in the office, you will focus attention on yourself in the best way possible. This indicates qualities of taking charge and leadership, the factors that will fuel your rise to the top. You can be a sheer genius at what you do, but by being inarticulate or excessively long-winded you may spoil your chances for success. Even if you think that talking has got little to do with your job, there will always come a time when you have an opportunity to verbalize your ideas. If such times are infrequent and speaking is *not* a big part of your job, it assumes a great deal of importance because of the impact you can make. Imagine that you are a laboratory researcher whose work is judged according to the results of written papers. Once in a while you will be put on the spot, and if you can explain what you are doing succinctly, it can help you in the right places:

> *"Barbara Bates told me about her work with annotinine after we had that budget meeting. She's a very articulate young woman. Smart."*

In fact, you may be no smarter than the researcher at the next bench, but you were able to provide a capsule account of your current project and make it sound interesting.

It is also a good idea to think about how you talk about your job to outsiders. I can come home after a very heavy day, even one that has been exciting and productive, but work will be the last thing I want to talk about. I go out to a dinner party or cocktails, and of course I get asked about my work; it is inevitable. We are what we do. In those circumstances I always have a stock response that I make in an effort to sound spontaneous. This is designed to bring my listener up to date in hard information but does not encourage the listener to delve deeper. Your "antenna" should be always on the alert for new job opportunities, so you must be prepared to deliver a sales pitch for yourself anywhere, anytime. In a couple of well-chosen phrases, present yourself as in control of your world but champing at the bit for new worlds to conquer:

> *"I've doubled the number of our commercial accounts at Bilge and Breakwater and what I really need is a second assistant, but the company is not prepared to expand."*

Follow these principles:

1. Use "I" as much as possible.

2. Use verbs that imply motion forward and up.

3. Use facts and hard numbers whenever possible.

Remember, numbers always impress. A pile of dirt is a hundred thousand grains of sand. A number, even if it has to be qualified, is always more impressive than phrases like "a whole lot."

There are two aspects to effective speaking. We have covered the points that relate to normal conversation in a work context, but there is a related form which is an *essential* personal skill that must be at your disposal if you are going to the top: the ability to deliver a speech.

Does that sound terrifying? Public speaking is the number one fear in this country, greater than the fear of death! I am not suggesting that you have to be able to tour the nation as I do, addressing crowds of people, but there is no way that you are going to be a success unless you can make an effective presentation to one or more people. There is no occupation that does not require this sooner or later. Your first approach, the job interview, involves a speech. If you want the job, you will have to do much more than provide monosyllabic answers to a stream of questions. You must be prepared to explain why you want the job, and that requires a speech. It may be short and sweet, but it should still adhere to the rules which I am going to outline. All forms of one-sided verbal presentations can be considered in this context. You make a speech during your job interview. You are hired. Two weeks later, your boss asks you to tell your colleagues that from now on the commissary closes at two. That means you have to give a speech. Next month the vice president comes through your department with a foreign delegation. You are asked to explain your section's work; you give a speech. Six months later you ask for a promotion—another speech. In sales now, you have to review the district managers' performance once every two months—a speech. You devise a new method for charting sales potential in new areas and present it to two department heads and the chief of corporate planning—a big speech. And so on, until you are vice president of sales and you rise at the board meeting to announce that you have accepted an offer from Dubbing Quilts, Inc. to be their new C.E.O. (Chief Executive Officer). Your last speech. For a while.

I am going to explain how to make your speech memorable. I shall assume that you are going to talk for fifteen minutes to a small group of colleagues, including your immediate superior. Whenever possible deliver a speech standing up. Start by making your audience literally look up to you.

The first thing to do is familiarize yourself with the setting. Take nothing for granted. If you can choose the location, pick a conference room or an office which is not a public area, where you can be absolutely uninterrupted by ringing telephones or people barging in to distract your listeners. Stand at the head position of a table. Plan who will sit where and arrange the seats accordingly. Decide toward whom you are going to aim for the most eye contact.

Are there ashtrays for smokers? Pencils and pads for taking notes? Check all the details. There is nothing worse than starting your speech to find that all the attention is focused on Charlie the Chainsmoker who is collecting ash in the palm of his hand.

If your speech involves visual aids, such as charts, maps, and diagrams, arrange how they will be propped up and secure them so that you do not have to hold them. You must be free to wander within a few feet of your position. See that there is enough space for you to do this.

When it comes to the content of your speech, plan very carefully. Come to the point. If your listeners do not know exactly what you are going to discuss, explain it in the first few sentences. Do not keep them in suspense. Structure your speech around big ideas. Perhaps there is only one; in fifteen minutes there should not be more than two. The first thing to do is cover all the ground in two or three key sentences. If you cannot do this, your objectives are vague and your speech needs restructuring.

Once you have your key sentences and your big ideas, take five 3" × 5" file cards and jot down your thoughts as brief points or phrases. Avoid any narrative and absolutely avoid writing the speech from start to finish, or you will be tempted to simply read it by rote and will give an impression quite the opposite of your intention. Everyone must see that you have a strong grasp of all the details.

Now take your file cards and shuffle them. Select an order that you think best carries the thrust of your argument and keep it logical. If there are conditions, ramifications, or side issues, save them for the end of your speech. Define the big ideas as clearly as possible from the start; *then* show off all the homework you have done about the related issue.

For the final step you need either a friend's ear or a tape recorder. You must talk through your speech over and over again. Listen to yourself on tape or pay close attention to a friend's reaction. Your reasoning must be comprehensible and your facts clear. Paraphrase and summarize as much as possible. Every word must hit home. Avoid labored analogies and cumbersome metaphors. Make an impact with your very first words:

"Sales are worse today than ten years ago."
Pause. "Measured against the cost of goods."

Even if your first statement strikes your audience as absurd or untrue, it has impact and you qualify it with a point that takes you to the heart of your big idea.

Earlier I encouraged you to use numbers as much as possible in your conversations at work. In a speech try not to fire a barrage of statistics at your listeners if you expect them to retain them in order to grasp your big idea. If you are dealing with an issue that can only be understood with reference to figures, use a large chart or diagram. Make it bold and clear; you want maximum comprehension.

Use *inductive* reasoning. First present your evidence; then state your conclusions. Do not start with a generalization and work backward.

Once you have made your point and touched all the bases, wind down as quickly as possible. Plan your ending so that it is not flat or half-hearted. You are making the speech in order to get something accomplished, so return the ball to your audience in a way that they can manage:

> *"Those are the reasons that I would like to see less sugar and more calcium in our cranberry cookie line. We should start on the first of next month. Are there any questions?"*

It is a mistake to be too light-hearted or to tell a joke. Even if you are capable of getting a good laugh, it will ultimately detract from your presentation. Above and beyond generating interest in your big idea, your aim in a speech is to identify yourself as:

Responsible
Firm
Creative
Outspoken

You may want to memorize your entire speech, but it is probably better simply to cue yourself with notes. I type the main topics of my presentation on 8½″ × 11″ bond and keep it in a folder. Type in capital letters or print large. You may find that, like me, you rarely have to refer to your notes, but it is both professional and smart to have them on hand.

When you rehearse, be aware of the time. If your speech is to be fifteen minutes long, you should be reaching your conclusions at the ten-minute mark. If your listeners are restless and if you sense their attention is wandering, never be afraid to pick up the pace, skip details, and get to your big idea immediately.

The ability to stand up and make an effective presentation is critical to your career. You do not have to study oratory, and it is not a matter of winning votes. For a Black woman it is a question of being able to register to her audience and to *herself* that she is not afraid to speak out.

The psychological advantages of knowing that you are able to do this are so overwhelming that it is well worth finding an excuse to give a speech just to enjoy the satisfaction it will give you. This may sound like sheer unadulterated masochism to those of you who shrink from the public eye, but believe me it is the one way to achieve instant self-esteem. Start with a small community group and address them about an innocuous topic. You will be invigorated and very surprised at your innate abilities.

LISTENING

That is easy, right? You just listen? No. Listening is a skill. There are two ways of listening. *Directive* listening is when we ask a question and, expecting a particular answer or type of answer, we hear only that. Example: I ask if you can meet my plane at Kennedy Airport so we can discuss a project on the way into Manhattan. You say "I'll try." What I hear is "Yes." What you mean is "I doubt it." The directive listener has a goal in mind, and the questions she asks suggest the answer she wants to hear. This is not always the most efficient way to work. I suggest that you consider the following techniques for *nondirective* listening. This means encouraging communication without steering the conversation or interjecting your own emotions. This is far more likely to provide you with information and insight than directive listening. A good psychoanalyst is a full-time nondirective listener!

1. Eliminate distractions. When someone wants a word with you, turn off the typewriter and close the door. Move away from your desk if it is cluttered with distracting papers.

2. Make the speaker comfortable. Get a chair; offer coffee. This is to show the speaker that it is all right to talk and that you will listen.

3. Be responsive. Nod your head; keep your posture in an alert position. Encourage the speaker with neutral questions or directions such as "Really?" and "Go on."

4. Withhold judgment. No matter what is said, do not betray your opinions prematurely; it may only impede what is already getting sticky. If I say to you, "I've been thinking about asking you to work late on Tuesday," and you immediately interrupt and say you cannot possibly do it, I am going to meet that challenge by asserting myself. If you say *nothing* or

merely a noncommittal "Hmm," I am more inclined to move back on my position by saying, "Can you do it, or should I ask Clare?"

5. Empathize. Make an effort to understand, even if the presentation is lousy and the logic, jumbled. If you wince and grab the aspirin, you will lose your speaker entirely and will perhaps lose the grain of a good idea.

6. Listen for what is *not* said. Pay attention and, instead of feeling compelled to jump in and agree or disagree, just follow the flow and listen for the holes. These holes may contain the most important pieces of information. A colleague may bring you an idea that is ostensibly to benefit your area of interest but may omit any mention of personal credit or profit; be suspicious of this.

7. Use the power of silence. It can be very compelling. When your speaker pauses or stops, you do not have to fill the gap with a conditioned response, possibly one that would not be an accurate reflection of your thoughts. There may be a final, very important fact or issue that your speaker feels dubious about presenting. If you stay silent for a while, the speaker will decide to bring it out and you will be better off.

8. Verify. If something is said that you do not understand, it does not mean you are at fault. Ask for clarification.

9. Let the speaker finish. After the final silence say, "Is that all?" And if it is, you are free to respond or not as you see fit. In a case where someone simply wanted to blow off steam or try out an idea, he or she will probably be happy to finish and leave, and you will have performed a very important function without uttering a word—just by listening.

When you listen well, you encourage creativity and monitor conflict. It also helps you when it comes your turn to speak out.

How you move (body language), how you speak, how you listen —all these are indispensable weapons in your arsenal of personal skills. They all involve extroverted functions of the body and for that reason are easier to handle than less tangible skills like *problem solving* and *decision making*.

PROBLEM SOLVING

There are definite techniques for solving problems, especially ones of a nonmathematical nature. Not every problem has a single, correct answer. In work we encounter problems that are logistical, technical, and that arise from human conflict. In all cases the easiest, most obvious solution is not always the best, but never abandon it until you have found a better one.

Since women are supposed to be able to comprehend matters *contextually* to a much finer degree than men, our technique for problem solving should rely more on examining the area in which the problem lies than in the knot of the problem itself.

Example: I announce a large promotion for a new "Naomi" bath oil at Macy's on May 1. Newspaper advertisements are run; models are hired; my staff and Macy's spend a lot of time and money on the introduction. Suddenly word comes from my suppliers that the boxes have been printed with an error and there is no way that a new quantity can be ready on time. I tell *you* to solve the problem. What do you do? I refuse to cancel the promotion.

A man would be likely to focus on the printing-error aspect of this problem. He would argue with the jobber and perhaps attempt, at considerable cost, to get a new company to print up boxes overnight. That is a solution which would:

a) Involve added expense.

b) Still result in a less-than-perfect product.

Here is how you could best solve the problem. First, verify that the printing error is a major defect and tell the jobber that he will not get paid unless he reprints immediately. Then you turn the inconvenience into a virtue. You ask Macy's for all the shallow baskets they have in the store, and you buy dozens of cymbidium orchids. You work all night with Macy's display team creating an extraordinary counter with just bottles of the bath oil casually heaped in the baskets with the flowers. Every woman who makes a purchase is given a flower, and the promotion is a hit. No one misses the boxes.

Was that too easy? Sometimes the problem involves a conflict between two people, neither of whom will budge. Men think they are born diplomats and often try to solve this type of loggerhead situation by talking the parties into a settlement. My approach is to use time as much as possible, especially when temperaments need to be diffused. Let it rest, focus attention elsewhere, and perhaps one of the combatants will unilaterally come around. This often happens if the spotlight is removed from such a situation. No one likes to be seen backing down from a strong position when the whole office is breathlessly waiting to see who will win. But once the curtain is halfway down, a day or two later, it is easier to unravel the controversy. But always give yourself a real deadline and stick to it.

MAKING DECISIONS

A woman cannot make up her mind. We have all heard this. Even by traditional standards this claim is absurd. Take a so-called non-working wife and mother. She budgets, markets, cleans, cooks, cares for children, and organizes her own and her family's time, but somehow we are supposed to believe that she does all this without making any important decisions? The fact that she is sometimes honest enough to admit that she cannot choose between a red dress and a green coat has nothing whatsoever to do with decision making in a work context. The strategy of the male is to simply avoid a decision altogether, the ultimate in indecisiveness.

Most women are trained to make multiple decisions all day long. Decisions are so natural for us that when a problem is packaged or presented as inherently more important (i.e., as is often the case in business) than a homemaking decision, we often believe that we have never solved a *real* problem in our lives. If it is true, as initial studies suggest, that our brains are more highly developed than those of males in areas that relate to gathering and integrating "bits" of information, it stands to reason that we should be good at making decisions. But the male is supposed to be capable of a narrower focus, so perhaps our ability to take all things into consideration may to some degree inhibit the decision-making process in its classic (i.e., male-oriented) definition as "either/or." By examining a potential decision-making situation in its entirety, we might well come to these conclusions:

a) A decision is not necessary.

b) The premise of the situation is faulty.

Example: You work in an advertising agency. It is an extremely busy day, and you are looking forward to a long-standing lunch appointment with a prospective client who has great potential. It would be a feather in your cap if you got her business. At 11 A.M. you call and confirm the lunch date. Fifteen minutes later your telephone rings and it is your boss:

"I want you in the conference room at one, Deborah. Bob and Julie and I are going to run over the No-Fat Fizz campaign, and I think your input would be valuable. We'll have a sandwich lunch on the job."

Gulp! You have been doing routine work for weeks, and suddenly two Big Breaks threaten to cancel each other out. What do you do? You are faced with a very tough decision. If you cancel the lunch appointment, it is very likely that the client will evaporate and not give you another chance. On the other hand, how do you explain to your boss—especially since you never mentioned you were chasing this client because it is a private project of your own, not central to your job? You have very little time to make up your mind. Wisely, you simply said "O.K." to your boss and did not let your voice betray any hesitancy.

You seem to have two choices:

1. Cancel your boss. Never a good thing to do, especially since this is your first high-level meeting.

2. Cancel your would-be client. You lose a chance, but you are the only one to know that.

Most people would most likely take the second choice on the argument that a bird in the hand is worth two in the bush. What if you took the lunch date but failed to get the account? Then you would have lost all around.

Actually I believe that you have more than two choices. The following is what I would do, using my female capacity to see all around a problem.

I would drop into the boss's office at noon and explain that a friend of mine who just happens to be the account executive for Wilson's Widgets is going to stop by in about an hour. You tell the boss that it might be a very good idea if your friend saw how your agency functioned, and you suggest that she be allowed to sit in on the No-Fat Fizz meeting. What can happen?

1. Your boss says "no" but is at least aware that you will have a potential client on your hands at lunchtime. Then it becomes his idea that you take your friend to lunch.

2. The boss says it is a terrific idea; you call your friend saying that lunch is on you at your office and that as a treat you will also provide a sneak preview of your new No-Fat Fizz campaign.

Of course, if you have a very shrewd boss he might cancel the meeting and take your friend to lunch himself! That is why it is so important to know the people you work with, so you can predict how they will react in different circumstances.

The first thing to do when faced with a decision is to re-evaluate *the terms.* Is it really an "either/or" situation? Can it be turned on its head? Is it a situation that requires the separation or integration of ideas?

How do you make decisions at the moment? Do you fall into one of these categories? Be honest.

1. The Agonizer.

   This woman worries about every detail and believes herself to be very conscientious. In fact she may be subtly withdrawing from the decision and hoping that it will be taken out of her hands.

2. The Plunger.

   She jumps right in on the spur of the moment and hopes for the best, having done little or no calculating in advance.

3. The Stargazer.

   This woman believes in Fate: "If the next person who comes in the door is wearing yellow, I'll go left. If not, I'll go right." She also consults the *I Ching*.

4. The Rationalist.

   She creates a very impressive array of lists, charts, and graphs. Often this obscures the decision.

5. The Evader.

   She procrastinates until the decision is out of her hands.

Is there a right way to go about making decisions? Definitely. Consider these steps:

A. Ask yourself:

1. Does the decision need to be made?
2. When is the deadline?
3. Why does the decision have to be made?
   (i.e., what are its objectives?)

B. Go into action:

1. Collect and collate information.
2. Define the possible results. I prefer the word "results" to

the word "alternatives" because I do not like to be restricted by "either/or" thinking.

3. Articulate, on paper if necessary, the pros and cons of every possible result.

4. Evaluate and choose.

5. Sleep on it.

6. Re-evaluate and check to see if there is any additional information available that might change your mind.

7. Take the plunge.

Never try to sidestep a decision. There is a boomerang effect, and it will be much harder the second time around. Decision making is a sought-after quality in the work world, and you should always take the responsibility for the decisions that you make. This is not just a matter of integrity, but even if not all your decisions turn out to be correct, you will get a reputation for decisiveness which is synonymous with achievement. People admire someone who is not afraid to take a tough decision onto his or her shoulders. Make sure you are going to get the credit, even before the decision has been judged right or wrong.

In both problem solving and decision making, a capacity to outline the relevant facts and marshall them in order is essential. This is a basic skill which can be learned and with practice developed to a high degree. In order to move away from the crowd, it is important to develop a personal skill that is traditionally considered to be a woman's prerogative: *intuition*. Men have hunches, but we have female intuition. Is it a myth that the ability to *feel* that something is right or wrong is greater in women than in men? I think it is neither myth nor magic. If you are a swift and accurate judge of character, it can carry you very far in the business world and many other fields. In science brilliant discoveries are made that began simply as intuitive guesses.

I am sure that many times you have disliked someone on sight, and later events justified your intuition. Does this mean you have ESP or second sight? Should you rely on that to make job decisions?

INTUITION

Dr. Jerre Levy has done most of her research about this issue and has the following to say about a woman who seems to know a great deal about a person after just a ten-minute conversation:

"There is considerable scientific evidence that women surpass men in verbal fluency, in noting details of experiences that

*may be incidental to a particular directed task, and in under-
standing the meaning of facial expression. Possibly, this
means that women are particularly sensitive to a whole range
of social cues and especially skilled at social interactions. The
proverbial 'female intuition' may reflect an integration of
meaning derived from both verbal and nonverbal communication and from the richness of contextual information
present in any social situation."*

Quite obviously we have a profitable talent that must be encouraged. It is not a question of guesswork or some ethereal capacity
to *know* without information. In fact, the information is always there.
It is just that we have the proper equipment to gather and analyze such
information and men do not. The farmer's wife knows the weather is
going to change. She is always right. Does that make her psychic? No,
it simply means that her brain is an efficient meteorological station,
gathering information and drawing sound conclusions. She may not be
conscious of the process, but this makes it no less valid. When you take
your instant dislike to a particular individual, the culture conditions
you to believe that this is an emotional response and perhaps even to
be distrusted. In some cases you might be inclined to overcompensate,
out of guilt, and might get involved in situations that your first instinct
was to avoid. You give the undesirable individual a chance because,
not wanting to be unfair, you deny your intuition.

In fact, it is your desire to be fair that is the emotional response,
one unfounded on any empirical data. On the other hand, your intuition
was based on a wealth of empirical data. The person you met, in just
ten minutes, gave you a wealth of information about himself. He may
not have given you any verbal communication concerning his past or
present activities, but his manner of approach, level of eye contact,
nervous gestures (or lack of them), facial expressions, and tone of
voice all combined to provide you with a profile that your brain instantly compared with those of all the other people you have ever
witnessed, and the result was a warning signal. A lie detector merely
measures *one* physiological change. Your brain is capable of assessing
a much wider variety of potential change. You say to yourself:

"This man is lying; I know it."

That opinion is not based on thin air. His voice may have altered very,
very slightly as he spoke, or his eyes, or his body language. Something
took place that you noticed.

Men have intuition, though not to the same degree as us, but they
use it in business all the time. The banker boasts:

"I don't have to see a man's file. I can tell just by looking at him whether or not he's a sound prospect. I have never been stiffed yet!"

Are these just empty words? Not necessarily. But he may have started his career by being "stiffed" so many times that he finally learned to read the silent signals of a dishonest man.

Intuition should never replace the need to examine all the available information about a given situation, but it should be combined with all you can find out. Think of your intuition as a practical tool, not a mysterious element in your judgmental process that is somehow less than just. You may say to yourself:

"I intend to give Joe the benefit of the doubt and even though I know he is going about his project the wrong way I'll wait to see the finished results."

That is being *fair*. On the other hand:

"She seems very nice, but I just know this new supervisor will do all she can to replace me. I don't care what she says; I am going to be very careful."

That is being *intuitive*. And practical.

EXPRESSION AND REPRESSION

Most of us would consider it advantageous to be able to *express* ourselves but not to be able to *repress*. To me both expression and repression are important personal skills, and all that counts is your awareness of what is being expressed or repressed and *why*. You have to develop the capacity to do either at will.

We all have the desire to express our better nature and repress that side of ourselves which we do not like. Unfortunately there are a number of things about ourselves which we have been erroneously conditioned to believe are dislikable, and these we repress to our detriment. For instance, the white male world tells us that it is acceptable for us to be:

Sensitive
Creative
Gracious

and to be *hurt* when things go wrong.

In addition to this, most of us were conditioned to believe that it is quite inappropriate for a Black woman to be:

> Strong
> Competitive
> Assertive

and to be *angry* when things go wrong.

The consequence of this is that when we strive for success, we consciously and unconsciously *repress* the very qualities that are essential ingredients for making it. It is ridiculous for anyone, male or female, really to believe that strength, competition, assertion, and anger have a gender! But we have been bowing to that creed for far too long. If we continue to accept this version of sexual differentiation, we will remain on the bottom rung.

It is not easy to reverse centuries of conditioning in a few years, especially since most of the information relayed throughout the world supports the old, traditional order. Many of us go to work, do an excellent job, repress all our attitudes, desires, and feelings, and come home wondering why we feel terrible. Some of us have found ways to compromise:

> *"Of course I know I'm actually much stronger and more decisive than Ted, but he is such a male chauvinist and I have to work with him, so I let him imagine that he is making the decisions and I play dumb half the time. That way at least we get the work done."*

This is common but specious reasoning. It fosters the female Svengali syndrome, that of the woman behind the throne. Both the man and the woman in this situation are deluding themselves. In time they both become crippled. He only *thinks* he is standing on his own two feet, but in fact if his female partner were to leave, he would be overwhelmed by the job. The woman is equally convinced that *given the chance* she can do everything herself. In fact she never gives herself the chance, never takes it, and so never develops all the skills necessary if she is present herself as the one person doing all the work. Even if she is actually doing all the work and Ted is simply good at *appearing* to do it all, he is the one that will get the promotion!

We must learn that we can *show* our strength, *show* what we want to do, *show* that we want to win. It has nothing to do with being masculine or feminine. Jewel Lafontant is a Black woman at the very top of her field. She is senior partner in a major law firm and the director of many corporate and public-service boards:

"I was recently appointed to probe the taxi industry in Chicago. Writers in the media kept asking 'Is she tough enough?' Even after I'd practiced law for thirty-two years in every court in the land! It's the old cliché that a woman can't be tough because she's a softie. I don't like to be considered tough. I'm strong. *Tough often means you're going to do a hatchet job, or you can't compromise or be reasonable. I'm* assertive *and highly* competitive, *but that doesn't mean I'm abrasive or devious or lack tact. Women will be making a big mistake if they try to pattern themselves to follow the so-called manly way of doing business"* (*my emphasis*).

Personal skills that are useful for the working world are encouraged in men from birth and emphasized in their education. A lot of these skills are equated with male behavior, and we shrink from them. One of the most powerful tools of success that a man is "allowed" to use and which we go to great lengths to suppress is *anger*.

ANGER

When threatened, a man feels anger and more often than not expresses it. When threatened, a woman feels anger and represses it. Perhaps, if she is overwhelmed by the injustice, she cries. This particular type of expression, a perfectly legitimate one, is *never* accepted in the business world. Neither men nor other women like it, and no one is prepared to say they understand it. It confuses most people and makes them extremely uncomfortable; it is counterproductive. So women repress their anger *and* their tears. By expressing his anger, a man deals with the threat. A woman has to deal with both the threat and her repressed feelings. Anger can be very healthy from a psychological point of view, and it is simply a very important part of our response vocabulary. Mothers are not afraid to express honest anger at children who repeat what they have been told not to do. If you are late three days running, you might well consider that your boss has a right to be angry with you. But how do we deal with our own anger at work? Here is a typical scenario as described by psychiatrist Dr. Harriet Lerner:

"Jane" worked for an executive in a high-powered law firm. She was one of three women at her level. One of them received a promotion that Jane wanted and felt she deserved. She was convinced that her boss's decision was not based on factors that had to do with the actual quality of their respective work. Jane decided to confront her boss. At first he listened, but after she had made her point he seemed clearly to be irritated and had obviously not listened to her in an open way. He brushed aside the main points she had made and instead started to criticize problems in her work which were quite unrelated to the issue of the promotion. Jane now became inarticulate and helpless. She could not argue or clarify her position. She started to cry and told her boss that she felt very hurt and unappreciated. Her boss stopped being irritated and instead became responsive and sympathetic. He told her the office could not function without her. Jane was relieved by his praise and her tension decreased. She left his office glad that she had not alienated him. A few days later she told Dr. Lerner that she was no longer angry and that the promotion was "no big deal." She even made a case for the advantages of *not* being promoted. But she was visibly depressed.

Dr. Lerner says that one of the factors that stopped Jane from being able to articulate her position was her fear that "a real fight" might ensue which would make her work situation difficult. But according to Dr. Lerner, Jane also had deep unconscious anxieties about fighting that interfered with her capacity to assert herself. This is what Dr. Lerner says:

> *"Why did Jane so dread the thought of fighting with her boss? In part because she feared she might lose control of her anger and destroy everything. Like many women, Jane had irrational unconscious anxieties regarding her own destructiveness and the vulnerability of men. (Women have been taught that they must be nonthreatening helpmates and ego-builders to men, lest men feel castrated and emasculated.) It was as if she feared that the full venting of her outrage might cause the entire office building to go up in flames. Also, like most women, Jane had little practice in expressing her anger in a controlled, effective fashion."*

I have learned that one of the least productive things to do in a work-related problem of confrontation is to gloss over the friction. There are always two issues at hand. One is the situation that exists, and the other is your reaction to it. By effectively expressing your attitude, even if you do not succeed in altering the situation, you will have demonstrated to yourself and others that you have a strong point of view, a capacity for anger, and a willingness to express it. This paves the way for much better relationships in the future. It will also win you *respect*.

Because women are not supposed to get angry, male workers have developed a set of responses that ascribe any outburst by a woman to be caused by her hysterical, female nature. Quite a paradox. If a man shows anger he is being masculine, and that is good. If a woman shows anger she is being feminine, which is bad. In fact, both men and women should express their anger in *controlled* ways. Always plan what you are going to say; try to imagine what the response will be, and know exactly how far you are going to go with an argument and when and *how* you intend to terminate the exchange. This will put you in charge.

Most of my work is done with a small group of senior executives, and they are aware that I am not often angry but when I am, watch out! For some reason my anger surprises the individual when she or he experiences it for the first time. I like to work in an atmosphere that is friendly but professional, and I do not encourage close relationships. Nevertheless there inevitably comes a time when an employee does something deliberately obtuse for the *third time* after having been warned, and I have to speak to the employee firmly but sharply. I get right to the point. I know what I am going to say and how I am going to say it. I plan to have the last word. Depending on the circumstances, I allow enough time for a response, whether it is an apology or argument, since everyone should have a chance to vent their feelings.

I frequently observe that when I have to do this with a new person they are initially much more surprised that I am being angry than they are upset at being criticized. That is the point. A woman is not expected to be angry. A male boss can project a sympathetic countenance ninety per cent of the time, but no one will be shocked if he shows anger when the delivery boy spills coffee over his desk. A female boss can maintain a neutral countenance ninety per cent of the time, but when the shipment arrives in Mexico City instead of Toronto she is expected to graciously excuse the culprit.

Your job can provoke highly charged emotional reactions. Some of these have to be expressed at work or else they will fester inside you, and eventually you will build up a huge negative attitude toward work and success will elude you. Even if it is utterly inappropriate for you to express anger when you are feeling it, you must make some effort to share your feelings with another person at work. Leave your anger at your job, even by sharing it with a sympathetic co-worker. In Chapter 9 I deal with the problems caused by taking it home.

Expressing your emotions, your drives, and your honest-to-goodness desire to succeed is a personal skill. If you show that you want to be a winner instead of hiding your light under a bushel, you stand a much better chance of actually becoming a winner. Articulate your very basic attitudes about where you want to go in your job, first to yourself and then to others. If it is all right for a man to tell his wife that he wants to be senior manager so bad he can taste it, then you go ahead and find a way to express your ambition. You *are* ambitious if you are reading this, but I bet there are people in your home and at your job who do not know that! Your ambition may be one of the things you are repressing.

Develop and use the fourth key, your personal skills, to express your aptitude for success. You must be able to control your *body language*, your *speaking voice*, and your *listening ability* so that you will be perceived as:

> Responsible
> Firm
> Creative
> Outspoken

This marks you as one who *will* succeed. As a woman, trust your *intuition* and learn to approach *problem solving* and *decision making* by considering all the information and especially the *context* of the information. Finally, ignore the taboos that have been used to keep us back and use every opportunity available to show that you are not afraid to advertise the fact that you are:

> Strong
> Competitive
> Assertive

And when you are *angry,* let it out!

When you have a triumph, large or small, blow your own horn. This is what Marilyn Lamarche, vice president of the second largest bank in the country, has to say:

> *"I'd say you have to be assertive, purposeful, and dedicated in business. You have to have a little bit of "street smarts." If I bring in a substantial piece of business, I let people know it."*

✞✞✞✞✞

4

Moving In

"Getting hired is not a question of being the best person for the job but being the best at getting hired."

Naomi Sims

We now come to the final and fifth key: the strategy. This is what will *position* you, put you on the road to success, set the scene for your triumph. What you are going to do is:

Get yourself a new job!

It can be your first, second, or tenth; that does not matter. It might be doing the same thing as you are doing now but at the next desk, or it might be a completely new occupation halfway across the country. One thing is certain: you cannot succeed unless you get *moving*. This brings us right back to the first key: you must know your goal. Here is a checklist that might help. These are the reasons why you are going to make your move:

1. You are about to graduate; you need your first job.

2. You have had it with housework; after a hiatus of some years you want to get *back* to a regular job.

3. In your present position you are overworked and underpaid.

4. You have been passed over for a promotion you deserved.

5. There is no future in your current job.

6. Your work environment is unpleasant.

7. You simply have to have more money.

8. You have just been fired or are about to be fired.

Before you decide on a move *away* from your present job, investigate all aspects of your work situation. Assure yourself that your problems stem from circumstances that you truly cannot control, such as company policy. Exhaust all the possibilities for movement within the organization. If you are underpaid, find out if other places are actually paying more for your job and what qualifying factors are also a consideration—fringe benefits such as location, overtime, environment: will these be equal or superior to your current job? Look at the older women doing the same job as you within your company. Are they paid the same? Will you have only that to look forward to? Are there men earning more than you for the same job?

Have you made a formal request for a raise, promotion, or transfer? Do these first, before you decide to move. You may find that the reason you are stuck in a rut is that you are not making enough noise.

Almost half a million Black women will change their jobs this year. Women who change jobs every two to five years used to be considered frivolous job hoppers, but now it is all part of building a career. Some of these women move out of desperation, necessity, or simply for more money. Others move as part of a well-orchestrated plan to piece together a career record that will make their experience invaluable and ensure that they get a chance at the top jobs.

I know a woman who spent twelve years as the absolute cornerstone of a small manufacturing company in California. I will call her Laura. She enjoyed her work and received a raise every year until she was earning $26,000. She had started as a secretary and felt she was doing well. Everyone in the company, from the owner on down, respected her, and relationships were very convivial within the office. And so they ought to have been since she was the only person who kept things running smoothly. There was not a single job, including that of the owner, which she could not do in a pinch. Whenever someone was sick or there was a crisis, it was always:

"Laura, please help us out, you know how to do this."

Hardly a week went by when she was not told how indispensable she was, and her Christmas bonuses were handsome. One evening she and I had a long talk, and she admitted to me that she was very depressed and felt it had something to do with her job, but she really did not know what was wrong. It took her a long time finally to say that she felt she was being taken advantage of, and she tried to retract the statement as soon as she had said it. The company was *so* good to her, she said, that she had no right to feel ungrateful. But somehow, some-where, she knew she was not getting her due. The fact is: she was get-ting paid very poorly *for what she did*. Because she had started as a secretary and was now called office manager, she thought she had risen a long way; but even though she was respected, in subtle ways she still felt herself to be a glorified secretary, and most of the people she worked with subtly supported this idea. She was running the show but was not *in charge*. In the twelve years she had spent at the job, she had seen herself passed by other women, some Black and some white, who had moved into senior administrative positions with larger companies. She had always told herself that since she had no college degree and was getting a good salary in congenial surroundings, she had *no right* to complain. In other words, Laura was like a house servant always being told he was "one of the family" and being compared favorably to the field slaves. Black women are exploited like this in the job market, just as they have been for generations as domestic workers.

I pointed out to Laura that with no exaggeration she could write a résumé which would knock the spots off that of virtually anyone else in her office. She had never been offered a share in the business, even though there was a profit-sharing plan for the predominantly male sales force, and her magnificent salary did not reflect the "extra" time she put in when there was a seasonal increase in business.

When she told the owner that she was leaving and had found a job as marketing director with a much larger company, he went through the roof. First he accused her of rank disloyalty; then he offered to double her salary. It was too late. Now she works in an atmosphere that is less chummy, but she walks proud; and no one, but no one, asks her to fetch a cup of coffee!

So you can see it is not always a cut-and-dried reason that spurs us on to get a new job. And as we shall see later on, it is sometimes stra-tegically very clever to move down in order to move up.

CHOOSING THE JOB

Never let the job choose you. Even if you have a skill that can be applied to a variety of fields (if you are a computer programmer, you could work at the Library of Congress or for an agricultural combine), make sure that you do not simply drift where the wind blows or where the offer is highest.

With an economy that fluctuates as much as ours, job opportu-nities shift from year to year. Whole industries can rise and fall in a couple of years. Specific sections of the country experience a boom and jobs there go begging, while in other parts of the United States there are two hundred applicants for a single vacancy. As a double minority member, your career positioning can be strongly affected by government policies on a federal, state and local level. A change of administration at any one of those levels can signal a drastic increase or reduction in positions for which you are eligible.

It may be a blessing in disguise that computers and word-processing machines are gradually making low-level administrative positions obsolete because in the next ten years approximately sixteen million jobs will be created, one-fifth as many as there are now, and half of them will be so-called white-collar jobs. Almost all the new jobs require skills that are more specialized than related jobs at the present time. For instance, the overall number of secretarial positions will decline, but the need for legal and medical secretaries will increase.

Because the birth rate is declining, the need for teachers at all levels, college included, will be reduced, but occupations related to work itself (labor relations, personnel, and social work) will increase. Administrators will be needed in banking and health but not in school systems. One area that is already booming is the trades. Computer and machine repair, as well as construction work including carpentry and electrical engineering, are areas that expand annually. Black women are completely underrepresented in these fields, which have long been controlled by unions that were bastions of white male supremacy. Legislation in the seventies opened the door for us a crack, and these occupations now represent a very realistic way to move many of us out of the clerical and secretarial doldrums and into secure jobs at twice the salary.

Parts of the country that will have a lot of jobs in the next ten years are not those parts where most of us live: Alaska, Wyoming, Nevada, and Utah. The Sun Belt is growing very fast, but it has a very low Black population; New York, California, Illinois, and Pennsylvania are not going to increase job opportunities by more than three per cent.

Whether you are at the start of your work life or midway through it, you have to decide if you want to add to your skill in order to progress in a field that offers the most scope. Black women with only a high school education or even a liberal arts degree will find themselves shut out of the job picture that is going to emerge in the final quarter of this century. In Chapter 6 I concentrate on labor-related blue-collar jobs that can offer very substantial opportunities for the Black woman who is lacking academic qualifications.

When it comes to assessing the job market in terms of your particular needs, bear in mind that many areas are developing that will be ripe for entry if you have *combined* skills. This does not mean that you have to have two master's degrees, but the trend of the future in *all* categories is *technical,* and a Black woman with, for example, five years experience in retail sales who also has accounting or bookkeeping skills is much more than doubling her job prospects. We are overrepresented in all the customary "women's" occupations, the ones that opened up for us because they were an extension of the nurturing and creative facilities that we were assumed to have as a birthright. This means that many of us are heading toward a declining number of openings in humanitarian fields such as education and the arts. It is very important to steer yourself toward areas for which you have a natural aptitude and above all else to pick a job that you can *like,* but most of us are incapable of thinking along any but the most prosaic lines when it comes to job categories.

In order to help you visualize alternate possibilities, I have compiled a listing of job categories that offer the greatest opportunities for Black women (see the Appendix). This means that if you are qualified *entry* is easy because there is a need, and *promotion* is likely because either the field is new or it actively encourages minority participation. Above all, hard-core qualifications are worth attaining, even if it means two or three very lean years at college, business, or technical school, or in a training program. We cannot and must not rely on affirmative action to present us with golden opportunities if we barely qualify. We must ride the crest of a dramatic shift in political priorities if we are not to be left behind to languish in all the low-grade teaching and administrative jobs that we presently hold.

A world of rapidly diminishing natural resources that is experiencing a technological revolution will provide jobs that we can barely begin to imagine, but only to those who have the technical skills. New job categories offer Black women the possibility of rising in systems that are so new they have no traditional orientations and are not dominated by the mores of the white male.

In an effort to halt and reverse the economic decline that categorized the 1970s, all levels of government are reassessing programs that do not have a sound financial footing:

> *"The Reagan Administration would permit planned increases in support for basic research in the so-called hard sciences, such as physics and chemistry, but would sharply curtail support for programs in the behavioral and other "soft" sciences, according to proposed budget revisions circulating in Congress. The proposals would also eliminate federal programs meant to widen the access of women and minority-group members to careers in science and would heavily cut other programs in science education."*

> *New York* Times, *Feb. 9, 1981*

Whether or not I agree that such measures are appropriate from either an economic or human-welfare perspective, we cannot simply wait until Election Day to show our disapproval. Although some government action (or inaction) is undeniably based on the desire of the ruling white male elite to return the country to the status it and they enjoyed before we raised our voices and fists in the 1960s, I also believe that we have to face the fact that tomorrow's world of jobs for the Black woman is going to be one in which her specific proficiencies will be the determining factors, not her color or sex.

I have compiled the following career survey based on the current climate for job opportunities in various professional fields. It is by no means exhaustive, but it should serve to stimulate your imagination. Look beyond the old stereotypes and prepare yourself to be one step ahead of the thundering herd. Because we continue, especially as consumers, to apply pressure on private industry to hire minority workers, bear in mind that special educational programs are available in many instances. Avon Corporation is just one that has a training program for Black women with college degrees but no business background who want to enter management.

Job Categories

1. Medicine

Who wants to be a doctor? They earn a fortune, right? And think of the prestige! But what kind of doctor? I know of no Black female surgeons, but we are making substantial inroads in family practice, pediatrics, and psychiatry, areas that the white male medical establishment finds less easy to control than, for instance, anesthesiology. A qualified Black doctor still has greater opportunities *outside* the hospital system. As a Black woman you can choose your psychiatrist, family doctor, or pediatrician. If there is one available, choose another Black woman. If you have an operation, however, more than likely the personnel involved will all be white males because, after all, you had no choice. I would single out obstetrics and gynecology as the most promising specialties for the would-be Black female physician. They command average net incomes thirty-five per cent greater than psychiatry, second only to surgery in the gamut of specializations. If you are really interested in earning, study to be an ophthalmologist, who can bill $1,000 for a fifteen-minute cataract operation!

But you do not have to think of medicine solely in terms of doctor and nurse. Between the two there is a panoply of emergent fields, and these are the ones to watch:

A. Medical Technician

Electronics has entered medicine in a very substantial way. Life-saving and life-preserving techniques are increasingly based on the use of complex equipment that requires skilled operators. Ten years ago most patient care systems that were not directly handled by a physician could be operated by the nursing staff. That is not true today. Kidney dialysis, radiation therapy, and a host of now-standard procedures incorporate electronics, and one of the reasons that the cost of such procedures is high is that the hardware requires operation and maintenance by qualified technicians who earn substantial salaries.

B. Medical Administrator

Hospitals are Big Business. They require almost every type of management employee that a large corporation does. If you have a standard office skill, think of obtaining experience or training in hospital management so that your basic skill becomes a specialty. This is a very wide field, from the supervision of computerized billing systems to handling patient admissions. If you are an R.N. seeking new worlds to conquer, I recommend taking a master's degree in public health. That is what Florence Gaynor did, and she has held top management positions with major New York and New Jersey hospitals and is now director of the Hubbard Hospital of the Meharry Medical Center and College in Nashville, Tennessee:

> "You're doing a management job that compares with any in private industry. You work with professionals and nonprofessionals. You oversee programs that involve contracts with government and private industry. It's power; it's exhilarating and exciting!"

Before we leave medicine, I would like to mention that this whole field is growing at a tremendous rate and that there are expanding job opportunities in all the traditional nursing areas, but your salary expectations increase dramatically if you add a basic skill such as radiology, midwifery, or electrocardiogram techniques to your nursing qualifications. Trained therapists are needed in mental health care, and specializations like optometry and dentistry require similarly specialized assistants. College degrees are available in lucrative fields related to medicine, such as nutrition and chiropractic.

2. Law

Like medicine, a former bastion of white males, the arena of law has accepted Black women into its lower ranks, and the danger is that we continue to think only in terms of those types of legal practice that admit us the most readily.

The media pay a lot of attention to Black judges, and I am proud that many of us are now in a position to interpret the laws of the land from the bench of justice. Justice Alice A. Bonner heads the judicial council of the National Bar Association (Annette R. Hubbard, another Black woman, is president), and I recently saw my close friend Peggy Davis become one of the youngest Family Court judges in New York state.

However, most lawyers in this country seldom see the inside of a courtroom. Not only is the practice of law a stepping-stone to political office, but it is a tremendous asset to have a law degree when entering corporate management. Most large corporations require a full-time legal staff, and hundreds of thousands of small businesses and individuals depend on tax-specialist lawyers to help them deal with the IRS. There are specializations within specializations. Pension law, for example, covers all the bureaucratic territory that exists between labor unions, major corporations, and the federal government, yet it is just one of a hundred such opportunities for the lawyer of the future.

It is very important that every defendant be represented by a lawyer, whether a lawyer can be afforded or not; but all too often talented female Black lawyers find themselves overworked and underpaid in public defenders' offices across the country. It is a noble and desperately needed job, but it does not lead very far unless you have aspirations to become a district attorney. Large law firms have excluded women from partnerships and concentrated them at the bottom of the ladder, dealing with relatively unimportant research rather than allowing them to counsel major corporate clients. There are exceptions to this, but for the time being there are better routes to the top than joining a private law firm unless it is new and relatively unorthodox, such as those that have sprung up in states that allow lawyers to advertise. Once lawyers have to compete for clients, Black women will be needed by firms that orient themselves toward the public. There is a very large new firm in New York that advertises heavily on television and has branches in department stores. This is a far cry from the hushed corridors and wood-panelled libraries of Wall Street law firms, but it is here that a young Black woman will get a chance to handle *human interest* law, not just as a defender, and be able to carve out one area as a specialty. Be a lawyer *plus*. Plus a tax specialist, plus a real estate specialist, plus a management expert. This may sound like overkill, but if you have a law degree *and* a degree in business administration, you will not have to knock on doors. You may think that you will never really "use" your expensive legal education behind a desk in senior management, but it will always be a major factor in your rise to a position of power.

If you have a four-year college degree, there are over two hundred *paralegal* training programs in existence that you can enter. Within two to six months you can qualify to research and prepare legal documents for private law firms. A typical salary for this is $15,000. With the addition of managerial skills, you can become a *legal administrator*. This is not a lawyer but a person who is the office manager for a law firm. Salaries here can go as high as $45,000.

Everything associated with the legal profession requires extra training, but the pay reflects that: a legal secretary can earn twice as much as her counterpart in nonlegal work.

3. Finance

Ours is a mercenary society: money is power. As individuals and in their private lives, women handle as much money as men, and women *own* as much money as men. When it comes to managing money, however, up until recently women have been mere counters, human calculators keeping the books. But with more and more women in the regular work force, we have been able to demand better positions for women within the structures of the systems that handle our earnings. Now two per cent of all bank officers and managers are Black women. Obviously there is a great deal of room for growth, but it is a significant figure because outside of Black-owned banks there was no such thing as a Black woman in middle-management banking ten years ago. Over twenty per cent of the banking work force is comprised of other than white males, but most of this percentage are white women and Black men. In the financial world there are three basic divisions, and we will take a look at each. Skills and experience in one are easily transferred to another:

A. Accounting

This is a standard profession that requires an advanced degree. Once you are qualified, you can choose to be affiliated with a large organization or can practice on your own and have a flexible schedule. There are virtually no organizations that do not employ accountants, from museums and prisons to conglomerates and churches. An accountant who specializes in taxes works very hard from December through May, and quite a number of Black women who are accountants do not want to be tied to a nine-to-five schedule; they *only* work these months, but twelve hours a day, seven days a week! Because accounting is so identified with taxes, you may not be aware of other specializations such as legal auditing, payroll accounting, real estate, investment, and general management. Like having a law degree, if you are a CPA (Certified Public Accountant), you will find yourself sought after if you desire to enter management positions that do not specifically require (or even utilize) accounting skills, simply because the degree identifies you as someone familiar with money and how it works.

B. Banking

Banks are anxious to recruit Black women, especially those who evidence a desire to complete the necessary requirements for senior positions. The prospect of working in banking is so intimidating to many women that the field is open to someone who is prepared to acquire qualifications. Most women in banking today do not have college degrees and remain as clerks and tellers despite the fact that many banks have programs for their employees that involve on-the-job courses for advancement and college tuition refunds. Banking is reliable and relatively free from prejudice, at the local level. If you are prepared to get a degree in accounting or business administration but do not want to fight tooth and nail to make your way up the corporate ladder, banking may provide a secure haven with a decent salary and regular promotions.

C. Investment

Stockbrokers buy and sell securities for individuals, groups of investors, companies, and public institutions. The best way to become a registered broker is to train with a large brokerage firm. Most firms like to take on trainees who have a degree in business, economics, finance, accounting, or sales. Black women are a rarity in this field. A brokerage house will only take *you* as a trainee if you more than fulfill their requirements, even though they will hire a client's nephew who never finished college!

The investment world is the opposite of banking in the sense that it is performance-oriented. The amount you earn is directly related to your energy and ability, not the simple process of turning up on time and putting in a good day's work. Most brokers work primarily on commission, which means that the sky is the limit. Personality is a strong factor in success because you are asking your customers to let you take risks with their money, and you have to be knowledgeable *and* convincing.

There are plenty of jobs in brokerage other than sales, however, and stock analysis and office management are just two. Experience with a particular industry or commodity (automobile manufacturing, for instance, or breakfast cereals (*combined with* an accounting or business degree can qualify you for very high earnings as a market analyst.

Because the financial community is viewed as conservative, many Black women avoid giving it serious consideration when it comes to choosing a profession. In fact, I see it as a job category that requires creative thinking, an ability to make judgments about individuals, and a well-developed sense of organization. We excel at all these things; all we need are the college courses. And the work is far from dull! Money has a fascination all its own, and it is about time we started to assume responsibility for it at all levels.

4. Science

Female scientists used to have nowhere to go except back to school, teaching, or research. If you are fascinated by scientific thought and method and want a promising career, specialize in an area that has tangible applications, that is more than just the accumulation of knowledge. These are lean years for pure research. There are plenty of fields that are not only recession-proof but underpopulated. Paramount among these are those that try to provide some of the answers to the environmental and ecological problems facing the world. The frantic search for alternative food and energy resources is creating a great demand for fully qualified environmental scientists such as oceanographers, geologists, geophysicists, and toxicologists. Life scientists (biologists, botanists, zoologists) are also at a premium. Physicists and chemists are not quite as sought after, although the field of biochemistry is booming.

Although we tend to think of scientists as working for private research foundations or colleges, the place where Black women have a chance to surpass themselves is in private industry. Most of what we consume is dependent upon the life scientist in one way or another. Food, pharmaceuticals, and cosmetics alone account for over half of every consumer dollar spent, and those industries employ many scientists. What could be more basic than agronomy and forestry? All forms of energy production and conservation are founded on decisions that can only be made by trained scientists. Medical research is dependent upon scientific analysis, and government spending is highest for projects that are science-based. Science does not hold all the answers to the problems facing our world, but it is more likely to be the scientist than the soldier, politician, poet, or philosopher who discovers the principles for making daily life more durable.

But it takes a lot of learning! A bachelor's degree in physics or chemistry will just about get you a low-paying technician's job at best. A Ph.D. is mandatory for advancement in practically all fields, and it is very important to target your specialty as early as possible. At the doctoral level, the inequity between the sexes in terms of salaries and job opportunities begins to level off.

5. Engineering

This is one of the few careers that offers a higher starting salary to women than to men! Because there are only 25,000 women out of 1,250,000 engineers, affirmative action laws have hit the industry very hard, and all the employers that do business with the government are anxious to increase their roster of female engineers. It is probably the only discipline in which graduating women students can pick and choose from among competing job offers even before they get their diplomas. The largest employers of engineers are the energy industry and the federal government. The following engineering specialties will be trying to double their numbers over the next five years:

Agricultural Engineering

Biomedical Engineering

Ceramic Engineering

Electrical Engineering

Electronic Engineering

Industrial Engineering

Mechanical Engineering

Metallurgical Engineering

Mining Engineering

Petrochemical Engineering

A scientist can be described as a trained person who discovers the nature of things and an engineer as the one who applies that discovery to a productive mechanism. The engineer uses a combination of hard data and past experience to solve particular problems. An engineer has to be concerned with regulations, productivity, and new systems. Engineers design transportation systems, agricultural complexes, computers, mining operations, and artificial organs, to name just a few. It is undoubtedly one of the most personally rewarding and financially lucrative careers for a Black woman. In private industry an engineer has to be prepared to pick up and travel at a moment's notice because engineers deal with observable phenomena around the world.

6. Sales

Three out of five salespeople in this country are female, and growing numbers are also Black. Despite the fact that this might lead to the conclusion that the job category is glutted, I make a strong distinction between *retail sales,* where we are an overrepresented part of the work force and *commissionable sales* where we are underrepresented. The difference between the two categories is very great—the difference between being a glorified cash register and virtually owning your own business. The ability to make a sale is a very valuable asset, and if you possess it do not waste it by working as a salaried employee in a retail store. Think of the goods and services that you could be selling which would bring in a great deal more money as well as prestige. I will mention just a few of the more obvious:

> Automobiles
>
> Insurance
>
> Real Estate
>
> Travel

There are virtually no Black women selling cars, yet a lot of Black women are buying them. In real estate, insurance, and travel, you can either work as part of a large organization that provides you with both the prospective clients and the goods to sell or you can strike out on your own, part-time or full-time, as an independent agent representing a particular line of goods and services.

Unlike most of the other careers I have so far mentioned, the sales field does not place so much importance on academic qualifications; the emphasis is rather on performance. Some types of selling require a license which can be obtained by taking the requisite courses and a state examination.

The best salesperson is one who cannot be restrained—she just has to sell. This is not for the shy or easily intimidated. You have to be able to get along with a cross-section of the population and know exactly when *not* to take no for an answer.

Manufacturers' representatives sell products to other businesses, and wholesale trade representatives sell goods to retail stores. Some but not all selling involves travel. Selling is not just a question of being persuasive but of knowing your product and its market *inside out.* In real estate you have to help clients get financing; in insurance you often function as an investment counselor; as a wholesale trade representative you will be up against cutthroat competition.

If you are sufficiently adept in sales, the sky is the limit when it comes to compensation. Some firms combine a base salary with a commission scale, and others simply rely on commissions. Do not go into sales without some basic skills in bookkeeping, at least enough to be able to compare your effort to the return.

One great advantage in selling is that your merits are immediately made known to your superiors and are rewarded accordingly.

7. Management

How would you like to earn $125,000 a year? That is what Ruth B. Love is paid as Chicago's first Black general superintendent of schools. She will earn every penny as she tries to balance the loudly proclaimed demands of students, teachers, parents, the city council, and the school board.

"I'm not looking for a rose garden, and I'm sure I won't find one," she said upon accepting her appointment.

If you want to get near that dizzying salary level and are also prepared to do without rose gardens, consider management. It is an essential part of business, industry, education, and government. Managers are administrators who formulate and develop policy and programs, co-ordinate their execution, and supervise employees. Essential qualifications for top management positions include decision-making and planning skills and an ability to interact and work well with people.

The best qualification for a career in management is a master's degree in business administration (an M.B.A.). If you want to conquer the executive suite, you had better have that degree! If not, at least a solid background and college credits in accounting, data processing, public administration, economics, or finance. There are plenty of entry-level jobs in management for Black women with just a bachelor's degree, but no matter how exceptional your performance you will stay close to entry level if you do not have a postgraduate degree. Many women quit these positions just to be able to go back to school to obtain the requisite qualifications for promotion.

The most prestigious and financially rewarding management jobs are with large corporations. It is important for corporations to have highly visible Black women in middle management, but this tokenism does not mean that without the credentials you can penetrate to the board room and make a strong contribution to corporate policy and planning. General Brick & Mortar Corporation once promoted Martha Jones to the position of vice president for corporate public relations from that of executive secretary to the C.E.O. Thus she had an impressive title but a fairly meaningless job, and she was nowhere near the power structure. Now the same company wants to recruit Sharon Smith, who has an M.B.A. from Stanford and five years experience with General Wood & Metal, as its regional marketing director. They will make her vice president of marketing, a profit-line job that brings her right into the nexus of power.

According to the U. S. Bureau of Labor Statistics, these are the types of administrative fields that will provide the most job opportunities for qualified Black female management executives:

Accounting
Data Processing
Engineering
Marketing
Personnel
Public Administration
Public Relations

This means that companies dealing with these areas need management experts to keep things running smoothly. For instance, if you have an M.B.A. and accounting experience, you would be wasted simply working as an accountant. Your management qualifications suggest that you should be in charge of the accounting division of a major company.

One of the most pervasive myths about American business is that anyone can work their way up from the bottom if they just have "the right stuff." If this has ever been true, it was long ago when even the largest corporation was basically an extended family business and required a limited number of skills: manufacturing and selling. Nowadays business is so complex that it is ridiculous to imagine that a person can start in the delivery room and with no formal training work their way through clerical, data processing, production engineering, research, marketing, management, and corporate planning to the office of C.E.O.

Jobs are more specialized today than ever before, and they will continue to move in that direction. Executives can move within their spheres from one company to another, even though the goods or services of the companies may be vastly different. How can a senior executive for a home appliance company go to work for a liquor company? Simply because her particular skills are in the area of financial management and have nothing to do with product design or manufacture.

In order to make yourself eligible for this kind of lateral movement, start off with qualifications geared to a *type* of executive ability that is required by the majority of employers. Of course, product familiarity is an important part of any job, but being able to make people productive and to create winning situations is a managerial skill highly prized by every major corporation.

Today's multinational corporations and conglomerates often incorporate widely diversified empires: publishing, textiles, travel, and manufacturing, for example. Your expertise in any given area will be secondary to your ability to make comparative cost analyses in all of them if you expect to sit on the board that runs the operations of all the entities.

There is another kind of management which is more directly related to the traditional meaning of the word. The province of *service* management offers substantial opportunities for far lower academic qualifications. In this category I include hotel and restaurant management, theater management and apartment-house management. For years Black women occupied the very lowest jobs in these organizations, but with increased domestic tourism, business travel, and condominium living there is a great need for people who can be responsible for the day-to-day running of an individual structure that caters to the public.

Each industry provides courses and even college programs in specific skills.

8. Communications

Apart from the so-called glamor jobs (newscaster, actress, etc.), which really have very few entry-level openings for Black women, the communications industry is undergoing a quiet technological revolution that will result in a whole new series of job categories. I am talking about cable television.

Network television, like print journalism, is dominated by a system that richly rewards the owners and executive officers of the various local and national companies, partially because many production level employees are underpaid and even on-camera news correspondents are treated like hirelings, to be disposed of as soon as their popularity fades.

News gatherers, news finders, and news writers are, like many performers, involved in vocations as much as in careers. What we will consider in this section is the role of the intermediary in the process of bringing the information and entertainment to the public. At the moment it is by and large a very cumbersome business. Even the most modest program on television requires designers, production assistants, directors, producers, and writers, as well as a promotion and advertising staff and general management. Local stations are just as conscious of hierarchy as giant networks.

As a Black woman your best bet is a management position if you have an M.B.A. and some experience in journalism. If you have some acting experience and are generally deemed to be good looking, you might get on-camera as a correspondent, but only if you have a degree in journalism and if the station's demographics decide that the regional audience would respond to "a Black woman."

For my money you are better off breaking into the ground floor of what is sometimes called "Pay-TV." Cable television franchises are springing up all over the country and promise to become not an alternative television system, but an entirely new kind of communication wavelength.

For instance, at the moment most cable TV stations program movies, sports events, and general interest shows like stock market reports. What cable television *can* and ultimately *will* do is provide a *two-way* communications resource linking students with teachers; retailers with customers (for actual *sales,* not just advertising); and local government with voters. The possibilities are endless because cable television incorporates the capacity for the viewer to *respond* to a message and for that response to be processed. This makes it much more than a mere tool for dispensing news and entertainment. It will become an indispensable adjunct to the traditional fields of education, retail sales, and the political process. In the near future, opinion polls on specific public issues will be taken swiftly and concisely via the cable system.

All this means that at every level there will be a need for individuals who are familiar with cable television technology and who also have specialized experience in various spheres such as teaching. The system can handle over a hundred channels, and already local programming reflects local concerns: for example, English lessons in Spanish neighborhoods or crop price quotations for rural communities. To a large extent this means that programming is being returned to the people, not ruled autocratically from the thrones of network chiefs in Los Angeles and New York.

From public service stations run by City Hall to complex technical programs emanating from local universities there will be an amazing proliferation of small sources. Each source will require a programmer who is imaginative and technically skilled. Many roles will be assumed by one person who will be a producer-director-editor that runs an entire local channel almost singlehandedly, with the help of computer technology.

Because this is a video revolution in its infancy, there is no entrenched establishment to mitigate against the ascendency of Black women. Because of its community potential, this type of communications system will demand our participation in those areas of dense Black population. At the moment entry-level spots require little prior experience and rely on on-the-job training. A degree in communications will help you move faster, however.

Nancy Wood, a communications graduate of Philadelphia's Temple University, first tried to get a job in traditional broadcasting. She felt that many prospective employers perceived her as "window dressing," and she was probably right. Instead, she accepted the relatively minor position of traffic co-ordinator for a New York City cable system. She felt that cable television was going to be the communications medium of the future, and this position would get her in on the ground floor. Her duties gave her much insight into the industry with responsibilities running the gamut from shipping tapes, to insuring the smooth operation of twenty-six channels. Just two years later Nancy is programming manager. She supervises the twenty-six-channel system, produces the company's program guide, and selects and buys movies for the company's pay-movie service.

In addition to programming, cable television offers many sales positions, selling whole franchises to particular communities and selling the service in the community to individual customers. With commissions it is possible to earn as much as $40,000 annually in a metropolitan area. All down the line this system can provide us with good jobs in engineering, installation, and maintenance, as well as general management.

Other communications fields that show promise for Black female enrollment are advertising and public relations. These require the ability to sell concepts as well as products. There are minority student fellowships available in the advertising industry, but you should also be prepared to have a degree in journalism and a background in English and creative writing. We can be encouraged by a burgeoning Black press, but permanent staff positions on newspapers and magazines do not pay well and competition is fierce. To get experience, if you have the academic qualifications, head for a copywriting job with an advertising agency that wants to direct its clients' products to the Black consumer. We represent a very strong economic force, taken as a major group within the consumer profile of the entire country, and your knowledge of demographics and our response to media, coupled with a background in creative writing, could make you into a very desirable asset for an advertising agency.

SUMMARY

I have touched on some of the avenues that you can explore, and I have concentrated as much on job types as on specific industries. If you take an area like insurance, for example, you will find that there is a need for almost every position I have mentioned. Insurance requires people with medical knowledge and legal training; it is based on sound financial principles, and it involves the investment of large sums of money; it covers real estate and manufacturing, and its services are widely advertised and promoted in the media. If you are a qualified accountant or administrator, you will find insurance is a viable place for your skills; and of course the very essence of the insurance business is selling, either to individuals or organizations.

By now you are probably tired of my emphasizing the need for a winning combination of skills, but it is something I cannot say too often. We are educating ourselves in the arts and humanities, and as you can tell from my survey most of the good jobs for us are going to require technical training.

One of the fallacies of modern life is that women are not skilled in matters mechanical, mathematical, and analytical, whereas men are supposed to be born with natural abilities in these areas. So many of us believe ourselves to be helpless when it comes to calculations or peering under the hood of a car, as if God gave us brains for every contingency except rational thought. The fact is that biologically we have a reasoning capacity which is exactly the same as that of the male of the species, but we have been conditioned for so long that many of us are convinced we cannot understand technical matters—and that conviction translates into an actual inability. We are not encouraged at school in the same way that boys are; we are not *expected* to excel in science and mathematics as if, like football, they were disciplines designed exclusively for the male physique!

It is not going to be easy for many of us to revise our thinking and face the fact that with the right kind of training we are all able to comprehend basic technological systems. The psychological conditioning in all aspects of society is very forceful to this day, and the exceptions are used to prove the rule. There are some, but very few, Black women who are top mathematicians, scientists, or engineers.

This does not mean we are by and large incapable of becoming superior technicians, research scientists, engineers, and financial experts. It simply means that we have been kept out of those disciplines by tradition which custom has turned into a natural law that serves as an excuse for the lack of opportunity and for nonencouragement. Now that affirmative action programs are urging the employment of Black women in many of these technical fields, the age-old precepts of what women are and are not "good at" have backfired, and there are not enough qualified Black women for the available jobs.

I say run, do not walk, to your nearest learning resource—whether it is a regular college program, an adult extension course, or a training school—and take a basic course in accounting skills, just to convince yourself that there is no truth to the lie that we are not cut out for such skills. Only fear will keep us back. We have been told for centuries that we are illogical creatures unable to add two and two. Most of us have had to work miracles providing for an entire family with limited resources, but that sort of financial planning is not supposed to count. But we can count, and build computers, and analyze the earth's surface. You will be surprised just how simple some of these technical operations really are. And believe me, once we have mastered the basic math, there can be no stopping us!

In fact, Velda Jones, the first Black woman to receive a B.S. degree from the College of Engineering at the University of Delaware says:

"The most difficult obstacle for me was that out of 19,000 students there, approximately three per cent were Black. There were no Black women in any of my classes and no one to identify with."

She is now a civil engineer with ICI in Wilmington and plans to get her M.B.A. degree through an evening program. That is the way to go!

That more learning leads to more earning is a truism we have all been subjected to, but it has never been so true as now. You can be an excellent, experienced, and dedicated worker, and quite capable of scaling the heights *if you only had a chance.* A degree or a diploma will give you that chance. You have a perfect right to ask why you need to study trigonometry in order to make your living as an agricultural economist, and I am not saying that there is always a great deal of rhyme or reason to the system, but the importance of the experience is that you demonstrate your ability to learn, to organize your study, work, and leisure-time habits, and to interact with your peers in an atmosphere that is both competitive and group-supportive.

The first day you arrive for work, your M.B.A. degree tucked under your arm, your boss is quite likely to say:

"First of all, forget everything they taught you at college, Miss Jupiter; we do things differently here; this is the real *world."*

That does not mean your credentials are not impressive. Over and over Black women of every age tell me:

"After fifteen years I'm going back to school."
"I've decided to stay in college after all."
"I just wish I hadn't dropped out."

With a degree, you have freedom. You can enter the system or work outside it, take a regulated job or strike out on your own. If you have no degree, you will be forced to work ten times as hard as the next woman just to get noticed! On top of that, thousands of doors will be closed to you, to jobs for which you may be very well suited. It is not simply that with the right academic qualifications higher-paying jobs are available; it is that the range of available jobs is much wider, and you can better suit your personal interests. With an M.B.A., for instance, you might go through college determined to get that degree because you see yourself as manipulating takeovers for an international conglomerate. When you find out that international conglomerates are not hiring, you still have numerous possibilities and after a couple of moves may find yourself in the "perfect" job for you—as general administrator of a metropolitan hospital.

Try not to limit yourself by presenting limited credits. A liberal arts degree is simply not enough. That and a teaching diploma will get you to the bottom of the poorest-paying glutted profession in the country. It may be an unfair situation but it exists, and with a decline in the population rate teachers are going to be laid off left and right for another decade. Go for the *skill*-oriented degrees and the practical and technical courses. Ninety per cent of all top-paying jobs require this kind of education. So, if you are . . .

In College

Stay there. Get a master's degree. Pick a specific company you want to work for and apply to them for funding. Engage in as much extracurricular activity as possible that might relate to your future job. Even if not for credit, take a course in business administration or accounting, no matter what your major is, and spend some time absorbing the *basics* of computer technology.

Start thinking about your job *at least a year* before you plan to leave school. Gather all the information you can about the field; do not rely on the printed word; spend time with someone directly involved with the kind of job you want. Apply early.

Out of College

For one month or twenty years, think of going back. It may not take much to move you up to a much better sphere of influence. Remember that many colleges have a system of giving credits for what some call "life experience." If you have organizational aptitude but lack a skill, see if you can take night courses. Even your own company may be willing to help out if you show enthusiasm for self-improvement. They may be able to give you the time or lend you the money.

ATTITUDE

Never be afraid to indulge your wildest dreams when imagining yourself in another job or much higher on your current pay scale. But once you have pinpointed your goal, find out *exactly* how distant it is. Let us say you are a bank teller and you want to go into public relations. Ask yourself: Does this bank have a public relations department or use an outside firm? What do I need to apply? What skills do I need? Should I take an extension course in creative writing? With my banking experience, should I start in the accounting department of a large public relations company or try to go through the front door? Dream your dreams, but back your speculations by getting the hard facts. You may find this easier than you think.

Never take it for granted that the job you *read* about (even in this book!) will actually be that way when you reach it. The grass is always greener on the other side. Talk to someone in the job to which you aspire. If you want to be a department store buyer, a librarian, or an oceanographer, track one down and try to find out what they do, day by day. There is nothing like witnessing the work experience. It may make you realize that you are actually better off where you are or may inspire you to take that big risk, to go back to school and get the extra credits you need.

One final word before we move on to see just how to land the job. Once you have picked the job, take the time to put it in perspective in terms of the overall economy. Is it vulnerable to recession? Does it depend on basic need or is it tied to increased spending? Can it be terminated by action of a government agency, directly or indirectly? In other words: is it secure? There is no point in going back to school to study architecture when one third of all newly trained architects are being laid off. Also look at your chosen job in terms of its potential for advancement. Is this based on merit, on productivity, or is it merely related to the length of time on the job?

Have you covered all the fringe benefits? Is there a health plan? Will you have to spend more for clothes? For transportation? In some cases a new job with a higher salary means that you have to spend more money on the social aspects of the job. How will your new job affect your taxes? Can you deduct more or less than before? When you have calculated all the pros and cons, you can construct your target.

Your bull's-eye may change, but until you have exhausted all the possible employers the rest of the board stays the same. Then change your target, based on what you have learned in the hunt.

Once you have your goal, you can construct your target; you have completed all the credits; your personal skills are at a peak; now all you have to do is find the actual work, and your strategy will be complete!

FINDING A (NEW) JOB

The employment industry in this country is very large. Consider that there are 12,500 employment agencies alone. Add to that the millions of dollars a year spent on print advertising ("Situations Vacant")

THE TARGET

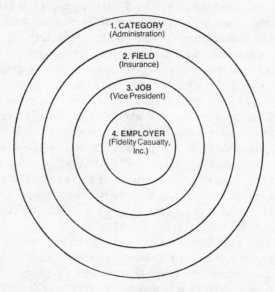

and the fact that there are two professions singularly devoted to job placement: career counseling and executive recruitment. Executive recruiters are often referred to as "headhunters."

It should follow then, as night follows day, that your obvious course is to contact all the agencies you can, send out your résumé, make an appointment with a career counselor, sit back, and wait. Right?

Once again, wrong! Despite the size of the industry, the employment industry is founded more on hope than necessity. According to the Federal Trade Commission, employment agencies have a success rate that is lower than five per cent! College placement services help fewer than twenty-five per cent of students find their first job, and the same is true of jobs found in the Want Ads. Consider this: four out of five job vacancies are known only to the employer who fills them by *word of mouth.*

Before this makes you completely and utterly discouraged, you have to understand that instead of reducing your chances it actually increases them dramatically. It means that there are at least four times as many jobs going "begging" than you could possibly learn about through conventional channels. How do you find them?

Personal Contact

It is "who" you know, not "what" you know! In fact, it is both that are important, but for now let us concentrate on the "who." We tend to think only in terms of close friends and even may be reluctant to "use" them. A fatal flaw. If you are lucky enough to have a close friend capable of directing you to the right job or even of introducing you to the right person, then you are not worth your salt unless you come directly to the point and ask them to help you.

Next, go through your address book with a fine-toothed comb and concentrate on all the people you have not seen for a while. It is worth a call just to find out what some of them are up to, especially if you suspect they might be in a position to help. Do not beat about the bush:

> *"I'm looking for a job" or*
> *"I want to change my job"*

The direct approach is always the best; you are not using someone if you state your purpose very clearly. Do not let any area of your life escape scrutiny: neighbors, your children's friends' parents, alumnae, high school friends, and (best of all) friends of friends:

> *"Don't you know Mary Carlisle, who works at Crumpet & Woof? Can you put me in touch with her? I'm looking for a new job . . ."*

We have a quaint tendency to think that this is not as professional as going the route of the agency or using "official" job-hunting methods. Take it from me, an employer, *how* you reach the right company is not the slightest bit of interest to them if you are the right person for the job. When you finally end up across the desk from your would-be employer and she says:

> *"How did you find out about us?"*

it is much more impressive to say:

> *"Mary Carlisle, in your sales department, told me that you were looking for the right person."*

which implies that you are not out of work, not forced to change your job, which would be the case if you had to respond:

> *"I was sent by the E-Z Jobs Employment Agency."*

Most of us start the job hunt by making one enormous mistake: we only look for a job where there is a vacancy. This sounds reasonable, but consider this: employers may not know they have a vacancy until they meet the person (you) who would substantially help them. In the majority of cases when employers hire someone, they are looking to sustain or increase productivity and profits. They measure the salary you will be getting against how much you can save or earn for them. The favorable impression you make can convince an employer to *make room* for you, to move someone else up (or out!), because you would be a better person in that job. Until you walked into the office, the employer did not know you were needed.

By *only* job-hunting through regular channels, you decrease your possibilities fivefold and establish yourself as a passive ("help me") rather than an active ("own steam") Black woman. By limiting yourself to people and organizations who make their living by putting jobs and people together, you are likely to spend only a few hours a day actually trying to get a job. You visit one or two agencies a day, leave your résumé, read the paper, wait by the telephone, answer five ads, and end up with one interview. On the average this means it will take you four or five months to get a job. Imagine (if you have the time) spending *eight hours a day* looking for a job and getting a job within two weeks to a month. That is what happens when you use the self-starter method.

THE TARGET PERSON

You want to work for Wimble & Sutton. You are a highly qualified production engineer specializing in vacuum gaskets. Wimble & Sutton is the fourth largest manufacturer in the country, and from gossip you *suspect* that they might be considering a shake-up. Do you call and make an appointment with the personnel department?

Not if you can help it. Personnel departments are rarely empowered to actually hire people. Their function is to screen individuals who have applied or whom they have recruited and to pass them along to "X." "X" is your Target Person. In an ideal world she or he would be married to your cousin. But you still want to approach on a personal basis almost as if that was the case. "X" is the person who will be your superior if you get the job, and "X" is the person you have to seek out for a job interview.

Your first undertaking is to get that person's name. There are a number of ways of doing this. If you have done your background research thoroughly, you will at least know enough about the job you want to be able to make an educated guess at "X's" title. Then you pick up the telephone and call the company:

> *"Good morning, this is Sheila Simpson. I'd like to know if Roderick Rosenberry (a name you invent) is production supervisor for the vacuum gasket division?"*

"Hold on please, I'll put you through. What company did you say you were with?"

You should not answer this, in case it gets back to your current boss; simply say:

"I'm the production engineer. Mr. Rosenberry knows me."

Remember to say *the* production engineer, not *a* production engineer. If the receptionist thinks you are looking for a job, she may divert you to personnel.

"Hello, this is gaskets. Can I help you?"

"Yes, I'd like to speak to Mr. Rosenberry, your production supervisor, please."

"Rosenberry? No one here by that name. Who is this?"

"I'm a personal friend. I was sure he worked at Wimble & Sutton as production supervisor."

"Well there must have been a mistake. Our production supervisor is Hannah Harrison, and she has been here for fifteen years."

"Thanks. Sorry to bother you. Good-bye."

Hannah Harrison. Now what do you do? Do you write a neat letter, enclosing your résumé? Only as a last resort. First rack your brains all over again and call your acquaintances in the business to try to come up with anyone whose name you can use for a personal introduction. If you have no luck, you should make a *cold call*. This is not easy to do, but it has a very high rate of success for getting interviews.

COLD CALLING

This gets easier the more you do it; you just have to overcome your fear of instant rejection. We would rather have a snooty type at an employment agency tell us we are out of luck than receive the news from the horse's mouth. I urge you not to neglect this powerful approach. Here's the scenario for one such cold call. Concentrate on the strategy and make the words your own:

"Good morning, this is Sheila Simpson. May I speak to Hannah Harrison in production?"

"Hold on, I'll put you through."

"Hello, this is gaskets."

"Yes, my name is Sheila Simpson, and I want to speak to Hannah Harrison, please."

"She's very busy now. What's it about?"

"I'm a production engineer, and I want to speak to her about a job."

"You'll have to talk to personnel first."

"No. Miss Harrison has been personally recommended to me, and it would be better if I spoke directly to her. I will hold on; I don't mind waiting until she is free."

(Wait.)

"Hannah Harrison speaking."

"My name is Sheila Simpson, and I have been production engineer at Weaks & Whipple for five years, specializing in vacuum gaskets. I'd like fifteen minutes of your time, please, at your convenience. When can you see me?"

"I'm sorry, we aren't looking for anyone new now. You can send in your résumé if you like."

"I have very good qualifications and first-class experience. Even if you are not interested in me now, it would be beneficial for the future. It will only take fifteen minutes, I promise. Can we say tomorrow or Thursday?"

At this point Hannah will either relent and give you an appointment or will stand firm, and then the worst that can happen is that when she does get your résumé, she will link it with a voice that was firm and decisive. Every experience is grist for your mill, and at least you may be able to use her name on another call:

"I've spoken to a number of people in the business, including Hannah Harrison, and I'm looking for a job. Can we make an appointment?"

There is a limit. Here are the rules:

a)   No outright lies. They will backfire. Do not claim relationships that do not exist. Do not say: "I have been recommended to Miss Harrison" if you have not. The reverse may be true—you recommended her to yourself—but stick to that and watch what you say.

b) When you have the target person on the telephone, be as brief and direct as possible. Forget about "How are you" and "Nice weather we're having"; just say "Hello" and get to the point.

c) Once your target says no firmly, accept that. Remain courteous and ask if you may send in your résumé.

It may not be possible to time your approach with accuracy, but if you are as acquainted with your future job as you ought to be, it is worth spending five minutes to see if you can calculate what time of day or day of the week would be most propitious for the target person to receive your call. Every type of job, every department, has its own rhythm, smooth or erratic. The first thing on Monday morning may be the absolute worst time; so might 4:45 on a Friday. Try to pinpoint a lull in the pace when your Hannah Harrison is likely to be at her desk performing routine chores.

THE WRONG WAY

I receive hundreds of requests for jobs. No, you will *not* get me on the telephone; do not even try! But I am amazed by the way in which young Black women who *do* have access to me manage time and again to ruin their chances by what I can only categorize as overaggressive coyness. This sounds like a contradiction in terms, but let me give you an example and see if you would do the same thing.

I am on the boards of a number of foundations. Because of my involvement with one in particular, I became acquainted with a woman who functioned as an administrative assistant. I was impressed with her efficiency, charm, and obvious talents. From time to time she would call my office to remind me about board meetings and other functions. She co-ordinated fund-raising activities in which I was involved, and we were on cordial terms as far as the relationship went.

She called my office one day recently. As usual I was on at least two other calls at the time, and I asked my secretary to take a message. "Yvonne" (as I shall call her) told my secretary that it was a personal matter and asked for me to call her back. I could not imagine what could be personal about the foundation business, but I called her back as soon as I could. Of course, she was out. My secretary started to leave a message, but before she could hang up Yvonne's boss came on the line, the head of the foundation. This man jumps at every opportunity to talk to his board members. He expressed surprise that I was returning Yvonne's call and did not know why she had called me. So, already Yvonne has:

1. Wasted my time and placed me in an awkward position with her boss.

2. Indirectly allowed her boss to find out that she called me on a "personal" matter.

Yvonne called my office a couple of times after that, but I was out of town. My personal rule is that if a person calls me once and misses me, and I call back and miss them, then I am not going to keep calling them no matter how many messages they leave. I'll take their call when I am ready. That may sound harsh, but time is the most precious commodity I have.

I make a very stringent separation between my home and my work. I work very hard, long hours, and when I am at home I want to enjoy my family. My business colleagues know that if they call me at home, it must be for a *very* good reason. When I pick up that telephone by my bed, I expect it to be family or close friends. It was Yvonne. She had access to her foundation's files and somehow managed to get my home number. That was her mistake number two. My home number is a state secret. I was not in a receptive mood. At all. But I listened to what Yvonne had to tell me that was so personal.

She spoke for about ten minutes. She is highly educated and articulate, but after she stopped talking I knew as much about what she wanted as I did at the beginning. The only thing she kept insisting on that I understood was that she wanted an appointment with me, but she was totally unwilling to state what the purpose of the meeting might be. I told her it would be much easier for me if she put her thoughts on paper and sent them to me and, in the meantime, not to call me at home. Mistake number three: having gotten me on the telephone (at the wrong place and the wrong time), she failed to say what she wanted!

A week later I received her letter. It was professionally typed and neatly presented on her home stationery. I had a searing headache by the time I reached the second paragraph. Yvonne wrote to me about her "possible career reorientation refinements" and her desire to seek "meaningful interpersonal commitments in work-related formulations." At the end of the letter, in an extremely roundabout way, she stated that she wanted to see me because she was thinking of changing her job and wanted my "advice." Naomi Sims, Free Career Counseling!

What it boiled down to was that Yvonne wanted to apply to me for a job, was in a much more advantageous position to do so than almost anyone else I can think of, yet she blew it completely. Why? Was she scared of an immediate out-and-out rejection? She presented herself as *desperate* to make a *casual* inquiry about a situation she failed to articulate yet which was vitally important for her future. Obviously she did not trust me to keep what she might say in confidence, and she concealed her request in language which was so high-flown as to be virtually unintelligible.

What should she have done? What should you do under similar circumstances? Remember, she is still at her present job and has not been fired; she knows I have a good opinion of her work and have more than once complimented her. The first thing she should have done was to decide exactly what she wanted. To work for Naomi Sims in any capacity? To ask Naomi Sims about job prospects in the beauty business?

Let us say that she simply wants to switch fields, from foundations to the beauty business. She has a particular company she wants to approach, mine. A couple of hours in the library would tell her what types of jobs might be available in a company our size, and she could compare her experience and credits with those required. In one or two hours she could make herself a résumé which is tailored to my needs. By making no assumptions about what I know or do not know about her experience, she shows me how *she* sees herself. Then she calls. I am on the telephone. Instead of saying "it's personal," this is what Yvonne should have said to my secretary:

"Please tell Miss Sims that I want to apply for a job as office manager or regional sales representative, and I am available for an interview at her convenience. I am still at my present job, and I would like her to call me at home if possible."

By leaving that message, she would have impressed me in a variety of ways. With her knowledge of my business, her directness, and above all by not presuming on our acquaintance more than to establish contact for a formal interview. Such an approach helps her to meet me on strong footing and have some *control* over the situation.

Above all be *direct*. Do not pretend that you are asking someone for advice when you actually want a job. There may be times when you encounter someone who can help you, and you may want to be discreet about your intentions:

"I'm not unhappy with my present position, but I'm very interested in your field and I've considered making a move at the right time."

This is the sort of thing to say when your encounter is *informal*. When you have initiated the interview or conversation, put your cards on the table.

One thing I cannot tolerate is when someone uses overtly convoluted language to mask their intentions. This is a trait among many career-oriented Black women and men. It is not the way to impress an employer with the fact that you are educated. Plain English will do, the plainer the better. What will impress an employer is your ability to use terms which are job-oriented. Otherwise say what you mean as simply and directly as possible.

SUMMARY

So far we have discovered that you must do the following:

1. Pick the job. Don't just look for vacancies.
2. Pick the target person.
3. Approach the target *personally*.

Your immediate objective is to get an interview.

If you research your market properly, you should be able to do all this yourself, and that alone makes a very favorable statement about your drive and abilities before you have even started to sell yourself directly. Nevertheless, circumstances will force many of you to take the "official" route; and in order to prepare you for the games that are played, here is a guide to the employment industry. We have examined the area of personal contacts. Here are the services that cost money:

Employment Agencies

The theory is that a person or firm becomes your agent with the task of presenting your credits in a favorable light to prospective employers so that you can get a job. In some cases agencies offer additional services, such as rewriting your résumé or providing you with practice interviews. The cost is based on a percentage of your starting salary. The agency is *usually* paid by the employer, but always check first to make sure that this is the case. You may be expected to pay a fee yourself.

Sometimes an agency will require you to sign an exclusive contract with them. This is rare; it should be for only a limited period of time and only with an agency working in a highly specialized field.

It is perfectly true that many agencies may have contacts that are out of reach to you as an individual. It is also true that ninety per cent of all agencies are concerned only with short-term profit. You may want a certain kind of job, but unless you are remarkably forceful they will talk you into taking "any" job. If you are just out of school or financially desperate, a job is a job and you must take what you can get. But if you are following my Five Key Plan, you know that ultimate success depends on ascending the right ladder. For instance, your ambition is to become a nonfiction editor at a major publishing house. You have found out enough about the business to know that such a position is attained from within by people who have worked their way up through the ranks from lowly positions for which they were probably overqualified.

"But Miss Henry," the agency tells you, "this position as a junior copywriter at Marbles & Malkin pays $13,000 a year. Hinkley House Publishing is not hiring now, and besides you would have to start as a clerk at $11,000 and you have a master's degree in English!"

Individual agents work on a commission basis, and they only care about their commissions. It is a question of body count, and they know the statistics better than you. If you qualify, they will send you on fifty interviews, and the odds are 5–2 that you will land a job within six weeks. That is all they care about, getting you on someone's payroll so they can get a commission. They are not necessarily interested in your long-range plans. To them you are just another ten per cent commission. Psychologically the job hunter is a petitioner, the employer is a monarch, and the agency simply a court chamberlain whose job it is to get as much work done in a day as possible. Hat in hand you approach the all-powerful agent.

Never look at it that way! The agent is working *for you*. By getting a job, you are paying their salary. Tell the agency exactly what you want and be specific. If they throw up their hands and say you are limiting yourself, then be prepared to reconsider—but only if they can give you concrete evidence. Find out what they are going to say about you to a prospective employer. They often exaggerate, and of course it is *you* who is on the spot when your employer asks where you received your Ph.D. in advanced electronics when all you have is a B.Sc. in computer science. Often agencies engage in mass mailings of applicants' résumés, and in some cases this means that your résumé may end up on your *current* boss's desk.

"There is no reason that you should look at, interview for, or be shown jobs that you have no interest in. If you feel you're not getting satisfactory treatment from the agency you're dealing with or you don't feel comfortable, go somewhere else."

Those are wise words from David Strachan, executive vice president of the National Association of Personnel Consultants.

Career Counselors

These are individuals or organizations that offer guidance, direction, information, and career resources. In few instances do they actually find people jobs. If you are able to follow the advice in this book, you probably do not need a career counselor. Their principal aim is to help the client evaluate their experience and credits, and to plot a future direction. Many counseling services incorporate mock interviews and extensive psychological testing. This may boost your morale, but it will not bring you any closer to your goal. If you are hopelessly at sea and have no goal at all, then counseling will help. It is good for people who cannot decide whether to change jobs or stay where they are, for students who are seeking as much information about the real world of jobs as possible, and for people who have been suddenly fired from jobs they were happy in and who have never given any thought to looking again.

Leila Jackson visited a job counselor because she was frustrated at being a dental technician and was convinced that she could do better in another area. The appointment took a full day to complete. Half of the time she spent being tested and half being interviewed; the total cost was $150, which is average. Afterward she was much better able to understand *why* she was unhappy with her present job and even to find ways to overcome that, but it did not help her specifically to identify alternatives. However, she does not feel that the money was wasted because it increased her self-assurance.

Headhunters

These are supposed to come to you, not you to them. They are hired by corporations to locate executives for top spots. Normally they are not interested in jobs with salary ranges below $30,000 and are paid by the employers. They are unlikely to be interested in someone who is out of a job, and they really concentrate on luring valuable employees away from their current jobs with extra incentives that the headhunter's clients are prepared to offer.

You may encounter individuals or companies who call themselves "executive recruiters" or "search consultants," but who are in fact employment agents and agencies simply trying to upgrade their image. Most true headhunters handle only two or three jobs at a time and are looking for people whose backgrounds match the jobs perfectly. The chances are very slim that you might approach one at the particular time when they are searching to fill a job for which you are exactly qualified.

But what if a headhunter approaches *you?* Do you leap at the opportunity? Is the offer serious or just a groping in the dark? Usually you will get a telephone call with the mention of a mutual friend or business colleague. You will not be told the name of the company that is recruiting but will be told that if you are interested further discussion might be fruitful. If you accept this offer, you will probably be invited to a lunch meeting.

First of all you might be worried that if you make this appointment your boss will find out and accuse you of disloyalty. After all, the headhunter does not care whether your boss finds out or not. In most cases your fears are unjustified. If you are worth recruiting, your boss either knows and expects this or it does not hurt for this to be known. Even if you have no intention of moving, the fact that you are sought after is good leverage for your next raise or promotion.

How do you handle the conversation at lunch? Let the recruiter do most of the talking. You do not have to sell yourself, express dissatisfaction with your present job, or otherwise compromise your neutrality. But always ask what the new job pays because this information is not always volunteered. If you are asked what you are making at the present time, add twenty per cent to your actual salary. The recruiter knows what range you are in, and it can only help for you to be at the top of that range.

At this meeting be yourself. There is no virtue in appearing either too eager or too uninterested. You are there, or you would not be interested; if you are absolutely yearning for the job, perhaps you are not as important as the recruiter was led to believe.

The next step is that the headhunter will ask for your résumé (in Chapter 2 I told you always to have an up-to-date résumé whether or not you are looking for a job), and then you will probably not hear anything for weeks or months, if at all, so do not celebrate prematurely. On the average a headhunter will call twenty-five people for a particular job. Of those, about fifteen will be asked to lunch and three, at the most, actually presented to the prospective employer. If and when you get a call back to meet with the employer, do not assume that the job is in the bag; you are not the only prospect.

One of the worst things you can do is "back off" your current job because in your head you already occupy that new corner office on Madison Avenue. Always keep working as if you intend to stay in your job forever; that is the professional way and the way that is fair to your employer.

THE INTERVIEW

Nothing, but *nothing* is more important than how you handle yourself here. Your credits have been accepted, or else you would not have the appointment. Your goal is within reach; your strategy is almost complete. Now it is up to your personal skills.

A successful interview contains all the elements of a good conversation: *be prepared to ask as many questions as you answer.* I have interviewed so many women for jobs who, when I ask them if they have any questions for *me,* simply smile politely and say, "No, I don't think so," instead of asking me if I mind their bringing their Great Dane to work! You can reveal as much, or more, about yourself by your questions as by your answers. You should also demonstrate that you can take charge of a conversation without dominating it.

Make No Distinctions

Do not automatically assume that if your interviewer is a Black woman, you can indulge in a greater degree of intimacy than if the interviewer is a white male.

The Questions

Yes, she may have read your résumé, and yes, she may be a close friend of your Aunt Nellie, but when she says to you,

a) "Tell me a little bit about yourself,"

answer in a job-related context.

When you are asked to describe yourself, *do not* respond with a capsule history of your entire life or with some vague remark like:

"I'm a hard worker and won't let you down."

Instead, give a brief description of previous jobs that you have held which demonstrate your ability to *get along with people.* This is what your interviewer wants to know:

"Are you flexible, easy to work with, or stubborn, a loner?"

Most people get fired because they are involved in personality conflicts, *not* because they are not working. It is essential that you spot the opportunity to bring forward examples of your successful involvement in group activities or decisions or close working relationships.

b) "What do you do in your spare time?"

This is another question that bears on your sociability. Try to frame your answer in a job-related context. Provide your interviewer with something that can be seen as a potential benefit to the company. If you are being interviewed for a position as recreational director this answer:

"I'm translating the Iliad *into Sanskrit"*

is very impressive *in general,* but it will not help you get the job. On the other hand, if you are being interviewed for a job in advertising or public relations and you mention that you are an amateur photographer, you present one more skill that can bear on your employment. Mention any community work you have been involved with, no matter how clearly it is stated on your résumé. If you are a joiner or someone who organizes events, from fund raisers to cat shows, it reflects well on the company that employs you and clearly indicates that you can get along well with others. It is not going to impress your future employer if you convey the impression that *nothing* is as important to you as your job, that you live and die for work, and that you have no spare time. Employers know that workaholics do not make the best employees and can actually decrease productivity by straining the office atmosphere. So if you are one, better keep quiet about it!

c) "What do you like about this job?"

Answer honestly. If you have done your homework and know the job inside out, here is a chance to demonstrate your grasp of its language and skills. This question, which is the same as:

"Why did you come to us in particular?"

is *critical.* You are being asked why you left or want to leave your current job. The best way to deal with this question is to stress the human factor:

"It gives me a chance to work with people older (or younger) than myself" or

"I work best as part of a team."

When discussing previous or current employment, *never* mention any trouble caused by personality conflicts. Even if you worked with someone everyone in the business knows is *impossible,* avoid being drawn into any admission that you did not get along well. Be positive. Stress that you want to change jobs because you are ambitious, because you want to get ahead and make full use of your potential. It is not easy to convey all this unless you are able to answer the questions as firmly as they are presented.

d) "What is your ultimate goal?"

Translated, this means:

"Do you intend to stay with this company if we hire you or to use us as a stepping-stone?"

Keep your ambitions within the scope of the company structure, but do not present a rigid strategy. The best way to handle this question is to prepare for it by finding out who else in the company held the job you are applying for, and then you can simply say:

"Like Joanna Barnes, I would like to head the public relations section one day."

e) "What are your worst faults?"

I assume you have at least one, right? But for the sake of the interview, it is a fault that you are in the process of overcoming in a constructive manner:

"Frankly, I get very angry with myself if I cannot solve a problem the first time around, but I am learning to have more patience. Now I'll move to another project for a short time and return to the problem with a fresh attitude."

Be prepared to give specific examples, from previous jobs, of problems that you have faced (and overcome!), but nothing that casts you in a negative light. What this question really means is:

"Can you take criticism?"

f) "Are you free to travel?"

It is not legal for you to be quizzed about your age or family status, but there are a number of innocuous questions like this that are intended to find out just how much time you are able to give to the job. If you do have family responsibilities, there is no need to be specific. You do not have to say, for instance, that you are divorced with two small children to care for. State that you have certain ties at home but that you would be willing to make arrangements if you were required to travel or work overtime on specific, important occasions. Indicate a degree of availability, but set limits.

g) "What is your present salary?"
or,
"What do you expect to make in this job?"

or any variation on this theme requires that you respond with a *specific figure*. Say:

"I am now earning $18,000, and I want to go to $19,500."

Before you go to any job interview, know exactly what you are going to ask for in terms of salary, decide what you will accept, and *stick to those numbers*.

Your employer may suggest a low figure just to measure your reaction and to see how you value your own worth. In most cases the difference will not be more than two or three thousand dollars.

If you find yourself having to negotiate your salary during a job interview, simply stick to your guns, politely. You may want the job very badly indeed, but *never* leave it up to the employer to:

"Pay me what you think I'm worth."

Wilma Cobb, a dear friend, called me from California for advice. She had been trying to get into motion picture production and found that the atmosphere was frustratingly casual. She had a number of contacts and ended up being included in some important meetings by an independent producer. The man in charge wanted to pick her brains and had indicated that there might be the possibility of a permanent job. Two days later he called to say that she had made a very favorable impression and:

"Dick wants to know how much you want?"

Wilma knew how much other people were getting for such a job and was so thrilled at the prospect that she replied:

"I'll leave that up to him, I know he'll be fair."

Now she was calling me because ten days had passed and no one had called her back. She was getting paranoid, convinced that she had shown such weakness by not negotiating her salary that she had been dropped from consideration.

I advised her to write a very brief, very firm letter to "Dick," stating that she wanted $18,000 and would start the following Monday. She got the job.

Now, what questions do *you* have for the interviewer?

a) *About fringe benefits:*

"Do you have a health plan?"

"How many weeks paid vacation are there?"

"Is there a stock option plan, a pension fund?"

A lot of women are afraid to ask these questions because they think the employer will imagine that they are *only* interested in these matters.

b) *About the future:*

"Are promotions and/or raises based on merit or length of service?"

"If I do this job well, what can I expect?"

Ask about fringe benefits and the future toward the *end* of the interview. If you are given a verbal promise of specific future raises at certain dates, then once you are in the job *get it in writing*.

c) *About salary:*

"I expect a salary of $19,500."

If no mention is made of salary, *you* must bring it up. Be specific. Do not make this a question but a statement. Never say "about nineteen thousand," because this means you will take at least fifteen hundred dollars less, an amount that means very little to the company if you are an asset but an awful lot to you!

REFERENCES

You should have the names and addresses of five people who will attest to your qualifications and indicate positive reactions to you personally. Have these typed and ready to hand over. If you do not wish your current employer to be contacted, then tell the truth; no reasonable person is going to blame you for protecting yourself. If you have been terminated, or you quit and your relationship with your former employer is not good, then make sure that the references you do provide are as strong as possible. Above all, never give as a reference someone whom you have not so informed. I do not believe in listing references on the résumé itself but simply in stating that "Excellent references will be supplied on request."

CONDUCT

A recent MIT study of job hunters showed a high correlation between those who got hired and those who during the interview spent about half their time asking intelligent questions about the organizations and half the time talking about themselves. Show that you know the company you want to join and reveal enough about yourself to be memorable.

No matter what is actually asked, bear in mind that these are the questions your interviewer has in the back of the head:

"Why are you here?"
"What can you do for me?"
"What kind of person are you?"
"How much are you going to cost me?"

If at the end of the interview you feel that you replied favorably to these issues (no matter what was actually asked and answered), then you will have had a very successful interview.

The Bureau of National Affairs, Inc., conducted an intensive study to determine the importance of the interview in job hiring. It turned out to be the *single most important factor.* The reason that the personnel executives who were polled gave as the major cause of applicant rejection was that those they turned down:

Did Not Promote Themselves Well

during the interview. Such a shame! Six years in college, three more learning the ropes, and it all goes down the drain in twenty minutes simply because you did not take the time to *prepare* and *rehearse*.

Black women are mortally afraid, with some notable exceptions, of *coming on strong*. That is what you *have* to do in a job interview, in a direct, intelligent, nondefensive manner. If you come across as self-assured and articulate, you will do justice to your years of study and experience. If you are insecure, unable to ask questions, and give the impression that you would rather be in a snake pit than answering these questions, then ten doctorates will be to no avail.

REHEARSE!

Use my questions to work with a friend or family member to rehearse for your interviews. Even if you think of yourself as capable and well spoken, there is nothing quite like running through the list a couple of times to make sure that you are actually saying what you mean; that you are not shading the truth just a little *too* strongly; and that you can "wing it" when a surprise question comes out of the blue:

> *"Tell me Miss Rathbone, I read your résumé with care, and it appears that you were out of a job from 1975 until 1980. Why was that?"*

Answer:

> *"I married in 1975 and started a family. I also organized a community day-care center still in existence, wrote three articles for our local newspaper, and took a correspondence course in bookkeeping!"*

PRACTICE!

If you have the time and the energy, and I sincerely trust you have the energy, it is very worthwhile to train yourself for major job interviews by going to preliminary interviews to companies that have jobs you are not particularly pursuing. You do this *only* to get the experience of handling different kinds of interviewers. Approach these as you would a "real" interview, follow my advice, and you will be surprised at how good you feel after two or three such dry runs.

It is important to demystify the process. Your interviewer is someone, like yourself, with a job to do, with problems and interests. Direct your conversation at the *person,* not the *job.* Avoid clumsy flattery:

"I like your dress/tie/hat/shoes,"

but wait for the interviewer to say as you're leaving:

"That's a nice sweater, where did you get it?"

Translated that means:

"You have made a very favorable impression on me, and you're a serious contender."

❦❦❦❦❦

5

Moving Up

"If you're not willing to take risks you don't get too far."

Joyce Colon, Assistant Vice President
Westinghouse Corporation

Your rise to the top starts the very first day at your new job. The reins are in your hands, and depending on your age and position you have to establish a five, ten, fifteen, and twenty-year plan.

For the sake of clarity, I am going to start you off at the bottom of the ladder in a corporate business, one in which you *could* rise, over a period of twenty years, to the top position. This is a model; in actual fact you may make several lateral moves. Although I will use mostly business terms to describe the various roles you will play, my advice is applicable to virtually *any* organization, large or small. The principles I formulate hold true for industry, education, government, and all subsidiary enterprises such as retail management, arts administration, and publishing.

The important factor to keep in mind is that you are engaged in an endeavor which can *only* function successfully and achieve its purpose if the individual human beings involved in that endeavor, whether they are five or five thousand in number, can interact as a *group*. The word "group" is frequently associated in our minds with a handful of like-minded people brought together on an equal basis. Forget that. A group is any number of people, most of them with different and possibly conflicting outlooks, brought together to form a structure which has its own internal dynamics and in which there are varying degrees of inequality.

As a sales representative, for instance, you may be at the end of one of the outer arms of your organization's structure. You may feel totally independent and beholden to no one but yourself. Day after day you approach different people, and only your own grit and determination account for your success. In fact, you may be closely connected with individuals at the home office whom you rarely see but who can help or hinder your job to a great degree. Are the goods you sell shipped on time? In good condition? Are your achievements measured on the same scale as those of your peers at company headquarters? Is the person responsible for your promotions aware of all the obstacles you have overcome? Your clients also, no matter how far-flung, also constitute part of your group. John Donne wrote:

"No man is an island."

No woman either!

THE LADDER

The task you have in your twenties is to build technical skill and knowledge. This must be done according to the rules of the organization and in such a way as to demonstrate your ability to function successfully with other people.

Later, in your thirties, you should begin to use your technical skills autonomously and to assume group leadership positions; you should be able to delegate assignments and make assessments which are acted upon by your superiors. This is the time when you can begin to be creative and to design new ways of doing things for your organization.

By the time you reach your forties, you should be in a position to run an office, a division of the company. You are approaching senior management and have large responsibilities.

If you are groaning aloud because you are thirty-seven already and just starting out or over again, calm down. I have used the age index for this ladder because it is graphic. In fact, such a timetable can be applied to a shorter span, starting at any age, so long as the organization functions on a merit basis and encourages upward mobility.

In any event, how you handle yourself at any stage will determine how fast and how far you go. We will begin at the beginning.

THE NEW JOB

What *not* to do:

1. Impress everyone with how hard you can work.

2. Suggest a major reorganization.

3. Invite your boss to lunch.

For the first months your motto should be "Work and watch." Be diligent, but not to the point of exhaustion. Your job-within-the-job is to determine the *real* (as opposed to given) lines of power and authority. Never take it for granted that office geography, job titles, or the length of time with the company reflect the actual power structure.

The way in which you will be able to present your qualities as a possible leader *at the beginning* is by indicating that you have gathered as much information about how the company works *inside* as about its public function and performance. Even though you are at the bottom, try to position yourself in terms of those that you are constantly contacting. Who did you replace? Did someone move up or out? How long have your colleagues been at their jobs? This is not the time to celebrate your new job by engaging in outside activities that could be distracting. Give a lot of thought to your placement and make an effort to be cordial to as many people as possible.

Your initial contacts should not go beyond cordiality. The introduction of a new person into a working group inevitably creates situations whereby some members draw themselves toward the newcomer and others move away, for reasons that may have nothing to do with the personality of the newcomer *per se.*

Especially as a Black woman, if you are entering a situation that is racially and sexually mixed, you will find yourself "rushed" by some people overly anxious to impress you with their lack of prejudice (watch out!) and treated casually or shunned by others who may be skeptical of your abilities or frankly prejudiced.

It is not wise to develop instant friendships at the early stage when you do not know the real lay of the land. Even if it takes a great effort, try to deal with *everyone* the same way, no matter how they react to you.

If there are occasions for coffee or lunch together, give every person a chance to know you; do not be afraid to approach the cold ones. They may be afraid you are after their job or simply, if they are older, discouraged by always being passed over by a succession of bright newcomers like yourself who always climb higher than they.

Respect *everyone,* and do not get drawn into any one "clique," even if it seems to harbor the smartest people in the office. If there is such a minigroup and it actively excludes you, this may be because the group members feel threatened. Take these social relationships easily.

Find out as much as you can about where your particular division fits into the larger corporate structure. Who are the people above and below? Even though you may be starting at the bottom, it is possible that the nature of your work vitally affects some other persons in the company not visible to you at the present time. Make sure that you are introduced to everyone in a superior position with whom you will be dealing and introduce yourself to everyone at your own level.

Reach out, at least once, and indicate that you appreciate other people's ideas and advice, but always follow your own judgment. You are starting your search for a *mentor* and laying the groundwork for establishing a personal *network*. We will examine these two all-important concepts later—when you are in your "thirties." Right now concentrate on establishing your territory and touch base with as many people in the company as possible.

How you handle your first success will be very carefully noticed by your peers and superiors. False modesty is just as inappropriate as a show of bragging. Someone will be jealous, and someone else will be genuinely glad you did well. Continue to act with restraint because soon you will make your first mistake, and that will be witnessed just as carefully. Analyze where you went wrong, make no excuses for yourself, and do not try to defend yourself to sympathetic co-workers.

"Speak no evil," but listen and watch. This is where your nondirective listening (Chapter 3) comes in handy. Others will confide in you, and you should be able to interpret that information without taking sides.

IDENTIFY THE STRUCTURE

Our instinct is to assume that all organizations are hierarchical and that merit, accompanied by suitable behavior, moves one up the scale. In fact, as the illustration indicates, there are three types of organizations.

This illustration was created by Warren Bennis, research professor at the Graduate School of Business Administration at the University of Southern California. He believes that comprehending the underlying system of the organization is much more a factor in success than most of us care to admit. Once you know how it functions in actuality, you can position yourself accordingly and relate to the system in a way that transcends imposed roles of race and sex.

Where is the power route in your company? Can you find it? Is the office where you work dealing with *line* jobs or *staff* jobs? A *line* job has a direct connection to the company's profits. This is where you want to be because the closer you are to the profits, the closer you are to the power. A *staff* service job can only route you to the top of your division. Staff service jobs include personnel, public relations, corporate communications, accounting, systems analysis, engineering, research, and customer relations positions. At the top of those staff jobs,

THREE TYPES OF ORGANIZATIONAL CULTURES

copyright © Warren Bennis

	FORMALISTIC	COLLEGIAL	PERSONALISTIC
Basis for Decision	Direction from authority	Discussion and agreement	Directions from within
Form of Control	Rules, laws, rewards, and punishments	Interpersonal group commitments	Actions aligned with self-concept
Source of Power	Superior	What "we" think and feel	What *I* think and feel
Desired End	Compliance	Consensus	Self-actualization
To Be Avoided	Deviation from authoritative direction; taking risks	Failure to reach consensus	Not being "true to oneself"
Time Perspective	Future	Near Future	Now
Position Relative to Others	Hierarchical	Peer	Individual
Human Relationships	Structured	Group oriented	Individually oriented
Basis for Growth	Following the established order	Peer group membership	Acting on awareness of self

you will be an advisor to top management, but you will not make company policy or occupy the chair of the chief executive officer (C.E.O.). The top of a staff division may be quite as far as you want to go, but it is important to know from the start where your road ends. If your goal is C.E.O. or a top management job, then get out of public relations! One of the insidious ways in which many corporations responded to affirmative-action rulings was to route women and Black employees into fairly narrow specialty fields that lead only to senior positions in those staff areas but do not lead to power jobs. Top management positions go to people who have had experience administering a number of different line departments, not to people who are experts at one particular function.

In your early days at the job, begin to build a picture of your organization and where you see yourself, eventually, in that picture. Ask yourself if you are on the right track, because no matter what your type of work, you will be rated by your ability to get along with others. I want to devote some time to this problem.

Getting Along With Colleagues

There are various stereotypes that we can observe quite readily in most offices. There is often a "bright young thing" (not, I hope, you) who is something of an office pet. She is brought to important meetings, and occasionally her advice is sought, but her chief value is as a "yes" person.

There is also the "old grouch," who has been in his or her job for years and has barely moved an inch. Such a person has a cynical "wait-until-you-find-out-what-is-really-going-on-here" approach to the newcomer. This is someone to listen to carefully but always objectively. There may also be a congenial mother- or father-figure in your office, as well as a gossip. But remember that it is easier to accept people as stereotypes than to deal with them as individuals. Give everyone a chance.

Jacqueline Fry works with a large architectural firm. She described to me her first days at work:

"I tried not to be intimidated, but I was the youngest in the group and the only Black. There were eight of us, and we were engaged in similar work, and all of us reported to a project manager. I was very shy at first, and some people thought I was being snobbish, especially since I had graduated from a 'better' school of architecture than any of them. After a couple of weeks, I learned to relax, and I was on good terms with

everyone except a white woman about ten years older than me. She seemed to go out of her way to ignore me or to criticize my work. But never to my face. I assumed that she was prejudiced or at least jealous of a younger woman in the group. Each of us worked on separate projects, so what I did had no effect on her in any way. Her attitude really began to bother me, and I would dread running into her.

One day I plucked up enough courage to mention this to Larry, one of our group with whom I got along very well. He couldn't think of any reason why she shouldn't like me, but in talking about her he did mention that she was an absolute genius at a particular type of concrete construction and that there was no problem she couldn't solve. Well, I soon found an opportunity to ask her for some 'help' in that area. It turned out that this was a sort of office tradition: everyone went to Celia for advice, and she was secretly very proud of her expertise. She had assumed, I suppose, that with my more recent and fancier education, I would not only not need her help but might usurp her position—it had nothing to do with age, race, or sex! When I did approach her she just melted, and gradually we became close friends. I guess you could call her my mentor now."

The importance of keeping your eye on the work cannot be underestimated. That is why you are in the office. Work first, personalities second. Never hold back on your work for fear of outshining colleagues whose friendship you value. Some people who cannot forge ahead relish the opportunity to keep others back. Do not fall for it. You are going to have to step on some toes, and there will be colleagues who resent you just for what you are, so learn to take it in your stride and sustain respect and cordiality.

Getting Along With the Boss

Until your boss emerges, if ever, as a human being, an individual with strengths and weaknesses, she or he will occupy a position in your life analogous to that held by all former authority-figures, including parents and teachers. You may react to praise and blame from your boss *as if* it were coming from a parent or teacher, and your reactions (overwhelming joy, burning resentment) may be totally out of proportion to the circumstances. Few bosses are perceived by their subordinates as being absolutely "fair," but if the organization is doing a good job, then the boss must be doing *something* right. Try not to think too much in terms of friendship and animosity, and never try to curry favor needlessly.

Realize that with your boss you are dealing with a human being, not a symbol. Your boss is not all-powerful and all-knowing, is not entirely stupid and incompetent—any more so than you yourself. It is a bad sign if you find yourself actively fearing or ridiculing your boss. There will be times when you are criticized unfairly, just as there may be times when you are singled out for praise that others should be sharing. Try to come to terms with your boss's personality on a human level. When you are told,

> *"My door is always open, I want you to talk to me any time that you have a problem,"*

only take it literally if the door *is* always open and there is a steady stream of colleagues in and out all day. Most bosses commence a relationship with such pat phrases, another of which is:

> *"I don't just want someone who agrees with everything I do and say. Feel free to speak out."*

Really? And are you to say:

> *"Mrs. Wilcox, what you just said was dumb, and if we do it we'll lose all the clients"?*

Of course not. But only "speak out" if you are sure of your ground and are capable of diplomacy:

> *"Mrs. Wilcox, I'd like to suggest just one other possibility before we do what you say . . ."*

When your boss says he will "try" to do something for you, do not count on it. That is often a euphemism for "not if I can help it." You would probably pick that up if it were anyone but your boss talking, but because it is your boss you want to *believe* it.

The boss may make a favorite out of you (and may do this automatically to every new person) or may hardly ever say more than "good morning," but that should not dictate your attitude toward the boss, your co-workers, or (above all) your work.

As you start your new job, as you prepare to discover as much as possible about how your organization operates, think in terms of sending the following message to everyone you contact. Do this not only by what you say but by how you say it:

"I am considerate and friendly and deserve your respect as you deserve mine, but my priority is work."

IN THE MIDDLE

This is part two of your career battle: the "thirties." I have leaped ahead ten years, or you have been rapidly promoted and now are in a managerial position. Within a limited sphere, you have autonomy. You have a budget and the power to hire and fire. Is this the end of the line? It is a far cry from where you began, and your family and friends already think of you as successful.

A lot of Black women are so grateful to reach middle-management positions that they concentrate on holding the job by digging in, rather than continuing to move. Of course, the going gets tougher every step of the way, but to me that is a challenge. Let us forge ahead together.

Support and Opposition

It is at this level that distinctions of race and sex really come to the fore. Only 1.1 per cent of management jobs are held by Black women, up from zero fifteen years ago. Theoretically, affirmative action should help us the most; any company that is court-ordered to improve its minority hiring practices should be *doubly* interested in a Black woman. But in fact, we are inevitably the losers in the minority sweepstakes that pit us against Black men and white women. At the moment white women are winning hands down; they occupy over fifteen per cent of all managerial positions. One theory for this is that out of the three groups white women "fit in" the executive structure the best, because they learned from their husbands, fathers, and brothers how to manipulate in that world. They only have to be assimilated on one level, that of the job, not also on a social and/or cultural level. The bonds between white men and white women are stronger in the executive suite than those between white men and Black men or white men and Black women. In other words, sex is less of a barrier than race, and a corporation wishing to promote up from the ranks or to recruit executives from outside will prefer white women.

That leaves us nowhere. Even companies that say they are actively seeking Black women to promote claim that they cannot find enough who are qualified. Too few Blacks of either sex have the M.B.A.'s required for management positions, yet the enrollment of white women in M.B.A. programs has risen 50 per cent in three years. Is this because they are more ambitious? I believe it is because they are more readily accepted into those programs than Blacks and that as a group they have greater access to funding, both private and public.

This means that the opposition gets stronger the farther we travel. Professor Bennis outlines three major factors for being what he calls "favorably placed" in the organizational structure:

1. Having the support of one's subordinates.
2. Having clear goals and a similarly clear path toward them.
3. Being empowered by the organization with appropriate means to punish and reward one's subordinates.

If we apply this to our situation, it is very obvious that a white man who has white male and female subordinates is in a much better position to enjoy their support than a Black woman. In *Black Enterprise* magazine Janice C. Simpson has written about the Black woman as boss:

> *"You have to deal with people's reaction to you as a Black person and as a woman and the assumption that you are less intelligent, less competent, less ambitious."*

Those are three strikes against us, the first day on the job. It is not easy to establish subordinate support under those circumstances.

Opposition is seldom overt:

> *"I don't like you."*

Often it takes the form of condescension and attempts at familiarity which no white subordinate would attempt with a white male boss. The only way to deal with this *from the beginning* is to crack a few heads. You do not have to do it loudly or crudely, but you will never get support from below unless you command respect, and you will command respect more by punishing than by rewarding—at least at the very beginning.

After a very thorough investigation of your department's operations, call out the staffers that you think are performing poorly. Remember, you are not in your position to win medals for being likable but to get a job done. In order to move up, you have to do the job *three times* as well as a white man because you are, at best, expected to hold down the job and in most cases to fail. If your staffers let you down because you are a Black woman, it is you, not they, who will suffer unless you make it very clear from the start that you will tolerate no nonsense and that you expect a vast increase in productivity.

Once you have initiated a Reign of Terror, give the office a week or ten days to recover; then take your staff aside one by one and assign them tasks that will match their strongest abilities. Your interest will be appreciated, and it will allow you and the staff to begin to operate on a more human level. Delegate as much as possible. This will be hard for you to do if you have moved through the ranks in the same company; you may not be used to telling people what to do, or you may suffer from the Naomi Sims Syndrome:

"I-know-I-can-do-it-better-and-quicker-than-he-can."

You convince yourself that it saves time and is much more efficient if you do everything yourself. Consequently your staff sits around drinking coffee while you exhaust yourself. Your job is to *supervise*. You design systems and delegate tasks.

The American Management Associations researched the attributes of a good manager, as follows.

Do you:

1. Initiate situations and anticipate problems and their solutions?
2. Build alliances, bring people together, and create networks?

Are you:

1. Adaptable, self-controlled, and perceptually objective?
2. Concerned with self-presentation, efficiency, productivity, and the development of others?

Can you:

1. Think logically, diagnose ideas, and communicate well orally?
2. Listen, be flexible, and assess the character of others?

The skills that these attributes represent are not necessarily discussed in graduate school, nor is it likely that many of us have learned them from our families. This puts us at a grave disadvantage to the white male and female, who belong to a heritage that subtly but distinctly imprints an awareness of these precepts from birth. We are at a cultural disadvantage. For one thing, it is not in our nature to react positively to power. Intellectually we understand the necessity of wielding power, but psychologically we consider power a negative force, having been subjugated by powerful structures for so long. That means we have a very ambivalent attitude toward it when it comes into our hands, and some of us reject it and are unable to assert authority when necessary.

We must learn to deal with power and to feel easy when doing so. Otherwise we are co-operating with everyone who wants to shunt us off onto a siding of public relations or staff administration. In those jobs we can see ourselves on neutral territory, not contributing to the corporate profit which is in itself power and which contributes to the powerful society that has oppressed us for such a long time.

You are the Black female manager of the future, and you must push yourself forward into line positions in the profit structure of your organization. You have to assert yourself at meetings, volunteer for assignments, and show that you are prepared to deal with problematical areas of corporate development.

One way that you can do this is by relying on your sex and color to give you high visibility. This is a great asset. The first time you speak out at a general meeting, everyone will be listening very carefully. Some of them will be expecting you to make a mistake. This low-expectation profile can be an asset if you are able to accomplish your work at a level well above average—which means twice as well as they anticipated.

The rules at this level are the same for interpersonal relationships as in the front office. Make no assumptions; jump to no conclusions about your staff until you have had a chance to experience their reactions to you under a variety of circumstances. No one is your friend, no one your enemy. Rena Bartos, senior vice president at the J. Walter Thompson advertising agency, says:

> *"If you're calm, if you're consistent, if you don't change your story, your message will get through . . . I also believe that the best game is no game. When people start being manipulative, telling partial truths, telling one story to one person and another to someone else, it gets so complex. It's a marvelous ploy to be straight. It's terribly important, too, to have one set of manners—corporate manners—for everyone you deal with. Some people behave one way with their superiors and another way with their staff. That catches up with you because today's office boy or girl is tomorrow's chairperson."*

You are going to be watched very carefully for signs of your private life. By and large men are not faced with the same problem of family involvement interfering with their job as we are, and it is easier for them to keep their personal lives away from the office. No matter how unreasonable it may seem, I suggest that you do not involve your family in any aspects of your job, that you do not discuss vacations, dinner parties, or the like with staff members. If the entire office knows that you are leaving early because your baby-sitter is sick, it will be held against you. Leave early, but for "an appointment." Do not conduct conversations with your children or husband or boyfriend that are lengthy and can be overheard, no matter how innocent the discussion. Try to maintain, at all times, a thoroughly professional attitude, much more professional, in fact, than a man in your position would have to maintain.

As you can see, the world is now much more complicated than it was a few years ago, when all you had to worry about was your tuition costs and getting good grades.

Now we will look at two common phenomena that grease the wheels of most career situations. They exist in almost every field of human endeavor, yet so far have been primarily responsible for aiding the male of the species. Both phenomena provide systems of relating workers to one another in a slightly or radically different way from that decreed by the particular career structure. They are additional, not alternative, ways of bringing the less experienced in touch with the more experienced and linking workers in one company with colleagues in other similar situations. Both go by many names, but we will call them by their most familiar: the *mentor* and the *network*.

The Mentor

You are a white male, twenty-six, just graduated from the Harvard Law School. You join the Wall Street firm of Whelks & Watney. You are assigned the worst hole in the office, and nobody speaks to you for a month. One day you are invited to lunch by Jack Wellworthy, a senior partner, a man you have never met in your life:

> *"It's good to meet you, William," says Wellworthy. "I was your Uncle Fitzhugh's roommate at Princeton in '53. How is the old devil? By the way, how are you doing in the dungeon? I remember when I started . . ."*

Although he would deny the title, Wellworthy has become your mentor, sometimes called a "rabbi" or "godfather." What does this mean to you? It means that now you have an unofficial guidance counselor, someone to show you the ropes. He is unlikely to become your boss in the regular sense, but he might call for your assistance on a particular project and point out your favorable qualities to one of the partners more directly in charge of what you do. Wellworthy has no desire to do your job for you, but over lunch once a month he will let you get steamed up about office problems, suggest solutions, and give you tips about how to handle difficult situations:

> *"Don't pay any attention to old Binnstable right now. His wife's suing for a divorce, and he's going to kick you 'round the office for a couple of weeks."*

What does the mentor get out of this? It varies. In some professions it is simply considered to be "the done thing," a way that makes the profession stronger, an informal method of bringing up talent. In the case of family ties, it is obvious that you would be eligible for discreet extra attention. Often the mentor looks forward to bathing in reflected glory once you have proved your mettle:

> *"I say, Binnstable, I see you are going to make young William a junior partner. I always told you he would be a credit to the firm. I was at school with his Uncle Fitzhugh, you know . . ."*

The mentor is an older and hopefully wiser person who provides encouragement and sometimes resources for the newcomer. Usually the mentor is over forty and the one who is helped is considerably younger. Because it is essentially a human relationship, sanctioned by the corporation but not part of its formal structure, it can go wrong. There is often a painful period of separation when, in our example, William will reach a level close to that of his mentor Jack. He no longer agrees with everything Jack tells him, and there may even be an open policy dispute. The mentor feels old and betrayed. So it goes. Often the mentor wants unconsciously to keep his young charge at a somewhat subordinate level, a contradiction if at the same time the mentor wants his charge to succeed. Jack wants William to rise so far and no farther, a step down from himself. The mentor can become possessive and jealous, unwilling to let William express admiration for other superiors or peers.

The business world has come up with an expression to explain this unorthodox relationship: it is called "sponsored mobility." Well, you say, that is all very well for William; I am glad he is a junior partner thanks to his mentor, but what has that got to do with me? How can I get a mentor?

The answer is really that the mentor gets you, if you are lucky. In a spate of "mentor mania," a lot of magazine articles have appeared in recent years, most of them inaccurately indicating that a mentor was someone you *had* to have in order to succeed and that there are tried and true ways of "getting a mentor." It is not that simple. For a Black woman in middle management, it is very unlikely that there will be other Black women in sufficiently senior positions to act as mentors.

Even if there are, the first wave of a minority that succeeds in a previously alien atmosphere is not always well disposed to those struggling along behind. Often their reaction is:

"I got here by myself and I expect you to do the same."

I am stressing the mentor phenomenon for two reasons. First, so that you can recognize it happening around you. It may account for the favoritism you are hard-pressed to understand. And second, so that if you are approached you will be aware of what is going on.

Of all the Black women I spoke to, about half admitted that they had been helped by a mentor.

There was no clear pattern of race or sex; some had been helped by other Black women, Black men, white women, and white men. What emerged from talking to them was that they considered the mentor more as a sponsor and that in most cases the relationship was casual. Some women expressed the fact that in a given job they had been helped by more than one person at a time. Others indicated that their boss had been their mentor. For a Black woman in a white organization, this can be a very confusing situation to handle. First of all, how can you be certain that the would-be mentor's interest is not sexual? You cannot. You have to be prepared to rely on your intuition and to deflect firmly the first improper advance that is made, if it is made. I cannot entirely discount sexual motivations, but my research indicates that in a corporate structure this is quite rare. Suspend your suspicions and give the mentor a chance to prove her or his intentions.

If you have been spotted by top management, they may even assign someone to keep an informal eye on you. Quite a few women I spoke to at first denied that they had ever had a mentor, but in further conversation it gradually emerged that at an important point in their career one person stood out who helped them along.

Obviously, if you are a good worker and you have an intelligent boss, it will appear that your boss is your mentor, someone who encourages you, praises your work, and points out your assets to others in positions of seniority. But remember that your boss may want you to stay where you are, thereby making him look good. If you move on up, with his help, he may not be able to replace you with someone nearly as competent. So an immediate superior does not always make the best mentor, because they may have too big an axe to grind; the best mentor has to be a relatively impartial colleague.

If you do excel at your job, if you are outspoken, if you take risks and keep your antennas bristling, you will probably attract a mentor. If not, then it means you can do without one; more power to you! If you see that a particular superior is paying you extra attention, establish from the very beginning what you wish to be the parameters of the relationship. That way your superior will admire your command of the situation. Never be afraid to ask the mentor for *guidance,* but always be sure that it is *you* who carries out the project. The mentor should not do your work or shoulder your responsibilities. The mentor should be a support, a guide, a sponsor.

Keep the relationship in the office as much as possible, to avoid the sexual innuendo that any such bonding can inspire. This means that if you lunch together it should be in plain view, where others from the office eat, not at a quaint waterfront bistro where you will be "discovered" by the office snoop.

Be loyal to your mentor, but not to the extent that you are persuaded to be part of interoffice political campaigns. This can backfire. When you tie your star to someone else, be sure that they are secure in their position within the organization. The worst stories about mentors that I hear all end the same way: the mentor tries a power-play and loses, and both persons end up on the street.

Some of us are going to attempt to attract mentors, and in some cases those advances will be misconstrued. Think carefully before you try to cultivate a sponsor. It may be lonely, being the only Black woman in your position, but value your independence. Cecilia Johnson is the director of the Human Rights Commission in Des Moines, Iowa, at the age of thirty-two. She says:

> *"I get a lot of support from Black men and white women and even from some white men, but there aren't many Black women who share my experience of running things."*

The important word in Cecilia Johnson's statement is "support." Instead of fishing for a single mentor who can magically raise you to the board, look for as much support as you can get from a wide spectrum of colleagues and superiors.

The Network

If you are an achievement-oriented Black woman moving up through the ranks of *any* type of organization, you *must* be part of a network. You are, even if you are not aware of it. If, as I suggested just now, you obtain support from a group in your office, that is just *one* network to which you belong.

Traditionally white male networks operate invisibly through family, club, and college ties. If you have an old family name, went to the right Ivy League college, and belong to an Establishment club, you have no need to join any formal business group because job opportunities, clients, and stock-market tips will come to you on the "old-boy" network that has done such an excellent job of keeping us out of the corridors of power.

Now we are at the threshold of pre-eminence in the business world, and we have to create our networks from scratch, deliberately. To clarify what a network is and does, let me first state what it is *not:*

A network is not a social organization.

The primary purposes of a network are:

1. To exchange information.
2. To support business endeavors.

A network is not a counseling center; individual members all have to stand on their own two feet. A network is not therapeutic. It exists not for the strong to help the weak; it exists for the strong to help the strong.

Try to identify the networks you already belong to:

AT WORK

The people with whom you exchange information on an irregular basis constitute a network. Friendships you have with your equals in other divisions or other departments; friendships you have with colleagues, superiors, and subordinates because of a mutual bond such as being Black or female or from the same city—these all constitute networks.

OUTSIDE WORK

The professional colleagues with whom you keep in touch, who work for other organizations; former school friends; all professional and business organizations—these too constitute networks.

For instance, that bunch of business cards you have been carrying around since your last trip to Atlanta—if you throw them away, you will be destroying part of a potential network. Network members patronize each other's businesses, pass job hunters along to each other, and make important introductions. Being the member of a network is an active occupation; every person that you meet, especially in your business life, is a possible contact who may become a member of your personal network.

We need networks to balance our positions, especially within organizations that have been built on old support systems to which we did not belong, systems whose members were not anyone like us. We have no role models. Few of us can look to top management and see individuals like ourselves in positions of power. We see white males, most of whom are from backgrounds totally unlike our own. We need, then, to be at least able to look *across* the spectrum of our professional life and to see other Black women, other white women, other Black men, other people in our particular line of work, with whom we can regularly correspond and whose mere presence gives us moral support. It is wise to participate in as many networks as you can handle. I list several formal ones in the Appendix. In addition to networks for Black women, you should join professional groups and alumnae associations.

If you want to further your career, making contacts is tremendously important. There are not many of us, and we need each other's encouragement. We need support from many perspectives, and we will get this by joining and *participating*. You have to *give,* and this means more time, often after work hours. But it is worth it. And if you expect to receive information, be prepared to give it as well. The strongest network is a mutual-use network with no weak links, a network in which each member has something to give to the others. A network is not necessarily the milieu for making the best friends; it is not a mutual admiration society but is more like a free-floating conference. Every network has its standards. There would be little point in an all-inclusive conglomeration of individuals, with little or no mutual ability to relate on a common level.

There are vertical and horizontal networks; both are flexible. The vertical network consists of the acquaintances you made during your school years and your first years at work. Some of these individuals may not be as successful as you, and some may have moved further on, but they all bear keeping in touch with from time to time. It is unwise to cut off people you think you have moved beyond, especially if they proved useful at one time; you may need them again, or they may need you.

Your horizontal network is the one you build now, with your collection of business cards, your informal exchanges with your peers at work, and your formal membership in business-oriented organizations. Go to meetings, speak up, *meet people.* Your situation can become a lot less lonely after an exchange of views with another Black woman in management, who is facing or has faced similar obstacles. Few networks have fixed or printed rules. The most effective networks are visible only to their own members—many of whom would deny the existence of a formal structure, preferring merely to think of themselves as a group of like-minded women in a profession.

I belong to a large number of women's groups, professional organizations, and charitable foundations. In addition, I am always meeting other writers and broadcasters as I travel to promote my products. The network that I use the most and that I am used by cuts across all those borders and constitutes an amalgamation of Black women more or less my age who run into each other again and again at similar functions. Although we never all get together in the same place at the same time (we are far too busy for that), we consider that we have in some respects grown up with each other. Even though we might mention aspects of our private lives:

> *"I hear you got married; congratulations"* or, *"How old is your daughter now?"*

we relate to each other as career women, not as social friends, and are comfortable in that role.

As women, we have a tendency to be inclusive in our relationships; many of us find it difficult to sustain contacts unless the ties are constantly reinforced by persistent contact or social events.

We must program ourselves to be more exclusive, in the sense that two men with relatively similar jobs might see each other once in a while over a period of years, have drinks, play squash, be mutually supportive in business, and never feel any pressure to get together with their wives or talk about their children or other matters that are best left outside the network.

Pamela A. Soden is chairperson of the Council of Concerned Black Executives (CCBE), and she has this advice for us:

> *"You should first determine what your long-term and short-term needs are before you pick an organization in which you can become active. Just as important, you should view your activity in any network as a necessary and legitimate career activity."*

If you are enthusiastic about establishing contacts with organized groups and if you create and sustain a personal network, it will have a very beneficial effect on your position in the company. Here are some pointers on how to manage a personal network:

1. Constantly update your name-and-address file with recent contacts and keep a duplicate file *at home.*

2. Go out of your way to approach and introduce yourself to anybody at work with whom you might have a common interest.

3. On a selective basis, join at least one common interest group of Black women; one of professional women; and one that reflects your business specialty. Participate in

meetings and volunteer for committees. Make yourself useful, visible.

4. Set aside at least one hour a week for reviewing your network. Is there anyone you should call for a lunch meeting? Do not be selfish. Some women only appear when they want something, and they are not as likely to get as much help as those that touch base regularly.

5. Show some concern for the aims of each particular organization. Do not propose new members just to impress. Only make recommendations when you know a person is reliable. A network is only as effective as its members' individual power and responsibility.

6. Try to be of service to network members before you ask them for information or a favor, especially if you are a newcomer.

7. When asking for assistance, facts, or an introduction, make sure it is well within the capacity of the person you are asking.

8. If a network member sends you another person for a job or to use your services or buy your products, always report back and let your contact know what happened.

It takes very little time and effort to maintain a list of contacts, and when you come across articles of interest, trade literature, or simply some amusing commentary, it is worthwhile to make several copies and mail them to a few members of the network.

Those of us who have been, at times, "the only Black woman who . . ." may develop a strong antipathy toward reaching out to others, whether they are Black women, Black men, or whites. We think it is going to be construed as a sign of weakness, especially if we have developed a reputation for being outstanding as individuals. But even if no one was there to help you when you needed it the most and even if only now that you are halfway successful do you find others taking an interest, this is no reason to shun contacts and try to "go it alone." If you work in any way—even free-lance, at home, or whatever—you are part of a system. Someone pays you for what you do; there are some other people doing a similar job; there are commonalities that deserve to be shared. You will simply calcify and grow into your present desk if you refuse to pursue contacts with your colleagues.

For centuries men have been building their networks "out there," while many of us worked at home or were restricted to a tightly knit, segregated community. Men in business are not even aware of the networks they use all day; they never stop to question "why" they know so-and-so. Believe me, a network has no gender; but this does not mean we have to be like white men. Any network is a natural *human* instinct for survival and success.

RAISES AND PROMOTIONS

This is the final part of the fifth key: strategy. You are in a management position, doing good work. You have initiated a number of new procedures that have benefitted the company, and your team of subordinates is made up of hard workers. You have been getting automatic annual raises since you were promoted to management, but that was four years ago. Now you are restless, inflation is shrinking your income, and you know you are ready for bigger things.

Matters come to a head when you are told that E. Willis Haddock has been named senior vice president in charge of sales with a total E.C.P. (executive compensation package) that amounts to well over $100,000 annually. You are incredulous because Haddock came into the company the same time as you but has shown all the signs of becoming a prime dimwit. Why him and not you?

First of all, he is on the fast track: he is in sales, while you are in personnel. This means that the results of his competency appear directly on the company's balance sheet, but yours do not. His department held up fairly well during a period of stiff competition, and he managed to grab most of the credit for that. Actually, his salary is still under $50,000, but because he now heads a department that can show a profit, he is entitled to stock options, stock appreciation rights, and a shadow asset base that brings him up to six figures. No matter how high you go in personnel, you will never be eligible for those "perks."

All right, you knew all that when you decided to stay in personnel, and it is too late to switch. You decide to contact some network members and find out about job prospects with a big company in Boston. Meanwhile, you are determined to ask for a raise and a promotion. How do you handle it?

Strangely enough, most of us consider "asking for a raise" to be a job-threatening procedure, whereas men by and large treat it as a gamble that has no downside. At the very least, men think:

"If I don't get the raise, I'll increase the boss's respect for me."

Why do so many of us think that we will lose our jobs if we ask for a raise? This betokens tremendous insecurity, and it is rampant all the

way up the hierarchy, from the clerical staff to senior management.
Take it from me:

You are not going to get fired simply for asking for a raise!

Or a promotion.

Decide What You Want

Be specific. If you say:

"I've done a good job and I'm worth more"

you provide your superior with the opportunity to agree with you about
the well-done job and launch into a lecture about the state of the economy, ending with:

"I'll see what I can do"

which is the least promising response you could hope for.

Evaluate the possible options that you have. If your compensation
is only in the form of salary, then you might discuss your raise as a
percentage. Allow for the rate of inflation since your last raise, and
then increase by ten, fifteen, or twenty per cent over and above this,
depending upon your analysis of company policy.

Find out as much as you can about what your colleagues are earning and when they received raises, and make comparisons with your
own progress. If you can draw attention to the fact that a white male
with an equal job history is earning more than you, it strengthens your
case. Dig hard to get all the information you can and rely on that (network) friend of yours in accounting! No one is going to ask you *how*
you know that Joe Blow is making twice as much as you; your superior
will be too busy trying to think up an excuse to keep you where you
are.

If your organization offers fringe benefits, evaluate them carefully.
If you move into a higher salary bracket, do you diminish or increase
your fringe benefits? How much are they really worth? Some organizations try to make their employees feel very grateful for small favors.
Use your calculator and figure out what your benefits are worth, in case
you have an opportunity to say that you would rather ditch the perks
and have a fifteen per cent raise. That is if you have done your homework and figured out that the perks amount to less than five per cent of
your remuneration.

What to Ask For

What are the chances of getting a promotion *and* a raise? What is the policy:

> *"Well, Susan, you are doing a magnificent job, so I'm recommending that you be moved up to Sarah Flynn's department. The pay is the same, but you will be an associate vice president."*

Thanks but no thanks. Unless you are moving onto a much faster track (from staff to line, for instance), it is better to have a raise and no promotion than a promotion *instead* of a raise—especially if it means more responsibility for the same salary. One way of handling this is to incorporate your own needs into those of your department:

> *"Mr. Grinch, here is my increased productivity report. I need another assistant and a larger budget. I have also included a proposal for a raise for myself."*

How to Evaluate Your Performance

Just as important as your ability to be specific about the amount of your raise is your ability to indicate exactly why you deserve it. It is quite legitimate to bring up the problem of inflation, since it devalues your salary so that if you do not get an annual raise you are earning *less* every year. It is not, however, particularly apt to discuss external considerations such as your need for money because of hospital expenses, or buying a new home or car. Stick to the facts of your job.

Because you are going to be asking for *money,* gear your approach to the financial aspects of your job. Is there any way that you can draw parallels between your department's productivity and the company's overall profit picture? Even if you are not in a line job, this may be possible. Look very closely at your company's annual report and current financial prospects. Is there ammunition you can use? Give your boss as much hard information as you can, especially if she or he is not the final court of appeal but may have to apply to their superior.

Characterize your output as professionally as possible. What have you been doing in excess of company expectations? Have you acquired any new skills since you were hired or last had a promotion? Have you attended any training programs? Professional seminars? Conferences? Have you *saved* money for the organization? It may be easier to prove this than to link yourself to profits. Are you doing the same amount of work as your predecessor, but with a smaller staff? Have you reorganized in any way? Introduced competitive bid systems for purchasing? Marshal your facts and rehearse your speech. Make it brief and to the point.

How to Ask

This is often where we make our biggest mistake. Because we are prone to think of a raise or promotion as a *personal* matter, we drop all the rules of conduct. If it is your practice to make an appointment with your superiors in the following way:

"Mr. Grinch, could I see you tomorrow at four about the upcoming sales evaluations?"

do *not* pave the way for a raise by saying this:

"Mr. Grinch, could you, um, I'd like to discuss something with you . . . it's personal. Whenever you have the time, please."

Your raise and your promotion are business matters. Treat them as such:

"Mr. Grinch, I would like to see you tomorrow at four o'clock. I want to discuss my raise."

There. You said it. You have given him time to prepare an excuse, but face the fact that you will either get the raise or not, and having advance notice will not swing it against you.

Many of us do not want colleagues, and especially subordinates, to know that we are asking for a raise or a promotion in case we do not get it. There is certainly no point in broadcasting your business, but Grinch may be less likely to let you down if he is aware that this is not a matter entirely restricted to your ears only.

Once you are in the office, make your pitch succinctly. If you are told by Grinch that he will "think about it," ask precisely when you can expect an answer. If Grinch is likely to negotiate, then you must be prepared to fix the figure that would be acceptable to you, or to determine the other elements of compensation that you might be willing to take in lieu of a salary raise.

Be persistent. If you are given an excuse that is tied to the company's profit picture, be prepared to come back when that picture improves. Certainly you must indicate that if you do not get what you want now, you intend to ask for it again and again.

If you are denied a raise and given an excuse which you know is patently false (e.g., that your work has not been satisfactory when you know it has), then look for another job. Most women have no contingency plans for being denied a raise because they treat it as a gamble and are prepared to lose. If you know what your position is within the organization, then you must know what you might be worth to another company; and if that is more than you are getting, you should mention it when you ask for more. Indicate that you would consider a move. Either the company needs you or it does not need you. If it needs you, it should pay the going rate for your services. If it does not need you, then be prepared to be canned sooner or later anyway.

When to Ask for a Raise

Frequently. A month or so after you have taken on increased responsibility. Certainly no less than once a year. Every six months is ideal. Even if you do not always get the raise, you will practice asking.

Remember this: if you tolerate a situation whereby you are knowingly being underpaid, then you are demonstrating your foolishness to your superiors.

AT THE TOP

Now you have made it! You got the raise, you got your promotion, and you are at the helm—no more brown-bag lunches. What do you have to look forward to? The liabilities. In this section I am going to steer you past the pitfalls of risk taking, decision making, responsibility, procrastination, and fear of success. Let us start with what happens when you go too fast.

Burnout

A Black woman in any job that requires her to supervise subordinates and answer to a board is a candidate for job-related stress called "executive burnout." This is particularly true for high achievers, women who have made sacrifices to get where they are, who are the first in their families to reach executive positions and who also have to manage a husband and children. Training and ability are no defense against burnout. It is far more likely to strike the woman who does an excellent, innovative job than one who merely coasts along.

Burnout has physical symptoms such as fatigue, insomnia, alcohol abuse, and drug dependence; but it is a psychological condition which, if not treated, can lead to a mental breakdown.

One of the confusing things to most of the Black women I spoke to who have suffered from burnout is that they could not, at first, understand why they felt so on edge when their jobs were going so well. One of them spoke of not feeling "up to it" day after day; another said that she kept wondering, "What does everyone else have that I lack?" —despite the fact that both were at the time considered by their superiors to be doing very well.

What these women refused to admit was that their jobs were making emotional demands on them far greater than on their male colleagues. Why? First of all, the Black female executive works harder just to prove to herself, consciously or subconsciously, that she can do the job as well as any man. This creates a great deal of stress, especially if she is earning less money. Also, as we shall see in Chapter 9, she is likely to be experiencing pressures at home relating to her status at work, or if she is not married, she may be increasingly depressed over the conflict between her success at her career and her perceived failure to become a wife and mother.

You *are* under more pressure than the others; make no mistake about it. All eyes are on you, and you do not have the luxury of being average or typical. You believe that your mistakes are obvious and your successes minimal. The most important single factor in burnout is *isolation*. You may not have the same outlets as your colleagues—informal activities, sports events, or social contacts with your peers that do not demand that you have to be "on" the whole time.

If you lack a mentor, and especially if you have no network and are in a senior management position in an organization that has few Black women at your level, then you are a prime candidate for stress. You may have no outlet for grievances other than your family and no source for positive feedback for your accomplishments. It is easy for you to get discouraged under those circumstances.

It is not easy for you to maintain a professional demeanor at all times. This is a strain. Your contact with men, especially with male superiors, creates a great deal of stress because of your need to keep them at a distance. Casual interest in you by a male employee is something that can create complex and confusing situations that you have to handle *on top of* your regular job.

Some Black female executives find it hard to exercise power in a straightforward manner. We have conditioned ourselves to be inwardly strong while on the outside agreeable, pleasant, and apparently yielding. In order to maintain respect and establish credibility, we have to adopt behavior which is perfectly suitable for our positions in the company. It is behavior that is neither masculine nor feminine, Black nor white, but it is in conflict with the way we were brought up to behave, and this causes stress and burnout.

Black women working in poorly run organizations are very susceptible to stress. If there is general apathy, no strong chain of command, and weak communication links, then we tend to absorb an inordinate amount of the blame.

You may find yourself overworked and underused, in the sense that you are not allowed to make the most of your abilities and are unable to experience any sense of true accomplishment.

To Minimize Stress

1. Admit that you are under pressure.

2. Seek outlets on the job. Approach someone you can trust for regular bull sessions.

3. If you have a hectic life at home, give yourself thirty minutes after your job to unwind: exercise, yoga, or a calisthenics class *before* you walk in your front door.

4. Re-examine your goal and polish your résumé. Should you be thinking about a move?

5. Distinguish between the stressful aspects of your job that you can change and those that are out of your hands. Enlist the support of others to make the changes.

6. Delegate as many of your trivial duties as possible and keep your eye on a major goal.

7. Learn what "risk taking" is really all about.

Risk Taking

Whether mentioned as such or regarded in other ways, this is the most misunderstood aspect of organizational life, and women tend to understand it the least. We have a strong tendency to personalize many aspects of our daily work. When we hear the word "risk," we equate it with a *threatening* situation. We would not *risk* our child's life at the deep end of the swimming pool; it is *risky* to drive without snow tires; if I spend this much money on clothes, I will *risk* not being able to pay the rent.

This is deeply ingrained. To take a decisive step, any step that has a win/lose aspect to it, can be a source of anxiety to us. We are very afraid of *making a mistake*. Why?

First of all, business is serious; our work is serious. Is it just as serious or more serious than our home life? We imagine so. Therefore the same kind of thing will happen on the job if we make a mistake as will happen (or used to happen, when we were children) at home: we will get *blamed* for it. The mistake is *wrong;* we are *bad* for having made it. We need no outside reinforcement for this because we are adept at *blaming ourselves*.

Secondly, we are Black women. Someone, perhaps more than one person in the organization, is waiting for us to *make a mistake*. So they can say:

"Ha! I always knew they couldn't do this job"

and make us feel *ashamed* for our race and our sex, make us feel that we have let all Black women down.

One of the reasons that too many of us get stuck in a holding pattern at the middle-management level is that we are afraid to take risks so we avoid making decisions and play it safe. But decision making is an inimicable part of organization life. It involves risk, but that is *organizational* risk, not personal risk.

A successful male executive in senior management knows that if *half* his decisions turn out to be right he is doing well. He considers risk taking to be an impersonal part of the job, day to day. He is not unduly disappointed when a decision he has made turns out to be wrong:

"Well, I learned a lot from that situation. Next time I will tackle it with better information."

How many times have you really been told that your job is on the line unless you make a right decision? The consensus opinion among career counselors is that a person who is afraid to take risks, who does not like making decisions, is far more likely to be putting his or her job in jeopardy (actually *risking* the career) than someone who seems to be quite reckless, forever plunging in and trying out new ideas.

Do not imagine that you have got to win every time you go to bat. Think of it in these terms: take the risk; if you come out ahead, your try was successful; if not, you have accomplished two things. One, you have demonstrated your ability to move forward; and two, you have added to your store of knowledge about that particular type of situation.

Unless you are an entrepreneur, running your own business, there is no decision you can make which will actually threaten the stability of your company. In the corporate world there are no women, Black or white, who are yet in positions that have that much influence, sad to say. Most of our senior-management jobs involve the routine implementation of staff decisions that do not have a major impact on the company's profit or performance. It should be quite different in ten years' time, and then I will be able to write about executive stress brought on by our having to make truly earth-shattering decisions.

Fear of being wrong sometimes prevents us from making any decision at all. In the long run you may be safe *and* sorry. I say, keep hitting out with those decisions and take the risks, over and over. Get a reputation for being decisive. The law of averages is on your side, even if you are using a pin and a telephone directory as a guide.

Here is a very prosaic analogy. Imagine that your decisions at work have as much real risk involved as your decisions in the supermarket. Sure, you will buy something new, and it might not taste as good as you expected. But does your family die of botulism? The next time you shop you are a little wiser, but you still keep on trying new things because you want to enjoy the best products for the least cash.

Take that attitude to your job. Learn to enjoy taking risks, and after a few tries you will find that you receive much more attention, praise, and respect by trying and failing and trying again than simply by holding the fort.

Risk taking is an objective factor in your job, something to be relished, not avoided. Win or lose, the more you do it, the easier it becomes. Your superiors want to see how willing you are to make revisions, create new systems, and hire and fire subordinates; all these things involve risk.

More job-related stress actually comes from the effort to *avoid* risk than from the results of bad decisions. Built into any organization's structure is an allowance for innovation, and that means ideas that fail as well as ideas that succeed.

Fear of Success

A number of us have self-destruct mechanisms that lead to total burnout as we approach a certain level of achievement. This is found in all senior executives to one degree or another, but as Black women we have more conditions against which to guard.

One of the most widespread causes of this phenomenon is family background. If you are the first in your family to go to college or to earn as much money as you are earning, and especially if your background was not encouraging, then you may be heading for trouble.

Janice M. was promoted from a secretarial position to the advertising sales staff of a well-known magazine. Three months after she was promoted, her boss singled her out for a great deal of praise because she had more than doubled the revenues in the Classified section. Right after that, Janice was stricken with anxiety and her performance plummeted. In therapy, she realized that she was experiencing a great deal of subconscious guilt because her father, who was extremely religious but had no formal education, had indoctrinated her from an early age with his contempt for books, business and, significantly, people who went door to door *selling things*. Recognizing her own talents as a sales agent, coupled with the fact that she worked for a literary endeavor, was too much for Janice to handle.

Black women who have risen through the ranks in one company, and made good pals along the way, may try to prevent themselves from succeeding beyond a certain level because they do not want to sacrifice the friendship of their former peers; they want to avoid what they perceive as a lonely situation, away from the girls. Paula R. does not want to accept a promotion. Why? She has spent five years building a network of allies in the promotion and public relations departments of a major manufacturing company. Now she has been tapped to head a combined division which would effectively put her in charge of both those areas.

Paula fears that as soon as she is "the boss," she will be spoken about in the same way that she and her pals used to speak about the former boss. She fears moving away from one socially comfortable level into an area that is dominated by white male executives. She feels that she will be rejected by her former buddies and not accepted by her new peers. She does not want the responsibility, and she does not want to take what she perceives of as the risks involved in the new position —even though she is fully qualified to do the job.

The most potent trauma associated with the fear of success, one shared to some extent by all women who achieve in a male-dominated world, is the subconscious identification of success with masculinity. The reasoning goes like this:

"If I can do a job that was formerly done by a man or is mostly done by men, then it indicates that I am masculine."

In extreme cases the woman experiences a deeply buried but no less forceful fear that she will "turn into a man" by taking a "male" job. If you were brought up in a very traditional home and your mother did not go out to work but firmly believed that "a woman's place is in the home," you may fear hurting or betraying your mother and may experience a great deal of guilt over what you are doing. This can hold true even if, in later years, your mother has encouraged your achievements.

If you think that you may be your own worst enemy in this respect, that you might be sabotaging your chances for success by doing stupid things that damage your likelihood of being promoted, then you may be afraid of success. If this is the case or if you are just experiencing a great deal of anxiety that has no discernible cause, you should consult a doctor and consider therapy.

Responsibility

The adept manager, the shrewd executive, and the successful dean all know exactly where their responsibility begins and where it ends. Our vision of achievement often involves an ever-widening realm of responsibilities, awesome and terrifying. That is not so unless we choose to make it that way, which we do only to our detriment. The *significance* of that for which we are responsible may increase, but the *amount* is usually less the further we move.

Do you ever find yourself apologizing for things that are not your fault? At home, perhaps? If you pick a restaurant that is less than perfect, do you apologize? If you bump into somebody, and they are clearly in the wrong, do you automatically say "I'm sorry"? If you are working on a report at work and you are asked for it a week ahead of the deadline, do you say:

"It isn't finished yet, I'm sorry"?

According to writer Jane O'Reilly:

"Apologizing too much is probably part of women's fear of success. It reflects guilt, low self-esteem, a touch of misplaced arrogance."

The arrogance is that by apologizing for something which is God's fault (the weather), not our own, we assume responsibility for *everything*.

At work, analyze your area of responsibility and reduce it as much as you can; do not apologize for what is not under your control. Recognize what is your responsibility and what is that of your subordinates, and let them do their own apologizing. We have discussed autonomy. It is very important that you establish your territory and rule it firmly. This is impossible to do if part of you feels responsible for areas beyond your control. A successful executive knows precisely where those boundaries lie and if the accountability is elsewhere states so.

Procrastination

This often involves a combination of risk avoidance, fear of success, and a feeling of being overwhelmed by responsibility. Do you:

1. Always have too much to do and too little time, so that only the less important things get done?

2. Wait until all the facts are in, and then some more, before making a decision?

3. Get involved in so many projects that no single one gets your full, undivided attention?

4. Always plan ahead, set a date to start a project, and then find a good reason for changing the date as the deadline approaches?

5. Avoid confrontations with your boss or your subordinates, because there is something *more important* to be done?

A procrastinator is not someone twiddling the thumbs instead of working. A procrastinator is someone able to make a very good case for not doing what has to be done:

"Look at my desk. See how much I have to do already!"

Strangely enough, procrastination is a form of *control*. By putting something off, you are demonstrating your power; you are not simply a cog in a machine, a mere tool, but an adult human being capable of making your own decisions about what has priority and what has not. The unpleasant tasks, however, usually manage to slip down the list. Often we do this to avoid exposing our lack of ability or the possibility that we may, in a confrontation, be challenged and have to lose face.

I pride myself on being a *perfectionist*. Do you? Are you so demanding, so rigid, and so convinced that you can achieve perfection in whatever you do that sometimes you do nothing? For some of us the mere *best* is second-best because it is not *perfect*. Since nothing in this life *is* perfect, we can successfully avoid doing *everything* on the grounds that we are not willing to accept the second-best.

A wise woman accepts errors as part of her job. The procrastinator sees errors as a devastating reflection of her own weaknesses. To avoid error, postpone. At work, we are assisted in this by the increasing volume of information that is at our disposal. Computer technology can feed us reams and reams of facts and figures about virtually anything we care to be interested in, and it is in the nature of some of us to excuse making a decision because:

"I just want to gather a little more information. There is no point in being rash when I can make a couple more studies . . ."

In this age of electronic overload, that could take six months and could bury the office in printouts. You can also have so many good ideas that you are quite unable to pick one, the right one.

Do you see what I mean? Are you guilty of any of these maneuvers, to a greater or lesser degree? Here is how to overcome procrastination:

1. *Examine your motives. What are you avoiding? What exactly do you fear? What is the worst thing that can happen?*
2. *Revamp your work schedule into smaller, shorter periods, and accomplish one of the easiest objectives ahead of schedule. This will break your mental block.*
3. *If you are avoiding a confrontation, try to rehearse it with a friend. Your biggest fear may be that you simply have not planned what you should say.*
4. *Make up your mind that it is better to do* something *to the best of your ability than to do* nothing *perfectly!*
5. *Stay at work one hour late and clean all the petty nonsense off your desk so the next morning you will have no choice but to face the important issues.*
6. *Make a priority list for days, weeks, and months. Make it very graphic. Block out in red what you have done and leave clear what you have to do. Vow to increase the red area at least slightly every day.*
7. *Full steam ahead!*

All people who have reached the top by their own efforts have experienced failure. Avoidance of failure is not a mark of success but a sign of timidity. How you cope with failure is what will set you apart from the crowd. If you can deal maturely with rejection, disappointment, and even humiliation, you will be a success. Failure is simply a learning process, not a grade. It can spur you on to greater effort or plunge you into paralyzing gloom. Which is it going to be?

If you are constantly seeking to compare yourself with the achievements of others, you are secretly looking for excuses to stay where you are:

"Look at her! She is ten years younger than me and a vice president."

What is your next thought:

"I bet she isn't divorced with two children to look after like me" or
"If she can do it, I certainly can!"

Make your own schedule for success and keep your eye on the goal. As you make your way, try not to be distracted by those going faster; there are plenty going slower. What matters is to keep your strategy flexible.

The Struggle at the Top

Never imagine that you can get where you want without making enemies. The dream of easy camaraderie is only possible, if at all, in the lower ranks. The higher you climb, the more reasons you will give people to be resentful and jealous of you. This is understandable when it concerns people that you pass on the way up, but you may be puzzled by the negative feelings from your colleagues near the top and your superiors, when you know you are doing a great job.

Ambition and talent scare people, and just by doing a great job you may be a threat to your superior. Recognize the fact that just as some women can experience anxiety in a "man's" job, you may be causing the same kind of anxiety in a man by demonstrating that you can do his job! You are a threat to his masculinity, and he may derive a great deal of ego-support from his position; he probably equates it with his role as husband/provider, and he is not going to be happy when a Black woman proves she is just as able as he is. I am not encouraging you to feel sorry for him—far from it. Just ignore the poor fellow.

We were raised, most of us, to expect that if we are *nice,* people will like us. When we are the targets of totally unwarranted hostility, we experience a lot of repressed anger. I was amazed and baffled as a very young fashion model to find that for all the people that I encountered who were proud of my success, there were just as many, Black and white, women and men, who conveyed extreme hostility toward me on sight, before they had any chance to know me. I later came to realize that this was envy, pure and simple. You can waste a lot of precious time and emotional energy by being combative when faced with career envy. It is just part of the load, and the way to handle it is to be polite and firm, not hostile, in return. If you ever experience something like this:

"I hope you realize this is not the typing pool, honey; we are expected to work*"*

from a male colleague the first day at your new big desk, you should reply:

"Please do not call me 'honey.' "

That is all. Not:

> *"You are a sexist, racist male chauvinist, and if I have any-*
> *thing to do with it, you will not last long around here!"*

You can *think* that, and act on it when you have the chance.

Hostile aggression is not assertiveness; it is bullying and is totally unproductive. Be assertive, not aggressive; be persistent, not boorish. As a woman you have a great deal of experience in diplomacy, timing, and intuition. Use it.

Timing and Discipline

Your first attempt to get a raise or a promotion may meet with failure. Never say die. Go back again and again. You may have found up until this point that, as hard as it was, scholastic achievement and hard work led to a steady reward ratio. Now the rules seem to have changed. You may expect the reward sooner than you get it, and this frustration may diminish your capacity to do the job well. Do not let failure to move as fast as you want minimize your self-confidence. Plot your long-term goals and short-term ends that have to be met this month and the next. Be reasonable and tell yourself that if you have not substantially improved your position within a set period of time (six, twelve, or eighteen months), you will seek another job. Make no compromises and focus on the goal.

Reading

How many times have I heard:

> *"I have been so busy, I haven't read a newspaper in* weeks! *I*
> *don't know what is going on in the world."*

You may be so deluged with reading material in your job that you never find the time to read "for pleasure." The fact is, if you want to succeed, you *have* to find the time to read because I firmly believe that you must widen your grasp of technical, political, and business affairs *in the world* if you expect to move into top management. If you know only about your limited field, even if you are an excellent worker, you will never move beyond yeoman duty. You must have an idea of how your work in your organization fits into or participates with the social and economic picture of the city, state, nation, and world.

Some major corporations—General Motors is one, Abbott Laboratories another—provide their senior executives with news summaries and digests. You have to make it your business to consume at least one periodical a week that is not related to your job and the daily newspaper. My favorite happens to be *The Wall Street Journal* because it gives me local and national news, humorous comment, provocative editorials, and plenty of hard information that helps me in business. This kind of news is a *must* if you want to avoid being narrow-minded. Some of us make the mistake of only reading Black magazines or so-called women's magazines. Read them by all means, but also read *Forbes* and *Newsweek*. You will never broaden your abilities unless you continue to read hungrily after you leave college. It is a grave mistake to dismiss major publications because you are convinced that they are prejudiced against women or Blacks. I read some of them just to find out what my potential enemies think, how they think, and what they are planning! I have one friend who was taken by surprise when her company folded and she lost her job, but if she had followed the business section of her local paper, she could have figured out that it was going to happen six months ahead of time.

Reading about other businesses is fascinating because you find out so much that you can relate to your own experience. The products or services may be widely different, but system problems, department shifts, or management-procedure changes are often common to many different types of organizations, and finding out how other companies have succeeded or failed is invaluable information.

If you ever had any knack for writing and you find yourself with ideas or commentary, it does your career no harm to get published. You may have a company newsletter or a trade journal, or you may simply write a "letter to the editor" of your local paper and identify yourself and your organization. That kind of involvement brings you to the attention of everyone on the job and reveals your abilities and concerns. Reading and writing are precious communication tools.

Income Versus Status

> "In some ways we have bought the American Dream about job sta-
> tus and what women should be doing more than white women
> have. We are often discouraged from careers in the trades by par-
> ents and male friends who do not think it would be 'ladylike.'"
>
> Gloria Parker, Associate Director
> Women in Apprenticeship Program
> National Urban League

Joyce Phillips spent three years working as a secretary at an insurance company in Chicago. Conditions at work were excellent; she got along well with her co-workers, and she took pride in her appearance as she commuted every day to the downtown area. Her family was proud that she worked for a well-known corporation, and her mother was always asking her when she was going to meet "a nice young man" at the office.

For two years Joyce liked her job and took a great deal of satisfaction from the fact that she was not stuck behind the cash register at the local supermarket like most of her high school classmates.

In her third year Joyce became somewhat uneasy about her job. She was only making $11,500, and it was unlikely that she would ever make much more than that as a secretary. Her company did not encourage promotions from her level and expected secretaries either to leave and get married or to grow old in their jobs. Also, she had met no nice young man to bring home to her mother, partly because at twenty-three she did not want to get married and partly because in her office there were no Black men except in the shipping department.

Joyce lived at home and helped her parents pay the rent. After buying clothes and paying for an occasional long weekend vacation, she had no money for her savings account. More than anything else, she wanted an apartment of her own, but unless she found three room-mates, there was no way she could afford it.

One evening, during the rush hour, she bumped into a former school friend, Leslie. Joyce barely recognized her because Leslie was scruffy, wearing not very clean denims and carrying what looked like a tool kit. Leslie explained that she had just completed a training program and had a plumber's license. She was hoping to join the local union and, after a year as an apprentice, could make up to fifteen dollars an hour. Joyce asked her what on earth made her take up plumbing:

"First of all, I was broke," explained Leslie. "My dear husband left me with two small children, and there was no way you were going to find me on welfare. All the jobs I got offered at the employment office paid slave wages for back-breaking cleaning work, so I had to find a skill. As you know, I did badly at school, but one day the handyman in our building gave me an idea when he came to fix the drain under my sink and I was able to figure out the problem quicker than he was! I got a do-it-yourself book about home plumbing, and after struggling with it for a couple of evenings, I could understand almost all of it."

"But isn't it terribly hard work?" asked Joyce. "Don't you have to lift a lot of heavy pipes and stuff?"

"That's what I thought at first," said Leslie, "and quite honestly that turned me off. I'm five-three and a hundred and ten. I soon found out that my hands and nails were getting banged about, but I wasn't handling anything heavier than a typewriter. Men aren't completely stupid, you know. There is a tool for every operation; you don't have to be a weight lifter!"

Joyce could not get this conversation out of her head:

"I kept finding myself doing mental arithmetic," she told me. "For the next couple of weeks, I multiplied hourly wages until my head was spinning. All I could come up with was that it always came out to more than I was making at the office!"

It took Joyce six months to make up her mind. She saw more of Leslie and even met her on the job for a brown-bag lunch. When she told Leslie what she was thinking of doing, Leslie did not want her to have any false illusions:

"Most of the guys go out of their way to let you know they don't like you doing their job! The Black guys are often worse than the white ones because they act as if I am taking a job away from one of them. They try to make me ashamed of working hard, and they will try to prove you can't handle it too—even some of the instructors do this. I've been called a lot of names. But in the end, if you keep up, they respect you. I was lucky to get hooked up with a real old fellow. He couldn't have cared less that I was a Black woman, and he showed me a lot of the stuff they don't teach—the shortcuts."

Joyce asked Leslie how her family felt about what she was doing:

"At first my father was very angry. He couldn't bear to see his 'little girl' getting her hands dirty. He finally saw the light when I asked him if he was willing to support me and my children!"

Joyce's mother was shattered. Joyce told her that she was quitting her job and had been accepted in the same training program that Leslie had joined. Now Joyce and Leslie are working for the same company and talking about eventually setting up their own business, but Joyce's mother still cannot understand why her daughter could give up a prestigious job in a big clean office to be a plumber.

It is not easy for a Black woman to break into a lot of the trades careers. The opposition is very strong, from within the trades and also from the world outside. This is true for quite a few of the jobs I am going to describe in this chapter, jobs that are loosely described in our society as "blue-collar." These include construction, printing, welding, and truck driving, as well as "uniform" jobs in transportation and security. Both unions and employers alike have been forced to admit women and minorities, and this means that the *opportunities are there,* but as you do your basic training and apprenticeship, be prepared to endure a spate of undisguised hostility in some, not all, instances. Conditions vary enormously according to the particular trade and local behavior.

Why do it? For the money. Skilled and semiskilled labor pays much better than secretarial or clerical work, retail selling, and a lot of other jobs that do not force us to scrub down at the end of the day. With a license and a union card, you also have a degree of mobility, and this means freedom. Your skills can be employed anywhere in the country.

Job satisfaction is an additional factor that cannot be discounted. Once you take away the congenial surroundings, your job as a secretary may have very little bearing on the business of the company. You are utterly replaceable; the job you do can be done by millions of others. You are a dispensable cog in a very large machine. As a skilled worker, however, you may experience physical and emotional sensations of real accomplishment. You can take real pride in a job well done and completed for all to see. In many trades you continue to learn and to increase your skill and earnings over the years. If you are a member of a strong union, you have more job security than you ever could have as an office worker. With experience you have the opportunity to move into a supervisory position as a job inspector. Most of us dismiss the trades because we think of them solely in terms of manual labor, but if you lack a college education and you have a family to support, it may be the best way for you to succeed in an honorable profession—even if you have a college degree! The head of one of the nation's largest schools for tractor-trailer driving recently reported that whereas ten years ago all the students were male and few had high school diplomas, now they are more often than not women, and half his students have had a college education!

Most women convince themselves that trades jobs are out of the question because they are simply not strong enough or mechanically minded. It is just a question of learning and practice. Unlike boys, girls are not encouraged to be interested in carpentry and are not given the types of toys that boys start playing with at an early age, toys which encourage manual dexterity and building. This does not mean that we are not capable of assimilating this type of information; it simply means that we are victims of a cultural bias against women. Because you have never had to perform a particular operation does not mean that you cannot do it. Like changing a tire, when you *have* to do it, you learn quickly enough! There are women now working as longshorepersons on the New Jersey waterfront, one of the most notoriously tough work places in the world, with a heritage of excluding almost everyone except local-born white males from the lucrative jobs loading and unloading the freighters that dock in the harbors. They experienced great opposition at first, and in order to prove themselves they had to do the worst jobs. They realized that in fact this was a tradition that every rookie had to endure, although as Black women they were subjected to additional difficulties. But when they did not break down, when they showed that they could keep up with the guys, they earned respect and, in time, friendship.

Your attitude is more important than physical strength. The employer could not care less if the job gets done by a Black woman or a white man, so long as it gets done well. If you can think only in terms of lowering yourself to do a dirty job so that you can earn more money, you will fail. You must have a positive, constructive attitude and a desire to take pride in your work. None of the women I spoke to who worked in trades regretted that they had made the switch. Some had been on welfare and had hit rock bottom before they took their first class in vocational training; others had given up supposedly fancy office jobs that had been, in their eyes, dead ends. Thelma Waters lives in Washington, D.C. She had a job with the federal government, but now is a television repair mechanic. Her starting salary was what it would have taken her fifteen years to reach in her old job. She owns her house and car, and sends her daughter to a private school.

"Now I can afford the nice clothes I look forward to changing into at the end of the day. When I worked in an office, half my earnings went to keeping up my appearance on the job. I couldn't afford the cleaning bills, so as soon as I got home I had to change into messy things."

It is just as possible to be exploited by a situation that appeals to your conventional ideas about success as by an inequitable ratio of work to income. This is very true of Black women in white-collar positions. Relieved to have moved beyond our parents' lives of toil, we fail to realize that only the names have changed. At first it mattered a lot to Joyce that she could work in a clean, friendly office; it mattered more than earning a decent wage. By spending a nominal amount on carpets and upholstered furniture, her employer attracted impressionable young women who were willing to accept low salaries. I have mentioned before that the environment at work is an important factor in choosing a job, but it should not override the very hard facts of wages, and it is not worth accepting half of what you could earn in the trades just for the privilege of keeping your hands clean. Especially if you have dependents, you should reassess your personal values.

All over the country there are vocational guidance centers and counseling groups that will advise and teach you about the trades and provide information regarding local job possibilities and union openings. Not all jobs are equally well paid, and before you embark on a training course, make sure that the skills you learn are in demand in your area. One way of doing this is to check with prospective employers, read the "situations vacant" section in the local newspaper, and get in touch with union locals.

You may have to be prepared to subsidize your training or at least take a drop in salary. A friend of mine took a $1,000 cut in salary when she left her job as a secretary to become a housing fireperson, but now she is making more than she did in the office and, having qualified for an assistant superintendent's job, she told me that in three years she can double her present salary.

Your initial training may be anywhere from six weeks to six months, and you will have to be prepared to support yourself during this period. After that, from six months to three years may be required in an apprenticeship program, during which you can expect to earn six to eight dollars per hour until you achieve journeyman status, which means you are fully trained and eligible for ten dollars an hour and up.

Most trades training programs require a high school diploma or a G.E.D. (General Educational Development) Certificate, as well as testing and interviews. In the Appendix you will find information sources for various programs.

I have compiled a survey of the most promising types of trades, ones that I believe are opening up to Black women and which will experience progressive expansion in the next decade:

Building and Construction

If you are under twenty-five, this area offers the best prospects. The work is hard and the hours are long, but the rewards are considerable. You may have to alternate periods of ten-hour days and six-day weeks with slow periods of six-hour days and four-day weeks. Apprenticeship programs are from two to five years, and they combine on-the-job experience with classroom training. You may have to scratch around for nonunion jobs until you are accepted by a union. Federally funded rehabilitation programs offer the choicest nonunion work.

There are three categories of construction jobs, and I have italicized those specific ones that the Department of Labor believes have the strongest growth potential.

Structural

Blocklayer
Bricklayer
Cement Mason
Rigger
Operating Engineer
Boilermaker
Carpenter
Iron Worker
Rodman
Stonemason

Mechanical

Electrician
Millwright
Plumber
Elevator Constructor

Pipe Fitter
Sheet-Metal Worker

Finishing

Asbestos Worker
Carpet Layer
Dry-Wall Installer
Glazier
Gypsum Board Applicator
Insulation Worker
Lather
Marble Setter
Painter
Paperhanger
Plasterer
Roofer
Terrazzo Setter

Maintenance and Repair

Just check the labor charges the next time you have your television repaired or your car serviced! Some garages now have a thirty-five-dollar-per-hour minimum labor charge. Of course, no one earns that eight hours a day, five days a week, but maintenance and repair trades are potentially very lucrative.

Automobiles and home appliances offer the best prospects, especially in an economy that is starting to indicate that planned obsolescence may be on the way out. In hard times people are prone to repair their old equipment sooner than they buy new models. This also holds true for office-machine maintenance and repair. Just one example: major manufacturers of office copying machines have their own trained crews of specialists in every part of the country.

The public telephone system is another major employer in this field. Women are beginning to make strong inroads here because as a utility the telephone systems have to comply with affirmative action regulations. This means hiring Black women for nontraditional jobs.

Law Enforcement

In addition to the gun-toting policewomen featured on television crime dramas, there are a large number of jobs open to women in police departments. Some are civilian jobs or administrative desk positions, and others are uniformed positions such as investigator, vice officer, community-relations officer, and decoy. The more traditional jobs include matron duty for juvenile offenders and female prisoners. More and more Black women are being hired for high-visibility jobs in the patrol and traffic divisions. Ellen Fleysher, the deputy commissioner of public information for the New York City Police Department, says:

"The field of law enforcement is wide open—a new frontier that has not been thoroughly exploited by women"

and that when considering candidates:

"We look for certain human qualities; anyone interested in pursuing modern police work must be an intelligent, insightful, and perceptive person. She must be extraordinarily flexible, because her life is different from day to day, from assignment to assignment. And she has to roll with the calm, with the dull, and with an all-out emergency she has to be able to flow from one event to the next."

Is that you? You have to have a high school diploma, and if you want to move up through the ranks, a college degree. You have to pass written, psychological and physical examinations, meet minimum height and weight requirements, and undergo character and background investigations. In almost all cities, local civil service regulations govern the appointment of officers.

Transportation

As fuel becomes more and more expensive, local municipalities have to expand their public transit systems, and this means more jobs for Black women. Driving jobs require a chauffeur's license and some proven experience, although federal regulations require that women be admitted to all training programs. There are inspection and maintenance jobs in transportation as well as routing and office jobs. Civil service examinations are given at specific times of the year and must be publicly advertised. There are few Black women in national transportation (cross-country bus, train, and air services) apart from flight attendants, and there is only one Black female pilot, Jill Brown. This can change if we take advantage of the training programs that are available to us.

MAKING THE FIRST MOVE

The hardest part about entering one of these nontraditional (for Black women) blue-collar jobs is the psychological adjustment required to fend off the disapproval of friends and family and to put up with the hostility that every Black woman who is one of the first in any field must endure. Here are some tips:

1. Do not go it alone. Try to persuade a friend to join up with you. If that is not possible, make a big effort to get to know other females in your training group, no matter how they strike you at first. Sooner or later you will be thrown together, and opposition or negative reactions from male co-workers is best endured if it is shared in solidarity.

2. Take the time to explain to your family that your economic reasons are sound. Chart the progress you can make as a trained worker against that of your current job.

3. When you are an apprentice, do not be too proud to ask for help. Some women make the mistake of assuming that they have to figure everything out for themselves in order to prove that a woman can do as well as a man in a trade job. In fact, a mentor system exists just as strongly here as in management, but much more informally. A lot of women drop out of trade programs because they can only go "by the book" and never learn the on-the-job techniques more often than not handed down by example. The whole point of an apprenticeship is to learn from an experienced older person. Try to attach yourself to someone who seems to know what she or he is doing. Do not worry about initial reservations. Someone with a skill is sooner or later going to enjoy transmitting it to a newcomer. Not every situation demands that you go it alone. Teamwork is as important as skill. You see men on the job asking each other for help, whether with physical tasks or problem solving. Asking for help makes you stronger, not weaker.

Your social life is bound to suffer once you move out of the nine-to-five system. Especially as a novice, you will be required to work at odd hours, sometimes at night, and this will be inconvenient for your family and for sustaining relationships with people outside your line of work. I know women in trades who go to great lengths to conceal what they do from their friends. This is a big mistake. Taking pride in your job and being able to talk about it with interest is a vital part of handling any job.

If you are unemployed and receiving public assistance and you want to get into a trade, my advice is to approach the training program on your own, not via the employment office or welfare program. Most employers have a very low opinion of labor they receive from this source, and you will be burdened by that from the start. In part of the Southwest, very successful motivational programs have evolved outside the government system to encourage young Black women to go as individuals to prospective employers. It is always better to arrive under your own steam than to have been "sent" by another agency. An employer likes to see evidence of a take-charge mentality, and this is as true of skilled labor as it is of senior management. Enthusiasm will be met with consideration, but as a former welfare recipient you will simply be treated as a warm body and, since you are a Black woman, as one whom the employer regards as a potential dropout. Under those circumstances, everything is working against you, and your first error will be enough to convince your boss you are not right for the job.

Most fear comes from ignorance, which is why it is worth spending time to obtain all the information you can about a skill you want to acquire. Talk to someone who has been at it for five or ten years. Never forget that you have a *right* to work. Any job that you see being done by a man is a job you can have! The laws of equal opportunity are strict, but interpreted in different ways in different locales. Find out how they are practiced in your part of the country so that you can be fully aware of your rights. You will be kept back unless you *demand* what is yours under the law. Policewomen are bringing discrimination suits against local departments because, although they are better educated than most men entering police work, they do not get promoted as rapidly.

Opportunities in the Military Services

All branches of the military are competing for eligible Black women as officer trainees and specialists. Thirty-six per cent of the women in the Army are Black. Until a decade ago, women in the military were restricted to traditionally female posts in the administrative and medical divisions. This translates as secretaries and nurses. The situation has changed dramatically in recent years to the point that we are allowed to compete with men on an equal basis for *all* jobs with the exception of combat areas, which account for a very small percentage of military-related skills. This means that you can be paid to learn a trade, such as electrical engineering, which can provide you with the resources for a profitable career outside the military when your tour of duty is over.

Although the Marine Corps, which is primarily a combat organization, does require women to test higher than men in order to be eligible for enlistment, the Army, Navy, Coast Guard, and Air Force operate on an equal opportunity basis. In some instances you can complete your high school education while in the service and go on to obtain a college degree. Various financial aid programs are available in conjunction with your enlistment. The Army is currently operating a matching fund plus bonus system that can provide you with over $20,000 for a college education after just three years in the Army.

If you are interested, get in touch with your local recruiter (see the Appendix) and also talk to any friends or relatives with military experience. Whether you are interested in a brief period of enlistment or a full-time career, find out for yourself which are the skills you can learn in the service that will be most in demand in civilian life.

Life in the military is not a piece of cake. In exchange for a total-care package that provides you with food, clothing, and a roof over your head, as well as a salary and training, you are expected to abide by rules and restrictions that are not found anywhere in civilian life. Although a great effort has been made to bring working conditions more in line with those in civilian life and to provide recreational facilities and vacation time, you must be aware that you are under an obligation to obey commands that you might have a perfect right to question in civilian life. There are, however, established procedures for deterring discrimination and sexual harassment.

Because military salaries are lower than civilian ones, there is no point in signing up unless you are determined to use the experience either to learn a specific skill or to increase your academic credits.

❀❀❀❀❀

7

Be Your Own Boss!

"The key ingredients to starting one's own business are:
a. Expertise in a specific field. One must be able to offer some-
thing to people one is approaching.
b. A strong education and/or exceptional work experience.
c. Competent internal accounting personnel, as well as external
accounting or auditing work with a knowledge of your specific
business. Do not just hire a friend of the family but hire a
knowledgeable firm if necessary, who will have a working
knowledge of your particular business."

Ernesta G. Procope
President, Chief Executive Officer
E. G. Bowman Co., Inc.

Is it a dream come true or a nightmare of burdensome responsibility? How often have you considered owning and running your business? Is it something that seems very far removed from your experience or unattainable because of the imagined cost? Are you willing to give up the security of a nine to five job and step out into the unknown world of subchapter S corporations?

History forced many of us to fend for ourselves in ways that were actually entrepreneurial although rarely considered as such. Black women have been running "small businesses" for a long time, whether they knew it or not: laundries, bakeries, corner stores, beauty shops, and house-cleaning services. Segregated from the services of the larger community, Black districts were forced to develop their own small businesses. These took care of the individual from birth (the free-lance midwife) to death (locally owned and operated funeral parlors). Few of these operations were structured as formal parts of the business system in this country, but the few Black millionaires that we can boast about developed out of this grass-roots need for services that the white community was unable or unwilling to provide. Madame C. J. Walker, with her turn-of-the-century cosmetics sold in small beauty salons across the country, is just one Black woman of whom we can be proud in this way. Most Black fortunes have been made in insurance and in retailing, "service" businesses.

One of the casualties of the way in which Black people strive to move into the mainstream of American business life is that women who might formerly have been motivated (or forced) to run their own businesses now have as their goals the security and respectability that will keep them forever under the thumb of an organization which they do not own and over which they have very little control. For many of us it is daunting enough to face the prospect of stepping out into an academic world, fighting for an M.B.A., and then struggling to get a management job—why risk that effort just to be able to say "I own my own business"? Especially since six out of ten new small businesses fail within eighteen months, and banks are not exactly competing to lend seed money to Black women entrepreneurs. So why?

Quite often successful business ventures have been started by women out of necessity. A husband dies or leaves, and without access to a profession his widow makes money the only way she knows: floral arrangements; baking and selling cakes; taking in the neighbors' children. Men are inspired from their early years to pit their mettle against the system and forge new business trails. We usually end up in our own business because of necessity or displacement.

I never saw myself as president of a corporation; I simply wanted to make hair, skin, and cosmetic products that *I* could use, and it took so much effort and time and money that I had to recoup my expenses by making them available to all Black women. Most women who end up owning businesses start with just an idea; and in the course of making it into a reality, if they are intelligent and have good advice, they found a solid empire, like Ernesta Procope, the owner of a multimillion dollar insurance company. Albert Shapero, a professor of business administration at Ohio State University, believes:

"Women have always been entrepreneurs, overtly in some cultures and covertly in others."

He makes his case by citing examples of pioneer women who, having been left stranded by their men, started hotels and retail stores in the Old West. Necessity is the biggest spur. In this century waves of immigrants have arrived in this country, with no education or knowledge of our language and culture, and within short time spans have built business empires. Why have 14,000 businesses been started by Cubans here in the past twenty years? Proportionate to the per capita count, we have started only a few *hundred*. Why them and not us? A possible answer harks back to the question of assimilation. We cannot fight on all fronts, and for most Black women running a small business means staying in or near the ghetto rather than advancing out into the mainstream of American life which, despite the country's heritage, does not encourage small business. America is educating armies of technical workers (on all levels, from trades to executive management) who will toil for a small number of giant corporations whose ownership by public stockholders conceals a vast impersonality and a deadly lack of interest in the individual. By owning your own business, you can take charge of your own destiny.

If you are going to be the boss, you do not necessarily need a college degree or even a high school diploma! What *do* you need?

A. The Idea

B. The Resources

A. The Idea

Probably one of the most widely held misconceptions about going into business for yourself is that it will only work if you have a novel or new idea. First of all, there are not enough new ideas to begin to go around, and secondly, if you have a new idea and wonder why no one has ever thought of it before (pantsuits for pets, cars that run on air), the answer is that they did and went broke. Ask yourself:

"Who needs my idea?"

Then:

"What are they willing to pay for it?"

If your idea has merit, you can conduct your own market survey. Bear in mind that family and friends are not the best people to survey. They will be very enthusiastic until you are in business; then they will not only be critical but will expect to receive your goods or services for free. If you have no potential customers outside your group, you will not get very far.

Estimate the price of your idea to the consumer, and then work backward and make sure that you can make a profit. Packaging hot meals from a fast-food outlet and delivering them to nursing homes may be a very good idea, but if your profit is ten per cent and your transportation costs twenty per cent, it will not work.

The most sensible procedure for the budding entrepreneur is to take a concept which has been proven successful and refine it for the specific market to which they have access. For instance, you know that there are a number of very successful photocopying centers in the downtown business district, but none where you live. If you open one up in a local shopping mall, would it be successful? The answer might be yes—*if* you combine it with a T-shirt printing operation or a magazine stand.

It does not matter whether your idea is for a small-scale operation or something that will shake the world; you also have to look at the economic climate. Is your business seasonal? What will your monthly overhead be if you have to sustain your business through slumps of inactivity? Does your idea depend on government legislation, which might change? On zoning?

Above all, you have to investigate the *need* for your business in very concrete terms. It may *sound* like the one thing everyone wants and can afford, but before you plunge in you have to try in every way you can to obtain comparative studies of similar ventures. Read all the trade literature for the past two years and determine whether your potential business is of a type that is stabilized, declining, or making progress. How will your expenditures fluctuate? If you are processing a raw product, how stable is the cost?

If you have no specific idea other than that you want to be your own boss, then you have to assess your own skills objectively. If you are an older person with a degree of expertise and experience, then you may want to start a consulting firm; if you are young, with boundless energy, then setting up a retail operation may be the right thing to do. Realize this: as the boss you will be working night and day, even if not all that time is actually spent *at* work. The buck stops wherever you happen to be, on your vacation or in bed with a cold. Be prepared to relinquish the supreme luxury of being able to quit work on Friday afternoon and to put it out of your mind until Monday morning, no matter how awful the work week. I find that the majority of the time I spend at my desk goes into "running" the company, making decisions, and solving problems. All of the truly creative work I do, which is the *essence* of my business, is done during what for anyone else would be spare time. The owner of a business has no spare time.

The rate of success is far greater in some businesses than in others. Your interests, aptitudes, and your local needs and economic conditions are the most important factors in determining what your idea will be.

According to Mr. Andrew Brimmer, writing in *Black Enterprise* magazine, the top prospect for Black entrepreneurs is technical services. Any service business requires a smaller capital outlay than a manufacturing business, and the majority of Black-owned businesses have always been in the service category. But Black firms are usually committed to providing *personal* services (retail stores, catering, limousine-for-hire firms, funeral parlors), and general economic trends suggest a decline in revenues from these operations. On the other hand, Mr. Brimmer indicates that the outlook for new services to the business community (from cleaning and maintenance operations to management consulting) is very positive. The failure rate is low, and in keeping with what I have said about the job market as a whole, the need for technically based enterprise is very high. So, if you have the ambition and are prepared to work hard at lining up your resources but do not yet have a fix on your actual idea, consider these fast-growing areas:

BUSINESS SERVICES

Advertising

Computer and data processing

Management consulting

Public relations

Equipment rental and leasing

Credit reporting and collection

Blueprinting, photocopying, photography, art, and graphics

Commercial research, development, and testing laboratories

Economic marketing and research

Public accounting and auditing

ALLIED COMMERCIAL SERVICES

If you have some mechanical knowledge or have the opportunity to hire responsible skilled labor, you can make a very good profit by considering a business involving a technical service that may be lacking in your location. Any Black woman running one of the following services would probably not have to spend a lot on advertising; it would be a sufficiently unusual situation to create a lot of word-of-mouth interest:

Automotive repair

Contract truck transportation

Commercial distribution facilities

Electrical and electronic repair (especially air conditioning and refrigeration)

Furniture upholstery and repair

Building maintenance (especially disinfecting and exterminating)

I am not suggesting that *only* the above kinds of businesses can succeed, but given the present economic climate these are the most likely to find a market as Black owned and operated ventures.

WORKING AT HOME

If you are not in a position to set up a substantial enterprise but still do not want to be tied to an office, consider marketing skills you can practice *at home* or in space that can be leased quite inexpensively. For instance, are you a good *teacher?* Could you give lessons in something you know a lot about, such as dance, painting, photography, or cooking? If you have a reputation for keeping fit and have the figure to show for it, how about starting your own *exercise class?* Fifteen ladies three times a day at $5 per lesson is $225 a day, less your advertising and the cost of renting studio space.

Even if you have nothing more than rudimentary secretarial skills, you can go a long way. Mary Bryant is a young woman who spent five years typing form letters for a municipal government agency. When her husband decided to go back to school to complete his degree, she was forced to assume the burden of providing both for him and their two children. This was impossible on her salary:

"I was taking home one hundred and thirty-five dollars a week, and we would have done better on welfare and food stamps. My husband had been earning two hundred twenty-five dollars before he went back to school, and I encouraged him to do it because eventually it would mean he could earn much more. But until then, what were we to do? I put up a notice on the supermarket bulletin board that I wanted extra typing—that was all I figured I could do! My boss let me come to work an hour early and use the typewriter, and I would do outside work during my lunch break. I charged less than the standard rate, and I was soon making an extra twenty to thirty dollars a week. A month after that, I saw an advertisement for typewriter rentals, and I let a fast-talking salesman convince me to rent a second-hand IBM typewriter for one hundred dollars a month! I almost called back to cancel. I thought it was the most reckless thing I had ever done! But am I glad I did it."

Mary now runs her own at-home word-processing unit and has one part-time employee. She leases all the most up-to-date equipment and provides business forms, legal letters, résumés, and camera-ready copy for advertisers. She types manuscripts and doctoral theses and is a long way from $135 a week:

> *"My husband said the other day that even with his degree he won't be earning as much as me and thinks he should be taking typing lessons. But it is not easy. I am often up until midnight, and every client wants it "yesterday." But they come to me because I deliver on time. All I have is my reputation. What I am looking forward to is one day off!"*

B. The Resources

Once you have picked your idea, the trouble starts. Take out a pencil and lots of scratch paper. Answer in full each of the following questions:

1. Where is your market?
2. How will you attract clients/customers?
3. Who is your competition?
4. How are you going to beat your competition—i.e., through lower prices, better service, different services?
5. Where will your plant or office be located?
6. What equipment and supplies or inventory will you need?
7. Will you run the business yourself or with partners?
8. How much money will you need to keep your business going for one year?
9. What are your projected annual profits, after taxes, for the first two years? Five years? Ten years?
10. Where will you get the money to start—i.e., from savings, relatives, a bank loan?

Once you have been able to answer all these questions specifically, your job is to find the person or persons who are most important for the first stage of your enterprise: your advisors.

Advice

It is worthwhile polling your family and friends for their opinions about your new venture, but my experience is that most of the time you will receive either support based on nothing more than the urge to see you succeed or criticism based on nothing more than the desire to see you fail. You need to talk to professionals who have business experience, if possible to a professional with a good track record in the specific area you are about to enter.

Finding the right advisor is not always easy. Start with your local Chamber of Commerce and work your way up to the A.W.E.D. (American Women's Economic Development Corporation) in Washington, D.C. You will find their address and that of similar groups in the Appendix.

In some communities there are organizations of retired business people anxious and willing to give their time to advising new ventures, and none of this will cost you a dime. In the New York area, the organization is called S.C.O.R.E. (Service Corps of Retired Executives) and most metropolitan areas have similar groups. At this stage you have the opportunity to gather information which will not only save you thousands of dollars later on but may determine whether you succeed or fail.

Most business failures are avoidable and the result of decisions made on the basis of insufficient information. Keep telling yourself that you know *nothing,* not everything, and be prepared to fill dozens of notebooks with miscellaneous information about how you intend to operate. Never be afraid to *ask;* it is the smartest thing to do.

When I went into business, I did not know the correct technical or legal terminology for half of what I wanted to do, but I was not afraid to ask the same question ten times over so that eventually I would understand what I was doing. One of our biggest drawbacks is the fear that if we ask for advice or help, it will betray our inadequacies. The consequence of this is that we blunder around in the dark, make obvious mistakes, and sink, discouraged. Smart people ask a lot of obvious questions.

If you are having trouble trying to estimate your expenses and yours is a business that depends on suppliers (a wholesale florist, for example), then visit your future suppliers, tell them your plans, and enlist their help. They will want you to succeed because if you do, it means more business for them. No matter what business you are entering, it means a new customer for someone else. Find that person or firm, and you can begin to compute your overhead.

The next step is to write up a proposal. Even if it is only for your personal benefit, it will help; but you will probably need it to approach your potential backers or partners, even if they are people you have known all your life. When you write a proposal, be sure to include *all* the information you have, not just the most favorable. Try to describe the business in one or two paragraphs—why it is needed, where it will be located, and who will be its customers. Then follow with a breakdown of your annual expenses and projected earnings. Predict how these will change over a five-year period and how you want the business to grow. Now you are ready for the next big step in utilizing your resources: to decide on your *structure*.

The Structure

Yours might be a venture that only involves one employee (yourself) at home, or it might employ fifty people in a factory. You will only derive the most from your business if it is structured on sound legal and financial principles. Two people are essential resources: a lawyer and a banker. You must talk to each one at length and with perfect frankness. Even if you do not need a bank for financing, you are still going to use a bank, if only for payroll, and the local bank officer will be happy to give you the advice you need and point out the pitfalls. The bank officer can even point you in the direction of suppliers or customers you may need for business.

Do not be intimidated by the first banker or lawyer you interview. There are lots of banks and lots of law firms. It is worth shopping around until you find the lawyer and banker with whom you feel the most at ease. If they offer encouragement and constructive criticism, and show by their grasp of details that they understand *why* your business could succeed, then you have made a good choice. These are the professionals you will need from time to time every year you are in business. No business is trouble-free; even great success and expansion causes growing pains that can be minimized by these two persons, the lawyer and the banker. You must be able to call on them whenever you wish. I have employed three different law firms, successively, since I started my business ten years ago. That seems like a lot, but as my business grew I needed different skills from my lawyer. All have been tremendously important to me, but when I started out, I needed the kind of daily attention that only a relatively hungry young lawyer could afford to provide. Now I need a very large law firm that can instantly give me expert advice on such widely divergent areas as copyright, investment, real estate, and taxes.

Once you and your advisors share mutual confidence, then you are halfway to home base. If you modify your proposal on the basis of what you find out from your lawyer and banker, it is a very good sign. There should be considerations of which you were ignorant. Have you made allowances for employee benefits such as health insurance, accident liability, and social security? Do you have to pay your bills before your customers pay you? Most important of all: what about *taxes*?

As a corporation your personal liability and taxes can be substantially reduced, but it depends upon the scope and nature of your business. I know of many young women in my former profession of fashion modeling who reduced their taxes substantially by turning themselves into one-woman corporations. The law allows this; you simply pay yourself a modest salary (which is taxed), and a very substantial portion of your expenses (travel, clothes, and rent) is paid by your corporation, which writes it off as a nontaxable business expense.

If you are properly incorporated and for some reason your business fails, leaving debts, you may not be *personally* liable, even though you are the sole owner and employee. There are many aspects of this to consider. Other possibilities include sole proprietorships and partnerships. Each of these presents different tax benefits and obligations. There is one structure that best suits your particular business idea, and it is worth starting with this from the very beginning. Your lawyer should be able to give you specific advice along these lines; if not, go to someone else who can. You want the greatest degree of flexibility with the lowest rate of taxation. What you do *not* want is a partnership that allows your partners to spend money for which you are personally liable; nor do you want a business that makes hearty profits all of which go to Uncle Sam because you are "Corporation" and not "Inc." So even though you are impatient to get started and to see the money roll in, it is worth your trouble to spend the time and get it right from the start.

With the proper financial advice at the start, you can also make yourself eligible for retirement benefits and pension planning on a scale that is simply not available to you as the employee of a large corporation or organization. You can defer profits, put them into a retirement fund, or plow them back into the business. The laws of this country encourage business—such is not the case everywhere in the world—and are oriented in favor of business owners and operators.

Participate in seminars and in as many courses devoted to new ventures as you can find. If you have access to a college that has a school of business administration, do not be afraid to call and find out if they have an official or even an informal consultant service. Some of us imagine that there are tightly guarded secrets to running a business, secrets known only to a handful of bosses. In fact, everything apart from the actual experience of running your own business is available if you go out of your way to ask for it. The more contacts you establish in the business community, the better. If you approach your Chamber of Commerce for advice, they can put you in touch with persons running businesses similar to your idea, and you may substantially alter your plans on the basis of what you can learn from them. Shirlee A. Rousseau worked as a travel agent for twenty years, and when the owner retired, she bought the business for herself. She was smart enough to participate in two eight-hour seminars conducted by

A.W.E.D., and even though she had been in her business for a long time, what she learned radically changed her ideas for the future:

"I realized that because of the recession and inflation I was going to have to look for customers that would keep my company financially sound."

Because of the advice she received from A.W.E.D., Ms. Rousseau concentrated on increasing her corporate travel clientele, which had formerly accounted for only forty per cent of her volume. Now it represents seventy per cent, and as a result her business is on a very secure footing.

It is especially necessary to get advice if you are in a single-commodity business such as making knitwear at home. Jeanne Thibodeaux, for instance, sells her exceptional knitwear to individuals as well as to boutiques. She participated in A.W.E.D. seminars and learned to keep her prices high! You may want to know if you can control the resale price of items that you manufacture, or how much discount to give on volume orders, or what discount your customers might expect if they pay early. Nothing is quite as simple as it seems, and there may be some distance between what you have figured out on paper and what will actually happen when you start handling orders.

Some businesses, such as food processing, operate on very low profit margins that are only visible with a high volume, and the smallest fluctuation in cost can spell ruin. How can you guard against this? What sort of *insurance* should you have? Is your business affected by the weather? By the economy? A store that sells all kinds of do-it-yourself kits has a much better chance of doing well in a recession than in a period of economic boom. If you manufacture umbrellas, do you call them parasols and change the design to capture business in the Sun Belt?

From the start get used to asking one question over and over again:

"How much will it cost?"

Ask your lawyer how much he or she will charge for setting you up in business and what the continuing charge will be for:

a) basic legal services

b) general advice.

Ask your accountant (you *must* have an accountant) how much they will charge for filing your corporate tax returns. If you hire a consultant, establish exactly what service you will get and for how much, *before* the meter starts ticking.

Now you have your idea, your advisors, and your structure. The only important resource you still lack is, of course, money.

Capital

Whether you go into the money market to raise five million dollars or go to your sister to borrow five hundred, the same rules apply:

1. Make sure you can afford the loan or investment.
2. Know exactly what your bankers expect from you and you from them.
3. Put the entire transaction in writing.

These may all seem very obvious, but you would be surprised just how much they are ignored, in large undertakings as well as small, with predictably tragic results.

For instance, you may be able to afford a particular loan from a financial viewpoint (i.e., the rate of interest may be compatible with your projected income), but you may not be able to afford the constant interference of the individual who now has a stake in your business. It may not be worth an interest-free five thousand dollars if the lender thinks he or she thereby has the right to breeze in and out of your office all day long, offering you gratuitous advice, taking free samples of your product, or expecting free services. It may cost you far less in the long run to borrow the money at a fairly steep rate of interest from the bank, which at least will leave you alone.

It is not always a good idea to borrow money from family or friends because it usually means that you have unofficial partners who feel obliged to tell you how to run your business.

Before you accept money from an investor, ask yourself *why* they are giving it to you. There are three possible reasons:

1. They believe in you and want you to succeed; whether they make money or not is secondary.
2. They want to make a profit within a fixed period of time.
3. They expect to lose money, which will benefit them as a tax loss.

It may not matter to you which of these reasons is functional in your particular situation, but it is in your best interests to find out—especially if your investor is looking forward to a loss! Often people with very high incomes reduce their tax burden by investing in losing propositions called "tax shelters."

That is why it is important to have everything spelled out in writing. You should have on paper what the money is for, when it must be paid in full, what the interest rate is, when the interest is to be paid, and what this investment or loan entitles the lender to do with regard to the business. Are you issuing shares, a promissory note, or enlisting a "silent" partner? Each involves different legal obligations. What will happen if your venture is a wild success? Will your lender get the money back, plus interest, *plus* a share of the profits? What if it is a big bust? You have to protect yourself against this contingency, no matter how distasteful. Does this give your lender a right to take over your business? Sell the office equipment? Sue you?

Explore all the ramifications. Usually everyone is so enthusiastic and anxious to get started that important points are overlooked, and it may be complicated to unravel who meant what when all you had is a verbal arrangement.

Even if you accept a loan from your parents or husband, for tax reasons both you and they must sign a formal note that is notarized and which states the terms and interest rate.

It is often a wise idea to take out a bank loan, even if you do not need it. There are two good reasons for doing this:

1. To establish credit with the bank. Prove that you are a good borrower, and the bank will be willing to help you later, when you need a large loan for expansion.

2. Because the money you pay back will be worth less than the money you borrowed. Inflation shrinks the dollar.

Credit is a fundamental part of every business, and you must be prepared to borrow and pay back. If you are going to compete, there are two aspects of the money market that you have to cope with: capitalization and cash flow. Almost half of all new businesses flounder because they are undercapitalized. That means they started off with less money than they needed. When that happens, you often run into cash-flow problems.

Example: you start a doughnut bakery. You calculate that with $10,000 you can rent the premises, buy a delivery truck, hire two bakers and a driver, and purchase flour, yeast, sugar, and fillings. Things go well, and within two months you are billing customers about $1,250 per week. Your monthly expenses are $3,850, so already you are in the black. But are you? You may be billing $1,250 a week, but are your customers paying? Some are retail stores that pay cash on delivery, but most are hospitals and schools—notoriously slow payers. Some are taking over 90 days to settle a bill which means that you carry them for over three months. If one thing happens—the cost of goods rises, you need a $1,500 oven, or your truck breaks down—it could be disastrous. You have to keep paying your rent and your employees' salaries, which will not wait. Business is good, but you will not have enough money to really get it off the ground until receipts are current with expenses. If you had had initial capital of $20,000 instead of $10,000, you would have had enough to operate for three months with no receipts at all. You should have reckoned that your real receipts would not commence, and your business not begin, until your institutional customers actually *paid,* not when they ordered.

When I start a new venture, I am *very* cautious and like to have access to enough money to keep my venture going for *one year* with no revenue! Here are some additional tips:

1. *Avoid* get-rich-quick schemes. The type of "business" that can be found on a matchbook cover or in the classifieds ("Make $$$ at home in your spare time") is not going to make you a millionaire. The only person getting rich from that is the one that gets your dollar bill in the mail in return for a badly mimeographed sheet of homilies. If your eye catches a "business opportunity" advertisement, a business for sale, find out why it is being sold. If you are told that the former owners made so much money that they have retired to Florida, do not believe it. Franchises, for fast food or ice cream, can be very profitable; but unless your experienced lawyer reads the very fine print, you may still end up working for a boss—the parent company—and for very long hours at that.

2. *Test* your idea as much as possible. Circulate questionnaires, spend money on samples, or simply start on a very small scale. No business got off the ground without some trouble, and you have to expect at least one major miscalculation—but this can be minimized by judicious testing.

3. *Screen* your employees well. You may have no experience at hiring people. Over and over again, Black women have told me that when they started their businesses they overlooked this issue. You must be prepared to pay a decent wage, and in return you have the right to expect hard work and loyalty. Whether you are hiring people with specific skills or not, check references thoroughly and interview at least five candidates for every position—even if the first one that walks in the door seems perfect for the job. Avoid hiring friends or relatives, especially at the beginning. It

will only distract you. It is easier to establish your authority with a stranger than with close friends. A recent poll of small businesses reported in *The Wall Street Journal* cited "finding good employees" as the *number one* problem, way ahead of financing, government regulations, taxes, and slow-paying customers. The reason: bad employees are especially disruptive in a small organization. The article went on to specify that by a "good employee" the small business owners did not necessarily mean persons who were highly trained or skilled; they meant persons "having the right attitude for the job." When you interview for your first employees, look for people who are alert, able to take criticism, and interested in teamwork.

4. *Check* into government programs for aid to minority businesses. Although the indications are that this type of assistance is on the wane, you should explore as many avenues as possible. In your area you may be eligible for low-interest loans, subsidies for training minority employees, and grants.

5. *Know* your business inside out. There are two aspects to running any business, and the boss has to be on top of both. One is the nature of the product or service: you have to be thoroughly knowledgeable about that *yourself*. This sounds axiomatic, but I know plenty of people who have gone into retail businesses, selling antiques or flowers or gourmet food, who knew much less than their customers about what they were selling! As the owner, *you* will be asked the big questions; do not depend on the knowledge of your employees. Laura Marshall persuaded her mother to lend her the money to purchase a retail florist business in Baltimore. She had been a good customer of the former owner and thought it would be something she would enjoy doing. Everything checked out very well; the store had a good clientele and excellent credit with wholesalers, and Laura figured that within a year she would be making a lot of money. She was in debt within six weeks because she knew nothing about flowers beyond the names! Costs fluctuate with the seasons, and she never knew what to order. She was either understocked or overstocked, and hundreds of dollars were wasted on flowers that perished. But Laura did not give up. She closed the store for three months and took a job with a rival florist across town. What she learned in those three months helped her begin all over again on a sound basis, and now she is a real success. The

second thing the boss has to know is how to keep the business actually *running*. Many of us may know all about the goods or service but have no experience with balancing the books, dealing with creditors, or hiring and firing. It is not enough to assume that these are things you will simply pick up when the time comes, because they are just as important to your venture's success as your ability to create an excellent product or service. The product is worthless if it is not advertised properly or delivered on time.

EXPANDING A SMALL BUSINESS

The skills required for starting a business are not always the same as those needed to expand it. It is never premature to think about what your next step will be, because you are always building, whether you know it or not. Your venture may start out to be a one-woman show, with you in touch with all aspects of the business, able to do everything yourself whether you have to or not. Everybody reports to you in the beginning, and you have a direct relationship with employees, suppliers, and customers. If the business is even moderately successful, you will enjoy all the face-to-face contact with everyone involved.

An expanding business reaches a critical point when it can take a quantum leap into the "big leagues," but only if the owner is willing to take advantage of the timing and do what has to be done. Orders increase, word of mouth spreads your credibility far and wide, and after five years you have more business than you can handle. At this point you can raise new money and expand, or admit you do not want a large company and elect to control the amount of business you do. The obvious desire is to grow, but in a surprisingly high number of instances, this does not happen simply because of the owner's inhibitions. The expansion of a small business inevitably requires the owner to "let go" of certain key areas that may be very emotionally satisfying to control directly.

Martha Lewis is a young Black woman who started to manufacture belts for local San Francisco boutiques in the mid-seventies. At first it was just herself, at home. Within two years she had a small factory and ten employees. She added handbags to her line.

"I spent very little time in the office, such as it was," she told me, "I liked to be in the work rooms, designing, showing the buyers around, sometimes just spending the afternoon making a piece myself."

One day a friend in the advertising business persuaded her to place a small ad in a national magazine, and she was flooded with orders. She had to double her employees and appoint a floor manager to keep track of production.

"Before I knew it, I had three people in the shipping department alone, and I hardly knew their names. Then I was interviewing designers. Designers! The whole point of the business was that I was the designer. I found it very hard to leave the fun part and concentrate on my relationship with the bank, my ad agency, and my trips to buy materials. The first time I had to go to Italy to buy leather, I canceled my trip three times because I just knew the whole place would be a shambles when I returned. I was slightly upset to find out how smoothly things went without me. I guess that is when I grew up, but it was hard."

After concerning yourself with the nuts and bolts of your business, you have to turn to the support system and handle questions in which you may have little or no interest such as real estate, computers to keep track of inventory, or even shareholders. In order to raise the money you need to expand, you may have to sacrifice part of your ownership, may have to trade off a portion of control in order to triple the scope of your activities. Small business owners, especially Black women, tend to wait until they are pushed before expanding. Sometimes this is from being overcautious. Roxanne Long took a year to make up her mind to install a small computer to handle billing and inventory for her wholesale hardware business in Austin, Texas:

"I knew that when we made the changeover to the computer system there would be snags, delays, and foul-ups. For some reason I was convinced that all my customers would desert me and I would be left with a huge inventory and this horribly expensive machine!"

It comes back to the question of risk taking and being able to calculate the odds. If you know where your business fits into the marketplace, you can project future sales and anticipate growth problems before they appear. Part of this means evaluating your current status regularly and projecting future sales and expenses. Costs can creep up very quietly. Just by adding a new telephone line, hiring an extra part-timer, and taking a half-page ad in the local charity program moves your overhead up from four to five figures. If the business starts out on a very small scale, you may think that you are instinctively aware of your overhead but in fact have no way of keeping track. You may need just a few hours of a bookkeeper's time every week to keep you up to date about the status of expenses and receipts.

What I am talking about is *management*. The difference between a small new business started and operated by one person and its growth into a medium-sized or large company is that a certain point is reached when it becomes necessary to hire someone to manage the business, in part or in whole. Examine your function very carefully. At what are you *best?* You will not be able to continue to do everything as the business expands. Are you basically creative? Good at selling? Making people productive? *Delegate* what you are not doing well. Put someone else in charge of vital areas and make them report to you on a regular basis.

As a business owner your ultimate goal is to work yourself out of a job, knowing that the business will be able to flourish on its own. This is only possible if you have developed the ability to hire good people and remunerate them accordingly. Know what they want. Will you get more out of your management team by a system of performance-oriented raises or by a profit-sharing plan? One of the hardest things to do is to take yourself off the team you created. This may be necessary when you insert a management person or an entire management staff between you and the workers, some of whom may have been with you from the start. Which is more important—that you be loved by your employees or that your business expands? You may just have to choose. Martha Lewis explains:

> *"I was on very familiar terms with the men and women who helped me make my products. I knew their children's names, and they all called me Martha. After expansion, some of them came to resent me because I was no longer available all the time to listen to their problems, and they had to go to a supervisor who had not been there nearly as long as they had. There's no easy solution to this because I simply had to attend to important things and leave production problems to an expert. The whole place became more impersonal, but I guess that's one of the prices you pay."*

You have to be able to calculate what you cost yourself per minute. How is that money best spent? If your time is worth two hundred dollars an hour, can you afford to spend it doing something that an employee you pay ten dollars an hour can do just as well, or even better? What are the functions that *only you* can perform? Stick to those. Once your business is going well, continue to plan as thoughtfully for expansion as you did when you first set things up; go back to your advisors, talk to your lawyer, and talk to your bank manager.

If necessary hire a management consultant to look at your operation so that you can anticipate where your strengths and weaknesses lie so that the money you spend on expansion is put in the best place. As you grow, more and more "offers" will flood in, salespeople will offer you all manner of time- and money-saving devices, from coffee machines to data processing units. If yours is an "image" business, you may really need a new carpet, but do not sign the check for that if what you really need is a new delivery truck.

The entrepreneur-owner reaches a point where she or he makes the transition from a hands-on doer to an administrator/supervisor. In order to make your transition a successful one, anticipate it, prepare thoroughly, and take the plunge!

THE BUSINESS OF TALENT

If you are, or want to be, any of the following, read this section carefully:

> Actress
> Dancer
> Singer
> Artist
> Designer
> Photographer
> Writer
> Illustrator
> Musician

Free-lance careers in the arts are nothing more than one-person businesses. They should be considered in this light because talent in our society will not be rewarded unless it is nurtured by business acumen. Genius alone is not enough. Yours may be wasted while your talents languish unnoticed simply because you have not considered the need to approach the question of success from a sufficiently businesslike point of view.

It is not possible for people without talent to elevate themselves simply by being businesslike, but it is possible to apply business principles to whatever talent you have so that all possible applications may be explored. Take a paper and pencil, and write down your goal. For instance:

I want to be a ballerina with the Dance Theatre of Harlem.

I want to have a one-woman show of my paintings in a museum.

I want to be a photographer for Life *magazine.*

I want a hit record and my own television show.

Next write down your honest evaluation of your talent and the need for further training or experience. For instance:

I need one more year in ballet school.

I need to complete a total of twenty paintings.

I need a better camera and more experience with news stories.

I need to get used to performing in front of a live audience.

Finally, estimate how you can achieve the *immediate* goals. How feasible is it for you to get the extra training or added experience? Can you do it alone? Do you need financial assistance? Are there any local training programs that you can join which will help you to improve your technique or to give you professional experience? Have you ever performed before strangers or shown your work outside your circle of friends and family?

More than in any other type of profession, a mentor is essential to the budding artist. Talent needs encouragement and talent needs to be accompanied by firsthand knowledge of what the real world is like, whether it be the world of music, painting, dance, or journalism. Even though you have your sights set on Hollywood, before you board the bus look around to see if there is anyone in your town who has "been there" on one scale or another. Learn from such a person's experience.

There are two kinds of people who fail to become recognized as artists: those that have no talent and those that do have talent but are forever waiting for a Big Break. If you have talent, you can make yourself into a success by approaching your career in a businesslike way. *Never trust to luck!*

Take ballet as an example. Do you audition at every possible occasion? Do you rehearse eight hours a day? Do you follow the news about your profession in dance magazines? Do you know what is going on in the major cities, here and abroad, or who is performing in what ballets? In other words, are you able to discuss ballet intelligently or are you only able to dance?

Assume that there are at least five hundred people with a talent equal to yours and that you must stand out from the crowd. Learn how to present yourself, how to be persistent, and how to take defeat with equanimity.

Should you have an agent? How much will that cost? Where do you find one? What does an agent do?

An agent: 1. Finds work.

2. Takes a percentage of your income.

Do not depend on an agent for anything else, especially not for career planning. Unless you know what shape you want your career to take, you have no way of knowing whether the work your agent is getting is the right work for you or not. Agents rarely get involved with amateurs, so you have to produce evidence of professional experience. How much have you earned on your own? Have you ever sold a painting? Performed for money? Published an article? You have to prepare a résumé, just as you would for a regular job. Draw up a list of career goals, experience, training, and education. Is it time to make a move or do you need more experience at the local level? How are you going to support yourself? Are you prepared to work as a waitress while you take singing lessons?

Plan. Make a timetable:

This year I will stay in school, take lessons, and save money.
Next year I will spend six months in New York and audition.

Stick to your schedule. Make contingency plans; be prepared. How long can you survive without a job? What kind of a job will allow you to continue your career? Read as much as you can about your profession. How did other people get started? Are you prepared to do menial work just to get close to the heart of your profession? Example: Successful painters and sculptors often employ assistants who simply prepare materials, stretch canvases, lift and carry, and run errands. The work may have nothing to do with your talents, but such a job gives you the opportunity to observe artists' professional work habits, their way of handling dealers, galleries, and collectors. One day it may be politic to show your artist-employer your own work, and this might lead you to an introduction to a gallery.

There is no correlation between talent and unworldliness. It is conventional to depict great artists—be they writers, composers, painters, or performers—as unworldly, dreamy, impractical creatures with their heads in the clouds and no real idea of what day it is or where the next meal is coming from. Such are the exceptions, not the rule. If you want to succeed in the very competitive worlds of art and entertainment, you have to have your wits about you at all times. Read Chapter 6, concerning mentors and networks, and apply it all to your career-building efforts. The same principles apply. Even though you are not working in an office from nine to five, you are part of a business community. You not only have to serve the public, but you also have to operate in conjunction with a variety of legitimate capitalist endeavors: theaters, promoters, publishers, and agents.

It pays to understand the people who have the power to make or break your career. How do you get yourself *seen* by the right people? Through introductions. By knowing someone who knows someone who knows someone who knows the woman or man you must meet. That does not happen at home in front of the mirror or even in a rehearsal hall. You have to get out and put yourself squarely where the action is; this means keeping your skills in shape *and* looking for work at the same time.

What is your real ambition: to be the best jazz singer in Buffalo or one of the top three hundred in Los Angeles? With how much discomfort are you willing to put up? Articulate the answer to every one of my questions and read voraciously. Get out-of-town newspapers and all the trade journals for your field.

If you expect to be an overnight success, you may be disappointed —just as much as if you expect to earn, at the top of your career, as much as you read about.

Think of yourself as a small business. Make plans on paper. Give yourself two-, five-, and ten-year goal schedules, with contingencies. What will your equipment (costumes, art supplies, cameras) cost, and what will your living expenses be? Get as much hard information as you can.

Once you are earning money, ask yourself these questions:

1. Do I need a business manager?
2. Should I incorporate myself?
3. Am I on the right track?

Artists and performers, when they work, tend to work so hard that they have little time for the details of their careers such as contracts, tax liabilities, copyright laws, and all the things that can bring a promising career to a grinding halt if they are not taken care of.

Just two hours a week, the same time of day or evening every week, go over your plans, either alone or with a colleague. Examine your current situation, your income, and expenses; look at your goals, your liabilities, and your assets. This can save you a lot of grief in the days ahead and will deter anyone from taking advantage of you.

Whether you are a business entrepreneur or a talented singer, owning your own business means being in charge of your life. That is what this book is really all about. It comes down to the same set of skills:

1. Appraise yourself *objectively*.
2. Plan the future and be *specific*.
3. Gather and digest hard *information*.
4. Create a personal *network*.
5. Trust your *judgment* of people and circumstances.
6. Enthusiastically take *risks*.

You cannot go it alone. Encouragement from someone who has been where you are going can be the vital spark you need to get the wheels turning fast. Make yourself available to anyone who wants to help or has advice; judge that advice according to the giver's experience and keep the door open!

🎄🎄🎄🎄🎄

8

Pride and Prejudice: Who Is on My Side?

"I think it's time for Black women not to be afraid to stand up and say: 'Look, my experience has not been a white woman's experience; it has been a Black woman's experience. I have been at the bottom of every ladder. They have played me off against the white man, and now it's me against the white woman.'"

Gerri Lange, Host of PBS-TV's "Turnabout"

When it comes down to the real nitty-gritty, you cannot *legislate* equal opportunity. We can vote for the most enlightened politicians who can pass the most all-embracing laws giving all women, Black and white, and all men, Black and white, an equal crack at success, *but* unless the ruling elite (and there will always be—before, after, and during the revolution—a ruling elite) is fervently committed to the *spirit* of the laws, they will be valueless. Fight for your rights! This is a mighty slogan for a march on Washington, but how many of us are willing to put our careers on the line?

Let us say you are passed over for a promotion, and you can *prove* that it was on account of race or sex. Are you willing to spend the next year of your life under the spotlight, in and out of court? Win or lose, you will be silently condemned as a troublemaker, your job opportunities will be greatly diminished for the rest of your life, and you will be tagged as a spoiler. Employers will think three times before hiring the Black woman who successfully (or unsuccessfully) sued Wilbert's Widgets, Inc.

Any Black woman who relies solely on the legal system of the United States of America to guarantee her right to a job worth her education and to give her a chance to move up the ladder as fast as a white man is living in a fool's paradise.

Do you seriously think that after the government had to force them to accept affirmative action, a giant company like A.T. & T. was ready to do an abrupt volte-face and throw open all the doors of opportunity to Black women? No. They more likely calculated to the decimal point the *least* they could do to conform with prevailing policy and statutes. The very least. This means that in such a case you will be welcomed noisily in the front door, and then tucked away in an office about ten miles from where the major decisions are made. We are still very far behind. White people admiringly judge us according to how far we have *come*. They never realize that this is totally beside the point. What matters is where we stand now and how far we have to go just to be on a par with the average white middle-class American. It is pitiful that we have to rely on the federal government to force businesses to hire us. I suppose we should be thankful for small mercies. But it is obvious that government action is vitally necessary. The less influence the government has on a particular branch of employment, the less likely you are to find Black women in senior positions. There is still a conspiracy among the ruling elite to keep us in our place! We may have moved up a couple of notches since Reconstruction, but we are still being *controlled* and *allowed* to succeed in limited areas, rather than being *in control* or at least *sharing control* on a basis equal to our representation in the population at large.

This is a white man's world, and the fact that there are a few Black women legislators, judges, college presidents, and self-made millionaires does not prove that most of us are on the move. The majority have to fight pitched battles every step of the way up—first to get a decent education, then to get a job; and after that we must struggle to get income parity and promotional opportunities.

The issues become infinitely complex as soon as we move out of the ghetto toward the dominant culture. Do we want to stick together or to become assimilated? Do we have to choose between racial solidarity with Black men or sexual solidarity with white women? Can we trust either, as a group? Are we ever able to get ahead *because* we are Black or women, or only *despite* those attributes. Is our struggle one for racial parity or racial dominance, or is it simply the age-old class struggle? Could it be that what we really all want, deep down, is participation in the American Dream of a comfortable bourgeois existence, with the mortgage paid and the kids in college?

There are no easy answers. No two Black women share exactly the same perspective because no two Black women share the same life experience. Some tell me that they have never experienced any real prejudice in their lives and others that every working day is riddled with subtle put-downs. White people are just as likely to be confused as we are; a lot of them honestly want to do the *right thing* on a personal level, but they are hopelessly ignorant about our true experiences and aspirations and varied styles of living. The most common delusion among white people is that when we demand equal opportunity we want to emulate them. They assume that their family patterns, morality, and leisure pursuits are naturally the "best." Most of them are painfully obvious about their prejudices, especially when they are trying to be complimentary.

Carolyn Shelton, a career consultant and a flight attendant, is in a unique position to observe and be observed by white passengers and co-workers from all parts of the country:

> *"They would talk about how we live in shacky houses and are uneducated, and then say, 'But you are different, Carolyn.' "*

There is not one of us who has ever worked with white people for any length of time who has not been told:

> *". . . but you are different!"*

Are we *all* "different"? Different from what? From television parodies of Black life, like "Good Times"? From the Black janitor who never had a chance to go to school? From our white co-worker's housekeeper? Talk about identity crisis! Prejudice is deeply rooted in the American psyche, and it is not going to be eliminated by government decree. It will only decline if all us "types" are able to rub shoulders in schools, at work, and in neighborhoods on a human, personal level and if each of us find out for our Black or white, female or male selves that those who are different in some ways are not *necessarily* different in others.

In discussing prejudice at work, however, we have to deal with objective situations that apply to many types of organizations. This means that we are more likely to succeed in certain occupations because the ruling elite considers them safe places for us to spread our wings. Such places used to consist almost exclusively of the worlds of entertainment and sport. Now, some fifty years later, we are allowed to run offices, manage stores, and teach. The circle has widened very slightly. They made a big mistake letting us into colleges, of course; we can now earn the credentials that can force them to give us certain jobs not necessarily on the approved list, like mining engineer, merchandising director, law partner, rather than the impressive-sounding but often powerless positions like executive vice president in charge of human resources, or assistant vice president for community affairs, or the ubiquitous head of personnel—all staff positions.

It is always very convenient and satisfying to label an entire category of human beings (such as white men) as implacable enemies. It is somewhat harder in a real work situation to apply these conventional theories when the one person who seems to be opposed to your promotion is the one other Black woman in the company! This fouls up the neat equation. Who *is* your enemy?

First of all, before naming names it is appropriate to take a quick look at the comparative successes enjoyed by the minorities. One group above all was the outstanding beneficiary of the Black-inspired, Black-dominated Civil Rights Movement of the sixties: middle-class white women. Presenting themselves as an oppressed "minority" (there are more women than men in this country and most of them are white), they represented, in the eyes of the ruling elite, the most palatable method of complying with affirmative action statutes. Most of the white women that led the initial push of the Feminist Movement were highly educated, wealthy, and had much more access to sympathetic ears in the media and the government than Blacks, female or male.

Even though it may be basically a sexist stereotype, American men (white) have always admired the "no-nonsense" career lady. She is always white, a former housewife who on the sudden death of her husband strides to the board room in horn-rimmed eyeglasses and a Chanel suit, and informs the portly, sputtering executives that she intends to run Zenith Zippers herself. There is no corresponding myth, in fiction or film, that elevates either the Black woman or man to the same level.

So white women are out there, way ahead and running like blazes for the brass ring. Where does that leave us—to fight over the crumbs with Black men? How many of us are actually taking jobs away from Black men and why?

There is an obvious correlation between who gets the farthest up the ladder the fastest and who has the best education. As a whole, white women are better educated than we are, and we are better educated than Black men. By simply hiring the most qualified minority candidate for any particular job (and who could quarrel with an employer that hired according to that principle?), the odds are that the job will go to a white woman.

Should we feel guilty that we are better educated than our men? Should we deny ourselves opportunities? A syndrome that is growing at an alarming rate is that of the disparity between the backgrounds of Black women and Black men, and the growing possibility of isolation between the two groups. There is absolutely no reason why a Black woman with an M.B.A. and a management job earning $32,000 a year should not be able to remain happily married to a Black man who works for the Department of Highways and earns $14,500 as a semi-skilled laborer, but of course it rarely happens, and when it does it rarely ends happily.

What about those with equal qualifications? Let us imagine four individuals competing for promotion. Two men (one Black, one white) and two women (one Black, one white). The job consists of supervising a predominantly white female sales force. The decision is to be made by a white male. How does he analyze the situation?

First, he eliminates the Black man. He feels guilty doing this; he knows it is not strictly fair, but he is not comfortable putting a Black man in charge of white women. He rationalizes this as follows:

> *"After all, Joe is a nice fellow but he's too stiff and formal for those girls. They like to be jollied along. He just doesn't have the right personality."*

Personality. That is what will decide this promotion. And personality in terms of what? The mores of the boss. Next he eliminates the white man:

> *"Fred will get that job in marketing next year anyway. He doesn't need to get stuck with this bunch, and besides I can always say to both men that they were out of the running from the start because I wanted a woman for the job. That way Joe can't accuse me of prejudice."*

Neat. Now it is between Julie the white woman and Valerie the Black woman. After sixty seconds of agonizing, he decides on Julie:

> *"The sales girls are white, and so is Julie. It just makes sense that they will get along the best. I'm not sure Valerie would really be able to exert the right kind of authority,"* he surmises, thinking not of Valerie but of Roots.

It is a purely circular method of reasoning but one that is prevalent. If the boss defines "executive material" as a thirty-five-year-old white Caucasian with an M.B.A. from the Harvard Business School and at least three years experience each in marketing, finance, and production and is forced to choose from a group that does not include a Caucasian male, he will pick the next best, which is a Caucasian female, followed by a Black male, followed by a Black female. We are last.

Of course, this was a fictitious situation that I created to suit my theory because I could get no white executive to admit to me that this was how they would make such a decision. My hypothetical people do not have flesh and blood like Dr. Adrienne Williams, operations manager and psychologist with Pacific Management Systems, who says:

> *"You have to be realistic in knowing that racism exists. You can't be successful in a white male organization if you don't*

*accept that, but it doesn't mean you have to be a crusader or
have a chip on your shoulder. One of the most critical things
is managing your rage around racism and sexism you encounter. If you don't, you're the one who loses."*

It is perfectly natural for people to feel the most comfortable with
their own kind. There are many ways in which we can be "the same"
as another: speak the same language; live in the same apartment building; have the same income; send our children to the same school; share
the same gender; share the same race. Which pull is the strongest? As
I have emphasized, "getting along with others" is a big factor in almost
every success story. Our ability to get along with others is determined
by the degree of similarity that exists. If I sit you in a room with an
Eskimo who speaks no English and has lived all his life north of the
Arctic Circle, how long would it be before you were sharing a joke
with him? Two years?

Some white men may feel uncomfortable with white women in the
executive suite, but it is only the discomfort of displacement. They are
used to white women in a slightly different context. They have white
mothers, white wives, white sisters, and white daughters. White men
can feel uncomfortable with Black men in the executive suite, but the
male bond is strong. As soon as the Black man is willing to share his
views of the Monday night football game, the barriers start to tumble
and a rapport begins to be established on the basis of common male interests, one of which is often how exasperating women can be. If on
nothing else, they can agree that the executive suite is no place for a
woman.

Finally, between the white man and the Black woman, where is
the common ground? What does each know about the other as a species? What has been the sum of the white man's experience with the
Black woman? It is more likely that she can be comfortable with him
than he with her, because her higher education brought her into contact with many situations where white males predominated, and she has
learned to familiarize herself with different types and noted distin-
guishing features. But he is at a complete loss. He tries to relate her to
other Black women he knows about, but he fails miserably. We are not
like his cleaning lady, the woman at the supermarket check-out
counter, or cultural stereotypes such as Cleopatra Jones and Miss Jane
Pittman. If we do in any way resemble the attractive, organized, super-
efficient young lady who reads the nightly news to him, it is more likely
to make him feel intimidated than comfortable. His ability to deal with
us is hampered by a hodge-podge of misinformation that he is heir to.
He thinks of us as both maternalistic and sexually potent. Before he
can deal with you or me as individual persons, he has to struggle
against and reconcile generations of stereotyping.

So we are doubly cursed, having nothing in common with the very beings with whom we *must* co-operate. Unless we are able to construct a Black feminist counterculture of our own, we have no choice but to stumble on, aided by no one, not even by each other. A bleak prospect! Is this accurate?

Not entirely. There are plenty of white men and women willing to give us all credit where it is due and to allow us to rise on merit. Also, there is one mighty power in this society that we can enlist: the power of the dollar! At the moment a lot of Black women get jobs because they accept a lower wage than a white man. This is exploitation. We should be paid according to our productivity—more, less, or the same as our colleagues, according to our performance. Unfortunately some types of organizations measure performance on scales that favor white males. It is obvious that so long as everyone plays by the rules, organizations having more hierarchical structures are best suited to us: an organization that sticks to clearly stated rules relating compensation and promotion to performance is one in which we can climb. A collegial organization, governed by the less easily defined principles of consensus, will only benefit those of us that have an obvious ability to "sell" ourselves to the majority of the organization's members.

What we want, basically, is to be judged as individuals on the merits of our qualifications, to be given tasks commensurate with those qualifications, and to be promoted as we demonstrate leadership potential. We must guard against responding to our detractors in kind, by making sweeping assumptions about individuals on the basis of their race and cultural background.

1. Never demand special treatment

This is a tricky proposition. We surely *deserve* extra consideration to make up for all we have suffered in the past, right? Well, *extra* consideration is not necessarily *equal* consideration. Draw the line at the difference between *access* and *mobility*. Historically, we have been denied access to power; therefore it is our right to use every form of legal duress to insure that schools and employers which are required to grant us access do so to the fullest possible extent. We should make the fullest possible use of our double minority status to *enter* programs and to receive benefits which will put us *on the right track*. Once we are there, in school or on the job, cheek by jowl with everyone else, Black and white, male and female, we have to forge ahead *under our own steam*.

2. Make no hasty judgments

There are plenty of reasons why people do not get along with each other, quite apart from prejudice. If you approach your job in a predominantly white organization, convinced that you will be subjected to prejudice, you will prove yourself right the first hour of the first day, as soon as a person fails to return your greeting. We all need time to adjust to strangers. If you expect to be offended, you will be; and you will give offense by projecting an obviously defensive attitude. That is what Dr. Williams means when she talks about having a chip on your shoulder. I have seen intelligent young Black women walk into neutral situations tight-lipped and with blazing eyes, clearly expecting a battle and by so doing encouraging one. No one likes to be prejudged. Wait until you have solid evidence of prejudice before you make a federal case.

3. Speak your mind

This is the other side of the coin. We put up with too much and are often at pains to make allowances for the majority because, as we tell ourselves, "they don't know any better." What we really mean is that we are too embarrassed or afraid to speak up. We do not want to focus attention on those things that are obvious to everyone else: that we are Black and female. In most mixed groups, there is a wise guy (or wise gal) who gets too chummy too soon and is immediately making sly references to your race and sex. Nip it in the bud. Make it very clear to everyone in the office that you do not appreciate that kind of familiarity or humor. If you let things slide, it will escalate. It does not matter whether this comes from a subordinate, a colleague, or your superior. Make it clear that you expect to be addressed in a certain way, not touched, and that jokes about your race or sex are in extremely bad taste. Of course, it is far easier to do this if you have allies who feel the same as you, which is why you should make an effort to:

4. Stand together

Acknowledge the common bond between yourself and other Black women at work. Go out of your way to make friends with them. If they are older or younger than you, they may be inhibited from approaching you directly. Try to see that you all adopt the same attitudes toward office behavior and show as much mutual respect as possible, especially if you hold different types of positions. This goes for Black men too. It is important that we present a united front to the white world, even in the limited arena of the work place. We should be proud of each other, no matter how disparate our jobs. But keep this professional and within the bounds of dignity and respect. You do not want to foster an "us-against-them" attitude; you want simply to make it clear that you will stand up for your own kind.

5. Never underestimate your opposition

Believe what people *do,* not what they say. We live in a time when politicians everywhere daily mouth dozens of platitudes about their commitment to minorities. All they are committed to is getting our votes and staying in office. The one white person in your organization who seems to be the least friendly may in fact be the most fair when it comes to judging your work. The one who goes out of the way to impress you with the number of Black friends he or she has is undoubtedly nursing some deep-rooted prejudice or guilt. We all have tunnel vision of one sort or another; it is simply more pronounced in certain cases. Take a recent public statement by a prominent white female tax attorney:

> *"There's a good market here in the suburbs. Women professionals helping each other."*

On the surface this would appear to be a reasonable, innocent observation. In fact it is indicative of a trend among white career women to follow exactly the same patterns of self-interest as their husbands and fathers, patterns that are essentially exclusionary. In Houston there is a women's organization that actually forbids its members from patronizing any businesses other than those owned by fellow members. This is discrimination on a giant scale, but they are very proud of themselves as a practical feminist progressive club.

The Reverend Dr. Pauli Murray, lawyer, activist, poet, and Episcopal priest, was rejected by the University of North Carolina because she was Black, so she enrolled at Howard University for her law degree.

> *"For three years," she says, "I began to feel acutely what it was to be a woman in a man's world; to be excluded because I was a woman. The first day I attended class, a professor who was a very outstanding NAACP lawyer—and whether he said this in jest I will never know, but he seemed to be serious —said, 'I don't know why women come to law school, but since you're here we'll have to deal with you.' "*

These are important words to bear in mind because even though we may encounter superficial smiles and token acceptance, all too often the underlying sentiment is simply the same: since you are here, we will have to deal with you!

Isolation

In most occupations the more successful you become, the more the chance of loneliness increases. You outdistance other Black women, other white women, and other Black men and find yourself in an atmosphere dominated by white men, creatures with fundamentally different outlooks. At the same time, your job performance may increasingly depend on your ability to deal with people, people with whom you have little in common except the job. At these levels informal exchange is often more important than office memorandums. The more isolated you feel, the less you are able to compete with white men who share the same interests as the majority of the organization's clients, partners, employees, and top management: baseball, golf, female movie stars. A lot of important decisions may get made at bull sessions in a local bar after work. How do you fit in?

We are still a long way from line vice presidencies with any of the Fortune 500 companies, and business writer Janice Simpson acknowledges:

> *"The chance of seeing a Black female chief executive at a major corporation in the near future is slim."*

One reason, linked to that of pride and prejudice, is company loyalty. A Black female manager in a major company may have to face conflicting ethical questions. Ermal Little, now a free-lance management consultant, was head of personnel for a California tool company that went into partnership with a South African distributor:

> *"On the business level I could understand the merger, but I had to quit. As soon as they were criticized for the South African connection, I was pushed out front to face the press and argue for the company. They were simply using the fact that I was Black, and that just wasn't right."*

In a number of our major cities, large department stores have contributed to inner city decline by moving their prestigious stores out of downtown areas and into the suburbs. This follows the flight of their middle-class white customers. At the same time they are active in promoting Black women to senior positions as buyers and department managers, even while they shut their doors to Black customers. How much loyalty does the Black employee owe to a company that seems to be taking a direction which is unfavorable for Black people? No white employee ever has to face such a question, and it is simply one more factor that can isolate us from the mainstream of corporate life. We have to learn where to draw the lines between our personal commitments and our belief in the inherent value of our jobs.

The struggle to succeed within any organization is a political struggle, not a race in which the fastest always wins. If you nurture your intuitive skills and learn to be a good judge of character, you will learn the ropes. Never go out of your way to make an enemy. Simply ignore the people that you find are the most obnoxious or antagonistic. Carefully select a handful of *allies,* a tight network, a group of people that you are prepared to go to bat for just as hard as you would expect them to do the same for you. Ideally these allies should represent a cross section of the organization and should include superiors and colleagues, as well as subordinates. It should be weighted in favor of those you get along well with, especially other Black women; but if yours is an organization top-heavy with white males, you have to have at least one firmly on your side, one who believes in your abilities, period.

Building such a cadre may take two or three years. Take your time. Seek people who are performance-oriented and trustworthy. Do not keep changing your allegiances within the organization. If your allies' fortunes falter, stand by them. Then they will help you when the time comes. Above all you want allies who will speak up for you because they know you do a good job, not because you are a Black woman.

When to Make an Official Complaint

This should be done the second time a grievance happens. And only if you have solid witnesses. Otherwise you will be judged the guilty party. This applies both to racial prejudice and sexual harassment. Bear in mind that it is very difficult to prove racial prejudice unless overt statements were made in the presence of others. The Equal Employment Opportunity Commission has representatives at most major companies, and it is to that person that you apply with your evidence. Present a list of incidents, indicating the time and place at which they occurred. If there is no such representative, take your complaints to your personnel department or in-house grievance committee. If you belong to a union, see your local representative if you think they will be sympathetic. If you cannot pursue your problem through these channels, talk to a lawyer or call the local branch of the EEOC or American Civil Liberties Union (ACLU). Listings for these organizations are in the Appendix. The ACLU will also help you if you can prove that you have been denied access to a job or an educational opportunity solely on the basis of your sex or race.

RACIAL DISCRIMINATION

First of all it is important that you know what your rights are, and I will emphasize what I stated at the beginning of this chapter: you have a right to expect equality of opportunity, but once you are in the work place you should not expect unequal consideration or extra opportunity simply because you are a Black woman. If you are denied access to a program or to benefits which are enjoyed by all other employees of your standing, none of whom are Black women, you may have a case. If there is simply a hostile, anti-Black atmosphere where you work but no concrete acts of discrimination, I suggest you move to another job, if possible, rather than try to fight a general attitude.

SEXUAL HARASSMENT

The following guidelines were issued by the EEOC to define illegal sexual harassment:

1. When submission to sexual advances is a condition of employment.

2. When submission to or rejection of said advances is used as the basis for employment decisions.

3. When such advances have the purpose of interfering with the individual's work performance or of creating a hostile or intimidating environment.

A number of important studies have shown that Black women are twice as likely to be victims of sexual harassment as white women and that the instigators of such harassment were just as likely to be Black men as white men. We are not safe.

What can you do if you are not sure that contact in the elevator is a pass or not? Wait until the second time and *trust your instincts*. The following situations call for action:

1. Endearments such as "honey" and "sweetie."

2. Unnecessary physical contact.

3. Questions about your personal life, especially those with sexual overtones.

4. Suggestive compliments about your clothing or figure.

Beyond these, anything that is close to an obvious proposition, a pinch or a pat on the bottom, deserves a swift, direct response. If the man is a co-worker, not a superior, then simply make your lack of interest known immediately. You can do this best by stating that you would prefer the offender never to repeat the words or actions. Depending upon the circumstances, this may be done at once, in front of witnesses, or quietly. Many women are afraid, after such an incident, that they unconsciously did or said something to inspire the action.

If such is the case take the man aside, or even to lunch, and explain very matter of factly that the things he is saying and/or doing (be specific) are not to your liking and that if you two are going to maintain a professional friendship he must stop now, please. You cannot go wrong if you keep your head and remain businesslike.

If it is your superior who makes the advance, then your response may have to be different. To confront him in front of witnesses may not be diplomatic. State clearly that you appreciate his attention but that you have a very strict rule about not getting involved with people at work. If he is persistent, make a specific appointment with him and tell him that you do not appreciate him using his authority to make advances to you. Be prepared for him to be angry and embarrassed, but try to avoid an argument and leave quickly after having spoken your mind. He may accuse you of having provoked him by your style of dress or way of walking. Ignore this.

When the approach is ambiguous—bodily pressure, for instance— make it very obvious that if it was a message, you do not like it. Move away at once, even an exaggerated distance. The same goes for hands on the shoulder, the knee, or anywhere else. A male psychiatrist, writing about this problem, counseled his women readers to "keep a level head and a sense of humor." My advice is to keep a level head and drop the sense of humor; it can very easily be misinterpreted as flippancy. Be serious. Not melodramatic or hysterical, just serious.

Join!

You are not going to encounter any problem involving racial discrimination or sexual harassment that is new. The more successful you become, the less companionship you will have with which to share such problems. The antidote for this is to associate with as many Black women in your position as possible, and this means joining one or more of the organizations devoted to solidarity among working Black women (see the Appendix).

Even if you have always been a loner, now is the time to reconsider your need for bolstering your confidence and getting the new perspective that only others who are in your position can provide. A problem shared is a problem lessened, often a problem relieved. You may have become so doggedly stuck into your education and then your job that you imagine you are alone and unique. Come together with your sisters, pool your resources, and let out that anger, that frustration.

As the sole Black woman at work, or one of a handful, you may feel absolutely powerless when harassed, discriminated against, or passed over for promotion. But with the kinship of a strong group behind you, Black women who know what you are enduring and who have suffered the same and worse, you can fight your battles vigorously. Pay attention to these words from the great Fannie Lou Hamer, in 1971:

> *"Let's try to get together. And strive to be yourself and not someone else. You know, I've seen so many Black women throughout this country. Two years ago, they was very white. This evening, they are so Black that you don't know them. The only thing you have to be that's important in life—to make yourself, your husband, or whoever it is very happy—is just go on being your own normal, Black beautiful selves as women, as human beings."*

9

Managing Marriage and Motherhood

"Young Black women . . . tend to be very career-oriented, often at the expense of personal life and personal growth. I think I'm simply typical of that pattern. I've never stopped to marry, to take time off and raise children, to have anything other than a career-oriented professional kind of life. I think there is an imbalance in that. I've done nothing else for the past twelve years except work and develop."

Constance M. Carroll, President,
Indian Valley Colleges
Novata, California

The more we strive for success, the more money we make, the more prestigious our jobs become, the less likely we are to find a suitable mate. Black women and Black men have been fighting with each other for generations, overtly and covertly, because so many Black women have had to be both breadwinners and double-duty parents. If it is not the fault of the Black man that he is "behind" us in the struggle for success, it is certainly not our fault that we *must* continue that struggle. It is a question of economic survival: forty-one per cent of all Black families in this country have only *one* head, a Black *woman;* and her average income is $8,500—precisely *half* the average income for white families with only one head. In order to really understand why our men are so threatened by our success, we have to look at the traditional biological functions of the sexes because we are not going to undo in a couple of decades the conditioning of more than ten thousand years.

Ardent feminists will surely argue with this, but we are designed to have children and care for them, and men are designed to protect and provide for their families. In its basic, primitive form, this is not a bad design; it works well for many species of life. It only got out of hand when men began to take advantage of their roles and limit the scope of women's activities. Obviously, from the very start, the male was afraid that if we were given a chance to hunt for food, we might do just as well, or better, than they.

Ideology can be a strong spur to social change. Books have changed the course of civilizations: the Bible, *Das Kapital, Mein Kampf,* and others. However, I do not believe that the main reason women have invaded the work force in such large numbers is because we have all read *The Feminine Mystique* by Betty Friedan. It is because most of us needed money. Why? Obviously the men were not providing *enough.* Even by middle-class standards, two incomes are now mandatory if the family is to remain in reasonable comfort. Our society encourages divorce, extramarital affairs, and cohabitation. If women are not to be victimized by these new standards, we must simply have our own incomes.

On top of this we are still plagued by this awkward desire to propagate the human race, much more so than the male. Or at least his desire is quickly satisfied. In theory, if we are to assume the breadwinner's role, the male of the species should assume the child-rearing role. Since they are not about to do this on any large scale, women now have either to assume both burdens or to choose between them. We are compelled by our basic natures to seek marriage and raise children, and are impelled by social and economic necessity to earn money. Something has to give.

The male psyche is fragile and easily threatened. For a long time Black men managed to cope with our ability to hold down a job and care for the family because the jobs we had were *women's jobs.* They were extensions of our nurturing skills: nursing, housework, teaching. We were not ostensibly taking the Black man's jobs away from him. Neither he nor we had access to the world of *careers.* Discrimination prevented him from moving even as far as the semiskilled job market, so he remained uneducated and unskilled while we improved ourselves at work and raised the families. Then everything was turned upside down in the sixties when civil rights legislation *in theory* opened the doors for Black men to move into the career world. Instead, better prepared, *we* moved in.

Because of this the Black male is insecure. Instead of encouraging us to develop our abilities, he more often than not tries to assert himself in a traditionally *macho* manner that is not founded on personal achievement but fear. The more he sees the Black woman outdistancing him, the more afraid and threatened and belligerent he becomes, demanding extremes of loyalty and affection which are incompatible with our *need* to work and our *right* to strive for meaningful jobs. Black men demand us to make sacrifices in our careers that they would have no intention of making themselves. A Black man calls home and says:

"I'm going to be late tonight," and that is that.

A Black woman calls home and says:

"Honey, the conference is running overtime and I still have to present my paper, so could you please give the kids dinner and put Julie to bed. I'll be home as soon as I can. I'm sorry . . ."

and her husband consents to do the family the favor of helping out while he is intimidated by the importance of what has kept her at the office.

I am drawing this outline with very broad strokes because many, many women I have spoken to tell me the same old story, and one has only to glance at contemporary Black literature to realize that Black men and Black women do not always seem to be living on the same planet: for instance, *Black Macho and the Myth of the Superwoman* by Michelle Wallace and *For Colored Girls Who Have Considered Suicide/When the Rainbow Is Enuf* by Ntozake Shange.

There are Black men who encourage and support their wives' endeavors; there are Black men who happily share the responsibilities of child rearing; there are Black men who are strong enough within themselves to see that co-operation, not competition, is the answer. But not enough Black men like that! Not enough to go around, it would seem. Typical is this characterization by Rosemary Bray, at age twenty-four the associate editor of *Essence* magazine:

"Men are going to have to realize that for a lot of women, work and love are equal. I bring work home and drop into the office at bizarre hours. You can't explain that to a certain kind of man. He says, 'But don't you love me?' What's that got to do with anything?"

Unfortunately it has everything to do with the Black woman who expects to have both a successful career and a successful marriage. We have to ask ourselves: is it possible? The inevitable answer is yes, of course it is possible, if you find the right man! But since we have to deal with reality, not theory, we should consider these words from psychiatrist George Serban:

"Even women in positions of power relate to men who are more successful than they—you rarely see a woman doctor

marrying a male nurse or a woman executive marrying her
male secretary, though you see the reverse all the time. Be-
nevolent control is essential for the male; protection and
affection, for the female."

Why should we be denied protection and affection simply because
we are able to keep a decent job? Black men view us in a most ambiguous light, with admiration and acrimony. Most Black men were raised
in a matriarchal group. The mother did more than the father. The
mother held the family together; kept a job, cooked, and cleaned. The
mother held the purse-strings; the father was inadequate or nonexistent. Now the Black man grows up and is faced with the question of
marriage. What kind of a woman does he want? If he chooses a woman
like his mother, who is strong and hard-working, then it reflects the
inadequacies of his father, against which he rebels. Many Black men
make no secret of the fact that they prefer women who are "soft," vulnerable, and helpless. That is not the profile of today's Black woman.
Because of this credibility gap, three times as many Black men marry
white women as Black women marry white men.

Just to start out, there are very few eligible men, whether they
want "our type" of Black woman or not! Robert Staples, a sociologist
at the University of California at Berkeley estimates that there are five
eligible Black women for every Black male. If it is natural for us to
want to marry men who are as successful or more successful than we
are, then most of us are doomed to disappointment because there are
not enough Black men in that category.

Some of us turn that into a virtue and concentrate on our careers,
like my friend Audrey Smaltz, a fashion consultant:

"I never doubted that I would be successful, but being single
makes you more apt to be aggressive."

In her case it paid off because now she says:

"I do have a wonderful, supportive man who's proud of me
and loves what I'm doing. He's a big part of my success."

But we cannot all find men as extraordinary as Audrey's husband:
Lionel Hampton!

Dr. Serban elaborates:

"Women are in an extremely difficult position. They must go
to work and are able to become successful, yet that success
may compromise their ability to function biologically and
emotionally with a man, may threaten their happiness. On one

*level, a woman is not able to meet her marital obligations; on
another, she loses respect for her husband."*

There are no pat answers, but being aware of all aspects of the
problem does help to diffuse the more explosive aspects of the situation. Contrary to everything I have said about avoiding body contact at
work, one of the solutions is to marry a colleague. That is what Bobbi
Gutman did. She is now consulting manager with the Smith-Kline Corporation. She met her husband when they were both working at Scott
Paper, where he is research manager:

*"You can't miss if you're colleagues. I won't be Adam's Rib
to any man; working is a big piece of me. We know enough to
keep competition out of the house. I don't bore him when
talking about my work, as we're both in business and have
strong interest in it. Conversely, he feels free to discuss work
issues with me. One of the things men have been lacking in
their marriages is problem-solving—real help, that is, based
on work experience. In the two-career marriage, when you
ask your husband 'Can I help?' it means something more than
mixing a martini."*

But no matter how well you and your husband handle a two-
career family situation, you have to be prepared to make massive compromises between the way you are going to lead your life and the way
you were brought up to expect families should behave. In some cases
you may have to sacrifice having children. This is often agreed upon,
blithely, at the start of a "sensible" marriage, but in ten years time both
may want to have children and neither may be willing to endure the career interruption. Of course it is the woman whose career really gets interrupted.

In some segments of our industry, jobs are being created for
women that rule out the possibility that they can both keep their job
and raise a family. At General Motors, a graduate degree from the GM
Institute (where one third of the enrollment is female) is valid for only
six months unless the graduate is working in the field. GM never per-
mits leaves of absence beyond three months. If a woman elected to stay
at home to care for a new baby beyond that period of time, GM would
lose a highly trained worker (it costs $25,000 to train each graduate),
and the woman would have lost her chance to reach her career goal.

The Black woman who is young and single, or middle-aged and
divorced, or older and never-married, should realize that she is not
going to find the right man by making compromises with her career.
Examine the reasons why the relationships you have had did not work
out. Were they related to your job? Did your career not give you

enough time? Were you preoccupied with business? Would you blame a man for acting the same way? In fact, no one can shut out their job just by stepping out of the office, nor should they be required to; yet many Black women feel the need to downplay or ignore their career achievements in order to attract a suitor. Never hide your accomplishments or be reluctant to talk about your work. I know that we women are supposed to identify ourselves according to our looks, but men always identify themselves according to what they do; it is the first thing about themselves that they announce to a stranger.

We are fortunate to be in the vanguard of the movement toward real power for Black women, but we also have to suffer through all the growing pains that this transition creates. Our isolation increases, and our personal lives are deeply affected. Our men distrust us, and our mothers wonder what the world is coming to. Just promise me one thing: before you decide to get married and have children, think about the exact effect it will have on your career. Are you willing to give up your job? Does your husband-to-be have a positive attitude toward Black women becoming successful? Is he willing to share the burden of child rearing? If not, you have to be prepared to have the children, suffer the consequences in your job, raise the children, and earn half or more of the family income. Ask yourself what your intended husband will do. A man who marries a working woman has no right to expect to be able to luxuriate in the type of atmosphere that *might* exist if his wife had nothing better to do than to wait for him to come home so she could soothe his aching brow. Who is going to soothe your aching brow? And your children's?

Pregnancy

So you went ahead and did it! You got married, and now you are pregnant. How is that going to affect your job? It all depends on *you.* Pregnant women are becoming more and more a visible part of the work force, but it is still unusual for a woman to remain on the job throughout her entire pregnancy, leave for a couple of weeks to have her baby, and then return to pick up where she left off. But that is what you are going to do.

Expect hostility. It is amazing how quickly your office will divide itself between those who are happy about your condition and the rest, who consider it to be a deliberate attempt on your part to evade the responsibilities of your job.

I worked every day until I went into the hospital to have my son, and a number of my colleagues could barely conceal their acute discomfort—women as well as men. You have to realize that the image of a pregnant woman confidently giving orders in a work milieu is the ultimate superwoman threat to men. It demonstrates that we can do *all* things. It is not enough for us to have a career (like a man); it is not enough for us to have a career *and* marriage (like a man); we want a career *and* marriage *and* children (like a man). In other words, we want equal rights. It just so happens that we are equipped to give birth. And for this distinction, for this minor task of being the source of all life, we ask a few weeks off. Is that too much to ask?

Yes! According to colleagues, who see your pregnancy as a feminist statement. Yes! According to your boss, who is forced to remember that you are a woman. Yes! According to your male subordinates, who will become patronizingly solicitous as if pregnancy were a disease they could catch (if only!). Also you may find that even among the women who applauded your decision to keep on working after you got married, the announcement that you intend to return after having the baby brings forth the subtle hint that you will not be much of a mother if you do *that*.

So you are caught in all the old traps of conflicting roles. For some reason a woman with teenage children capable of getting up to all kinds of mischief is not criticized for working all through their critical years, whereas a younger woman who elects to spend only sixteen rather than twenty-four hours a day with her immobile newborn is a monster of insensitivity.

First of all, it may be hard to stay on the job because physiological changes during pregnancy may sap your energy, so do not try to be a Wonder Woman. As soon as your pregnancy is confirmed, your doctor should ask you for a work history; if not, be prepared to volunteer this. Give, in detail, what your work entails and make sure that you have your doctor's sanction to continue with any or all phases of it. There are certain types of occupations that are dangerous for pregnant women: for instance, jobs that involve working with lead, vinyl chloride, and radioactive material. If you are a librarian, you should not use ladders while pregnant. When telling your doctor about your work, describe how you spend the day: standing, moving, or sitting. How close are you to bathrooms, and how clean are they? If your doctor suggests that you avoid certain activities, make sure you know how long that avoidance should stay in effect.

The next step is to inform your employer. There is no ideal way to do this, and different organizations have different methods. The larger the company, the more likely there is to be a standard policy. I suggest that you make a verbal statement and follow it up with a written note, memorandum, or letter. This should be very brief, simply indicating that you will be absent from approximately this date to that date and that you will take care that your responsibilities are covered in your absence.

If there are medical reasons for you to be relieved of any particular tasks, then simply state that your doctor prefers you not to do these and provide your doctor's name and address. In 1978 Congress amended Title VII of the 1964 Civil Rights Act to specifically prohibit employment discrimination based on pregnancy, childbirth, or related medical conditions, so you cannot be penalized for being pregnant!

Expect to be less than popular with your colleagues when you delegate the work they will have to do in your stead while you are away. Leave as few loose ends as possible, but do not try to double your work load before you leave because pregnancies do not always go according to schedule. If you sense that one or another of the people at your job seem to be particularly put out by your condition, see if you cannot talk it through with them, quietly. You do not have to justify your pregnancy to anyone, but it is a condition that can inspire a lot of psychological problems, and if you are able to discuss it calmly with your co-workers, this will help you and them. The worst thing to do is to try to pretend "it" is not there or to treat it (if they do) as a sickness.

Technically—and this bears heavily on your medical insurance— your pregnancy is a "temporary disability," and you are entitled to *every* benefit that it is your employer's policy to give to any employee with that condition. Many state insurance commissions require that employers provide maternity coverage but *not all*. Find out what the requirements are in your state and check that your employer abides by them. Your employer is not required to give you preferential treatment, simply the same treatment as the company policy (and state law) allows for all temporary disability cases. These provisions only cover the time that you are *unable* to work and do not allow for time to care for the baby once you are physically recovered.

Your employer may continue your salary and may give you a paid or partially paid leave of absence or an unpaid leave of absence with employment benefits still in effect. If your employer does not have a temporary disability plan and is not so required by the state, then you may be eligible for state aid. Contact your nearest state insurance agency office and file a claim. Find out when you can expect to receive the money, weekly or at the end of your disability period. This may make a big difference to your financial planning, since having a baby is expensive. You should hear within two weeks of filing a claim.

As a person with a temporary disability, you have to be allowed back to work, and your other job benefits (such as accrued seniority, sick pay, or vacation benefits) should continue. By the same token, if your employer has a policy of assigning lighter work to temporarily disabled employees, then you are eligible for the exact same treatment. Many employers take the point of view that the pregnant employee has voluntarily created a nonaccidental condition that inconveniences the organization and costs the company money. Your job is to stick calmly by the rules and to explain your rights. If you have any doubts about the way you are being treated, contact your local or regional office of the Federal Equal Employment Opportunity Commission.

When you make the decision to have your child, make sure that you can afford it; and when you return to work, make sure that the provisions you are making for child care are adequate. Do not rely on vague promises from relatives. If you have a parent or sibling who is willing to care for your baby while you work, then make sure you discuss with them what you will contribute for food and clothing. If you are hiring a full-time baby-sitter or nurse, then interview them thoroughly and make sure that they are not just a warm body but a person experienced in baby care. If your husband is going to help care for the baby, draw up a schedule well before you go into the hospital. His well-meaning intentions may fly out the window when his boss sends him on a business trip. Planning is essential. The person caring for your baby must be able to contact either you or your husband or the baby's doctor at any time—preferably all three.

If you intend to take your baby to work, which is becoming accepted in some parts of the country, make sure that adequate facilities exist and that you are doing it because it really helps, not just as a social experiment. Think twice if your place of work is not geared for it; no matter how enthusiastic your colleagues and superiors are, it may not be fair to you, them, or the baby. If your husband is able to take time off, he should schedule it a week or two *after* you have the baby, at about the time you would be getting ready to return to your job. A few corporations give men "baby leave" but have found that few men actually use it to stay home caring for the baby. So it goes.

Leading A Double Life

Jim and Rosemary are in their thirties, with a girl of two and a boy of six. Both have management jobs, and their combined income is enough to allow them to have a housekeeper who works from ten until six, five days a week. Their son is in kindergarten until three every day, and the little girl has neighborhood playmates. Jim and Rosemary both have to travel in their jobs but never at the same time, and to all intents and purposes they share the burdens of providing for, nurturing, and protecting the family. The modern way. But do they *really* share? Let us look beneath the surface.

Jim helps make the breakfast and leaves the house at 8 A.M., confident that by having accomplished the task of buttering toast and pouring cornflakes for his unruly children and by admonishing them twice he has proved himself to be a progressive father, a feminist husband. He dismisses his family from his mind and concentrates first on the newspaper, then on his job. When he gets home at 6 P.M., he concentrates on the television news.

What about Rosemary? She takes her son to kindergarten and experiences a mild anxiety fit because, as usual, she has to leave him there fifteen minutes before the other children arrive, and even though the teachers never seem to mind, it makes her feel like an uncaring mother who cannot wait to get rid of her child. Then she takes her daughter (who sounds like she is catching another cold) to old Mrs. Flynn down the hall, who is delighted to have her until the housekeeper comes at ten. One day, old Mrs. Flynn is going to have a heart attack, and Rosemary frankly worries more about what will happen to her daughter if this occurs between eight and ten in the morning. Then Rosemary dashes off to work, running back home first for ten minutes to write a note to the housekeeper asking her to please do the laundry. So Rosemary is late for the train and late for work.

Rosemary does her work conscientiously, pausing occasionally to remember that she forgot to call her son's best friend's mother (what *is* that woman's name?) to see if the boys can play together after school. At lunch time she spends thirty-five minutes trying to get through to the housekeeper (the line is busy) to tell her to pick up both her son and his friend from school. Then Rosemary remembers the best friend's mother's name and gets her on the telephone to make sure she knows her son is playing with Rosemary's son. Then Rosemary chokes down a tuna salad sandwich in five minutes and is back at her desk for an afternoon of hard work, interrupted only by the need to make a surreptitious shopping list and plan the dinners for the week ahead. At the end of Rosemary's workday, her boss calls her in for a brief chat, just long enough to make her miss her regular train, so after shopping she arrives home to find the laundry all over the kitchen floor, the housekeeper having tea with Mrs. Flynn (has her daughter been there all day?), and her son's best friend howling with a huge bump on his forehead and the bathroom covered with squirted shaving foam.

Even if the working wife is not actually required to *do* all the housework, shopping, and child care herself, it is inevitably she who *oversees* all that work. This is a major management operation. Most husbands imagine that simply because they and their wives can afford help (baby-sitters, day care, a housekeeper), the buck stops there. In fact it is the working wives who have to spend their working days on the job, pursuing their careers but also remaining "tuned in" constantly to what should be going on at home, or what has to be done for the morrow, or worrying about what to do if the baby-sitter quits or if any number of domestic problems occur that are piled on top of her regular job—a job which could itself be just as pressure-ridden as her husband's.

It turns out to be one enormous struggle from morning until night.

The most fortunate of us belong to extended families that can pitch in and help, but others of us are separated from that support system and have to start from scratch. When my son reached the age of four, his social life became more complicated than my own, and virtually all of his friends' mothers worked. In order to co-ordinate after-school play dates and weekend visits, there was a constant telephone exchange between the offices of us executive mothers, our secretaries trying to get hold of us for top-level conferences about sandbox meetings. Some mothers are more conscientious than others. One sent her daughter to my home at 2:30 P.M. and came to pick her up at midnight. "I had to meet a client," she explained. Never again.

Some companies subscribe to a plan called Flextime, which allows workers to arrive at ten or leave at three, so long as they put in a minimum number of hours per week. If both parents can do this, it obviously solves a lot of problems. All organizations that have tried this report that it has helped business as much as the employees themselves, although I do not see it becoming widespread for many years, especially with regard to executive jobs. Usually the mother has to tailor her life in two directions, toward her job and toward the family, and both make very major demands on her time and energy. What does that leave for herself?

Something that I have observed among the group of working Black mothers that I know, which has been confirmed by professionals, is that those of us who are most organized in our jobs tend to be the least organized at home. Often the tasks are only different in name and scope, not in their basic natures. Take that of hiring a baby-sitter or a housekeeper, or that of finding a day-care center. Instead of applying the principles that we would use at work—for example, to hire an employee or to check out a production facility—we leap on the first candidate and beg them to take our child, whom we describe as perfect. We leave no instructions, neglect to pursue the references, give conflicting instructions, criticize prematurely (out of guilt that no one should be able to care for our children as well or better than we), and in essence ignore anything we have learned about judging character. I know women whose desks at work are the epitome of order, who chart their work schedules like clockwork, yet whose lives at home are mayhem and who keep all the receipts, old and new bills, check stubs, important telephone numbers, broken pencils, torn stamps, and rubber bands in one small broken kitchen drawer.

Are we afraid that if we try to organize our home lives, we will lose that warm feeling of constant crisis that knits the family together? Why do we allow our husbands to wander in and out as they please and embark on "more important things to do," while we come home from an awful day at work to utter chaos?

Organize, plan, and make time for yourself. Be selfish. First of all, make your husband responsible for certain specific tasks, not just the easy ones like making breakfast. How about putting him in charge of after-school activities on alternate weeks? One simple device for spreading the responsibility is to get a very large monthly calendar, one that gives you plenty of writing space per day, and hang it in the kitchen with the appointed jobs marked clearly.

Define your home management problems just as you would your job management problems. One of the prime solutions is always to delegate authority to those best able to wield it. This means your husband has to accept some authority, as well as whoever you are paying to help you in the house.

Learn to separate the physical tasks from the emotional ones. Most of us want to spend as much time as possible participating in our children's education, growth, and development. If you hire a baby-sitter who feeds your children candy all day to keep them quiet, you will have to come home and spend all your precious time disciplining them and in three hours try to undo the day's damage, instead of being able to spend the time quietly enjoying your family.

Eliminate everything that you do not *have* to do. I know that you *can* do everything, but not if you also have a career. Even if you think you can find the time to do everything, it is pointless to try because it will leave you an emotional wreck. You want to be emotionally fit so that you can give your children the best of yourself (and keep some of the best of yourself *for* yourself). Things like housecleaning, cooking, shopping, and the physical care of your child can all be delegated. What cannot be delegated are the supervisory tasks like selecting your child's school, attending events with your child, becoming acquainted with your child's friend's parents, teaching your child about religion or reproduction, or being available to your child for quiet times of simple communication to no particular purpose.

Most Black working mothers I know catch themselves feeling that despite the fact that they seem to spend all their free time with their children, there is always something going on, a move forward, an event to take the child to; and that they are not just simply "with" their children enough. Unfortunately our children are blissfully unaware of all the time we spend, not with them but in planning for their welfare, worrying about them, and seeing to them, out of sight. The child only cares about what he or she experiences, such as whether you have ten minutes to read a story or to listen to what happened at school or not. It is worth letting the dinner burn to do these things.

The most convenient type of child care *for you* is not always what is best for your child, and mistakes made when the child is an infant come home to roost when the child is older and unmanageable. Many working mothers want help with child care of a type that will not supplant their mothering role, which is a contradiction in terms. It is unrealistic to put someone in charge of your child for the better part of every weekday and not expect the child to treat this person as a surrogate parent. Any person who cares for your child on a regular basis—whether it is your husband, a relative, a teacher in a day-care center, a baby-sitter, or a housekeeper—is going to displace you temporarily. Face the fact and live with it, or quit your job and be a full-time mother.

Ideally your substitute should be responsible enough to do more for the child than simply keep it out of harm's way, yet not so authoritarian that they do not think you need to be informed about important aspects of your child's daytime behavior. When you take your child to a day-care center or hire a sitter, it is normal for you to receive, unasked, some feedback about your child, whether it is positive or negative. Silence is suspicious. In such cases it is worth coming home early once in a while, unannounced.

You cannot ignore your child's need for outside company, and even if this means approaching strangers in the playground, you should put together a network of neighborhood working women who have children of the same age.

Before the children came along, you probably enjoyed spending half an hour after work shopping for a couple of delicacies, finding a butcher, or buying fresh fish. This is the sort of thing you will have to sacrifice unless your boss will give you the afternoon off. Patronize supermarkets that will deliver and take pot luck. You cannot often serve gourmet meals and hold down a job. Your husband should help with the cooking, and the children too, as soon as they are old enough.

Once you become a mother, your status changes. You may be the vice president at work, but in your neighborhood you are "Elizabeth's mommy." If there are other women where you work that share this distinction, it will help you to get to know them. It is a common bond that can relieve the tension; you can exchange "horror stories" on coffee breaks.

It is unlikely that your husband grew up expecting his father to be home all day, especially in early childhood. But most likely you remember, or at least know, that your mother was with you all day every day until you were old enough to go to school. For your husband it is perfectly normal to be with the children at dinnertime and on weekends only. You, on the other hand, probably harbor guilt about not being home all day. If not actual guilt, at least you regret that you may be missing some of your child's important hours. Children grow up so fast. This is all the more reason to plan your weekends carefully. It is not good for a two-career family to have only one day when they can all be together, but if this is the case and Sunday is the only day you all can be together, try to avoid the syndrome that you have to do something *special* to "make the most of it." Both you and your husband may be dog-tired, and in the long run your children will value your presence much more just by being there, in the yard, in the playground, or going for a drive, than if you contrive always to create an exciting event which inevitably leads to someone's frayed nerves cracking. If you do a lot all week, do nothing on Sunday, but do it with your family.

Both women and men who have demanding occupations experience a period of confusion *every time* they come home from work. In *The Executive Parent* Dr. S. P. Hersh calls this "re-entry" and counsels us not to dismiss its importance or to deny that it occurs. He says we should start the mental shift from office to home as soon as we leave the office and should give ourselves time:

> *"If we fail to recognize re-entry as a real issue, our return home becomes a setup for misunderstandings . . . and even for hurtful behavior on everyone's part."*

This is not hard to understand. Your husband is coming from one direction, having had a frustrating day; you are coming from another direction, ebullient that you have completed an important assignment; at home your children are sitting zombielike before the television or are super-demanding. These three highly charged circumstances have an enormous impact, and such things happen *every day*.

Dr. Hersh advises families like ours to plan very specific "buffer times" when the family comes together for the one purpose of talking, listening, and *expressing*. Instead of saying:

> *"Not now, Mommy's had a rough day . . ."*

sometimes it is better to make the effort to get everyone around the kitchen table, including you with your headache, and to talk awhile about why your day was hard, to ask your husband, in front of the children, how his day went, and then to listen to your children tell you about *their* day.

Not everything can be planned to perfection; life at home is likely to be made up of more unforeseen circumstances than life at the office, but that is precisely why you should try to be as organized as possible. Make it a team effort; do not assume that you have to provide a pool of calm for your husband, even if he does earn a few thousand dollars a year more than you. Rope him into the psychological middle of family management crises; he does not qualify for any exemptions. We still believe that it is our job to nourish and nurture our families, but we must recognize that if we are managing these functions, even from a distance during the day, we are carrying the emotional responsibility and burden just as much as if we were doing the work ourselves *and* on top of a "regular" job.

Rivalry

I interviewed a number of two-career Black families that exhibited a disparity between the status and income of the jobs held by the wife and the husband. For example, Bob and Linda Gordon live in a New Jersey suburb and have three children. She is a production supervisor at a pharmaceutical plant, and he works in the maintenance department of the New York City mass transit system. Linda's response to my question about competitiveness was typical:

"I know that Bob is sensitive about the fact that he makes less money than I do, even though he never mentions it. I don't want my children growing up having no respect for their Daddy, so at home I make sure they can see that he's the boss!"

I asked her how they made family decisions about such things as saving money, where to go on vacations, or what major purchases to make:

"I let Bob handle all the important stuff. He's pretty good at it, although sometimes I get frustrated because I see him doing things I wouldn't do and I see us not getting as much for our money as we could. But when I grew up, I had to watch my father out of work, just hanging around the house while my mother had two part-time jobs and took care of us. I had no respect for my father, but that sure isn't going to happen here."

This is a familiar pattern but not a healthy one. Linda is so worried about her children's being influenced by an imbalance in the roles of the parents that she is suppressing her own abilities. In fact, their children know nothing about what Bob and Linda do at their jobs, nor anything about their respective incomes. Linda is trying to make it appear that hers is a family resembling an idealized one she never herself had as a child. It would perhaps be wiser to explain to the children, as they reach an understanding age, that this is what Dad does and this is what Mom does, as graphically as possible, and to teach them about the different types of jobs available, tell them about discrimination, affirmative action, and why it is important for them to get a good, complete education. Bob has no reason at all to be ashamed of his job, and I suspect that he is *not* but that Linda may be,

slightly. Keeping the issues partially hidden from the children only encourages the children to draw their own conclusions, probably wrong
ones.

By trying to avoid competitiveness, Bob and Linda are actually in-
viting it because they are committing themselves to an outlook that
creates a lot of inner tension. You may be a "boss" in your office and
your husband may be a blue-collar worker, but that does not mean you
are *his* boss! There is no need to compensate at home for a difference
in positions outside the home. No matter what you both do to earn a
living, you should co-operate equally as partners in the business of running a family. This means sharing the labor and the management decisions. Your children will grow up with appropriate value systems only
if they see both parents working on an equal basis to solve problems
and to look after the home.

This question becomes critical when one partner has to make a career decision which will affect the whole family, such as relocation.
Traditionally there is no question but that when the male is required to
move, the family quietly uproots itself and starts anew with new
schools and a strange neighborhood. But does it work the other way
around? The corporate world moves people a lot, often with little
regard for the effects on their families. Is your husband willing to look
for a new job in a new city because *you* may have to move? These are
questions to be explored ahead of time so that the family can have
some policy. The major problem is the unwillingness of business to be
sympathetic to these problems. There are organizations, like Catalyst,
Inc., that bring together corporate leaders and experts from the disciplines of psychology and sociology so that the business world can better understand the two-career family and help it to operate as a partnership, not as a lopsided rivalry.

If the husband is willing to relocate because his wife has an important opportunity, this will do no harm to his career if he can at least
move laterally, with no loss of status or income. For ten years the Harvard Business School has included a course about mobility and the
two-career family, and Brigham Young University recently instituted a
seminar series for graduates and their spouses that addresses these important problems.

Sex, Friendships, and Time

Many two-career couples end up living as roommates rather than
as husband and wife, simply because they are both too tired for sex. In
some cases the wife is not willing to admit this, and a great deal of
strife is the result. Often she feels that her ambitiousness or assertiveness may be diminishing her husband's interest in her, but often the

incidence of sexual contact is low simply because playing superwoman at work and managing the family at home leaves little time and no energy for sex. It is a question of *overload*. How much can you accomplish in one day and still be relaxed enough at the end of it to make love? A lot of working wives are desperate to get a few hours sleep before they have to get up and start all over again.

Although spontaneity can add a great deal to the pleasures of sex, unless you are aware of the need to plan you will never get the opportunity to be spontaneous! Couples drift into celibacy while they blame each other for a lack of interest, when in fact what is needed is a co-ordinated effort to find or make the time to be alone, to have a quiet drink or a dinner without the kids.

A woman who performs well at work and is determined to be available to her family will burn herself out because she is neglecting *herself*. Sex is part of being good to yourself, and unless you are good to yourself you will be no good to anyone else, not to your job or your family. When I asked Linda about this, she acknowledged that it was a problem:

> *"But I spend so little time with the children that I feel very guilty every time I pack them off to my sister's, and I know she feels I am neglecting them!"*

Linda is lucky that she has a sister to pack her children off to; I am sure some of us wish we could do the same. But however you do it, you must create a quiet time, for you and your husband alone, a time for which you have two rules:

1. No talking about work.
2. No talking about the children.

You will realize just how long it has been since you had a conversation with each other that did not revolve around one or the other of these topics and will think of all you had to discuss before you were married, before you had children! But you have to consciously *make* the time available; it will not come of its own accord. It is worth revamping your budget to keep a baby-sitter late just one night every week or two, just so that you and your husband can be yourselves again, not Mom and Dad or two working stiffs.

You need an escape valve that lies outside your work and outside your home. This is something you may feel guilty and selfish for doing, but treat it as an investment in your sanity. I asked Linda about when she saw her friends. Her reply:

"Hardly at all. In fact I don't know my neighbors except those that have children to play with mine. Look, I don't have the time! There are people at work I get along with, but none live around here. I speak to my sister every day on the phone, but we haven't been alone together since, I don't know, years. I guess I'd have to say Bob was my best friend; we get along real well."

But Bob, it turned out, was not quite so alone:

"Yes, a couple of nights a week I stop at a tavern with Rick and Louis, two guys I work with. We have a couple of beers. Weekends I'll go to a ballgame or watch it on TV with Charlie. He's a fellow I've known since I was at another job."

Linda told me that she never minded Bob's seeing these friends. He never stayed too long, she said, and it helped him to unwind. I asked Linda when she found time to unwind, and she just shrugged her shoulders. This can get out of hand, and husbands do neglect their families in favor of work and their drinking buddies, but the basic drive to have a "third life," a buffer zone between home and work, is a drive that working women cannot afford to deny themselves. Why does Bob have time for a beer after work while Linda is battling to get home on time so his dinner can be hot when he finally rolls in?

I suggested to Linda that she talk to Bob about her having one "late" evening a week when he would agree to be home by a certain hour and to give the kids dinner, even if it meant taking them out for a pizza. I told Linda that a working Mom needs her own time, just as much as a working Dad. I said she should go for a drink with her sister or with someone from her office. It seemed to her like a very strange idea. "I can't do that!" she said. But she really had no good excuse why she should not.

There is a big difference between giving your time freely and having it stolen. When a major women's magazine published a series of time "logs" that they had asked a number of exceptionally successful career women to fill out for a typical working day, it was graphically apparent that most of the women were prisoners of their own schedules, schedules which included an occasional hug with their husband or getting up at 5 A.M. in order to organize their children's clothes for the week.

Because they were asked to state how they felt at each particular juncture, they revealed that the most dominant emotion they experienced was related to a lack of time, the one thing over which they had the most control! So much to do and so little time in which to do it was the recurrent theme. Yet in terms of actual *work* (time spent talking to a client, writing, or treating patients), it amounted to the normal six or seven hours a day. How was the rest of the frantic time spent? Mostly at activities which supported the prestige of the participants, what I call "make-work." These women had little time for their spouses, their children, or even themselves, only time for their ego-as-perceived.

Are you giving your time or having it stolen? Are you in control? For the next month pick a day at random each week, and before you sleep that night record just how you spent the day. Where did the time go? Give yourself fifteen lines on a page and put down what you were doing each hour from 6 A.M. to midnight. Do not analyze the charts until you have completed four of them. Then compare. Does the day that looks the most efficient from a work point of view coincide with the day on which you felt the best? How great is the difference between the most and the least busy day? How can you improve your schedule so as to give *yourself* (not your job, not your family) more time? Where does the biggest chunk of time go on any given day?

Career women are just beginning to learn how to cope with the pressure of work that does not leave your head when you leave the office. We are prone to judge *all* our time on a scale of efficiency. This may be all right for work, where the output can be measured, but how can you measure the efficiency of yourself as a mother, as a wife, as a woman? Highly organized women, driven to perform all the time, are likely to substitute formula care of their homes for real involvement. For instance, the woman who rises at 5 A.M. to sort her children's clothes is convinced that she is spending the time efficiently, performing a vital mothering task, caring for her children. But what do they care about having neat clean clothes in careful piles if they are not going to see their mother until five minutes before bedtime? In her mind she is rationalizing that since she is too busy to be home for dinner four days in a row, she will make it up to the children by assuming a routine service for them.

Perfection can be measured in some jobs in the sense that the results of what you do are available at the end of the day, week, month, or year. When are the results of mothering available? Or of wifing? Or of how you have cared for your own emotional self? Not for a long time.

Be good to yourself and you will be good for your family and good at your job. Even if it never works out exactly even, strive for a tripartite division: one third of your time and energy for your job; one third for your family, and one third (and not just when asleep) for yourself.

Are You a Workaholic?

Do you say, "Thank God it's Monday"?
Are you always aware of the time?
Do you think about your job more than anything else?
Do you feel guilty if you sleep eight hours a night?

If you answered yes to any two of these questions, the chances are you are on your way to becoming a workaholic. This is a condition that is by no means fatal, but it is incompatible with a decent home life unless your husband is a workaholic about housework. Most of the symptoms of workaholism are regarded by society as admirable in a man and despicable in a woman. Workaholics spend as much time as possible on the job and try to relate everything that they have to do to their job. Samantha Richards works for a Black public relations firm in Atlanta and is a self-confessed workaholic:

"My clients run the gamut from clothes manufacturers to fertilizer companies, and I am so hungry for ideas that there is virtually nothing that I do during my waking hours that doesn't have some bearing on my work. If I have to go to the dentist, I consume the magazines and tear out anything that gives me an idea for promoting a client. I can't watch television for more than five minutes without grabbing a notepad, and if my husband takes me out to dinner in a romantic little restaurant, I try to get the owner as a client!"

But despite all the rushing around, the frenetic pace, and the constant drive, the workaholic does not necessarily do a better job than the person who frankly looks forward to quitting time, who hates Monday morning, and who believes there is life after work.

Most compulsive workers are very insecure. They fear social contact outside of the context of what they do because they feel inadequate. They *are* their jobs. They are also likely to be people with relatively short attention spans who switch quickly from one subject to another. They are not able to perform one task for a long period of time but have to create many varied problems in order to be able to have an excuse to be constantly on the go.

At a certain point in one's life, this kind of behavior is appropriate, if not required, if you want to be a success; but if it persists beyond the early stages of a career, it can become pathological, especially if you find yourself nervous when not at work. Often the workaholic works to avoid contact with her family and, ultimately, herself. She is not happy alone and has to justify her existence by constant activity, which she convinces herself is productive and therefore warranted. Workaholism is one way of saying:

"Look at me. I must be alive and well. See what I am doing!"

There is a big difference between the quality of your work and its quantity. In our society it is easy to confuse the two. I know a stockbroker who sets herself a profit goal each day and quits when that has been achieved:

"Depending on the state of the market, I'll say to myself that today I will increase the portfolio by x per cent. Sometimes I reach that by lunchtime; sometimes I am behind when the market closes. But if I achieve it by ten-thirty in the morning, that's when I go to the movies!"

Her opposite number, the workaholic, will be in the office hours before the market opens, will juggle all day buying and selling, and will end up being no more productive than my easygoing friend.

By constantly working, the workaholic is advertising the fact to the world; it is simply a ploy for attention and praise. Many workaholics *know* that the quality of what they do could be better, and the fact that they do not stop is an attempt to compensate. Employers are not fond of compulsive workers because sooner or later something snaps. Workaholics sometimes develop into alcoholics, develop drug-dependency problems or nervous breakdowns.

ALCOHOLISM

This, and drug abuse, are not uncommon among Black women who are striving to become successful. As they are pulled in one direction by their families and another by their jobs, they seek refuge and emotional release. It may also happen that drinking becomes part of the job. As Samantha Richards has written:

"I did not realize how heavily I was drinking until about a year ago, and I never drink at home! It was all on the job— lunch with clients, cocktails with clients, even breakfast meetings, which would be bloody marys. Once I realized that I needed 'eye-openers' four mornings a week, I decided it was time to get help and quit."

How can you tell if you are an alcoholic or a potential heavy drinker? Some doctors feel that there may be genetic predispositions;

children of alcoholics are twice as likely to become one themselves as the children of nondrinkers. If you need a drink to *face* a situation rather than to *relax* after a situation, then you are starting to get your signals twisted.

With a lot of pressure from a job, it is very easy to get into the habit of having a couple or three drinks at lunch to brace yourself for a hard meeting in the afternoon or to have a few swift cocktails to deaden the pain of having completed a particularly grueling day in the office.

Some Black women have told me that they did not realize they had a problem until they found themselves having two or three glasses of wine every night at bedtime, just to help them sleep. All of these apparently harmless nips are dangerous when they add up to a regular habit.

No one ever forces you to have a drink, and once you manage to scrape through a couple of hard afternoon meetings without any help from alcohol, you will be exhausted enough to sleep without any "extra help" either! Never be taken in by other alcoholics who need your company. We are subject to a lot of peer pressure but I defy anyone to tell me that their job depends upon their ability to drink and that if they stopped they would be fired. You should not have to prove you are "one of the boys." No woman has to drink in order to make a good impression. Here are some tips:

1. How many drinks do you have in a week? Count them. Write it down. A lot? More than you thought? When did most of the drinking occur? Why? Always with the same person or group of people? What would happen if you avoided them?

2. Start off by saying that you will drink only every *other* day, and never alone. Stick to business occasions and never drink for private relief.

3. Experiment with tangy, nonalcoholic "cocktails" like grenadine-and-soda or Perrier-and-lime; this may be enough for you to feel part of the crowd.

4. Learn to say no with a standard phrase such as: "It makes me sleepy and I have to work" or "Too many calories; I'm on a diet."

INSOMNIA

We recognize this very quickly in terms of "not being able to get to sleep," but there are other forms of insomnia from which we may suffer that are job-related and less obvious. You may wake intermittently throughout the night—never for very long, but long enough to disturb your rest. You may fall asleep easily but may wake up at 3 or 4 A.M. to ponder the next day's problems. Insomnia can be an insidious barrier to job performance and part of a cycle of depression that includes alcohol and sedatives. Sleeping pills more often than not aggravate insomnia because their effectiveness is short-lived and our bodies build up resistance.

Sleeping aids:

1. Keep to a regular schedule of work, play, and meal times.

2. Exercise lightly in the late afternoon or evening to relax the muscles.

3. No coffee, tea, cola, alcohol, or over-the-counter sleeping pills.

4. Keep your bedroom well ventilated and at between 66 and 68 degrees.

5. Warm milk. It contains L-tryptophan, an amino acid fundamentally related to sleep!

The Single Working Mother

Hundreds of thousands of Black women find themselves in this position: widowed or divorced (or perhaps never married) with small children and the desperate need to work. Is it possible to become a success under those conditions, or merely to survive?

It is possible to become a success as a single working mother, especially if you define your goals in terms of a unity between work and family responsibilities. You are not going to be able to compete in the same types of jobs that can be held by single women with no obligations, by married men, single men, or married women who have husbands that help with child rearing. Marcy Lawson is a young single mother who thinks she has it made:

"My mother takes care of little Pixie all week. I see her on weekends and we have such fun! In my job I often don't get home until nine at night, and there is no way I could look after Pixie. This way I can also date. I mean, I'm only twenty-six!"

Marcy is a corporate sales representative for a high-powered travel agency in Washington, D.C. What she has not reckoned with is that she is a favorite aunt to her daughter Pixie, not a mother. This may be a very convenient arrangement for Marcy at the moment, but when Pixie is old enough to compare her experiences with those of other children —when she goes to school, for instance—Marcy may be in for trouble. No matter how loving Marcy's mother is, she is a grandmother to Pixie, not her real mother. What would happen if Marcy got married and wanted Pixie back, full-time? At that point, if Pixie is old enough to articulate her needs, she may want to stay with the woman she regards as her true parent.

Almost all the professionals I interviewed agree that standard day-care facilities do not provide adequate nurturing. Being in a safe, sanitary room with ten other preschoolers looked after by a responsible adult is the lowest common denominator, no substitute for mothering. By midafternoon most infants are exhibiting strong signs of parent need; they are cranky, whining, and generally distressed. If your child is left in a holding facility all day long during infancy, you may have to be prepared to deal with anything from a withdrawn to a wildly antisocial teenager later on. The fact that your child is cared for does not mean that she or he is *valued*. That sense of self-worth cannot be measured in terms of convenience.

If you are able to leave your job by midafternoon and spend a major portion of the rest of the day with your child, or if your child is cared for in the afternoon hours by a loving relative in a home atmosphere, then you are not depriving the child. Only a few occupations give you this flexibility, mostly ones that have a traditionally female bias, like teaching and nursing. Most jobs in business and industry are determined by the availability of a man, and the average man wants to work from nine until five.

Working at home offers one solution to combining mothering with making money and pursuing a career. In Chapter 8 I described former typist Mary Bryant, who operates a word-processing business out of her own living room. Investigate what you could do in the home. Most free-lance writers I know churn out their articles amidst the confusion of a squabbling family, but the children grow up in a warm atmosphere, even if all they hear from their mother is "Close the door!" and "Turn that television *down!*"

Balance is, of course, the most important concept. If your child's father is available, it might be only your own prejudice that considers him unfit to help out. No matter how your relationship with him terminated, he may be available to do some baby-sitting during the week, not just on the weekend when it suits him. Judge all the possibilities on their merits for the child and for your peace of mind. There is no victory in being a great success at work (where you spend the least amount of time) and a loser in your own home, with children you cannot relate to because they barely know you.

Going Back to Work

Most women have fractured careers. Not all of us have an unbroken series of jobs from college graduation until retirement, as a lot of men do. We get married, have children, work part-time or full-time, and tend toward a less ordered job history. Many of us return to the job market in midlife out of boredom (the children are all in school) or necessity (if these bills are going to get paid, I'll have to get a job). It is not an easy decision to make, and the biggest fear for anyone who has been out of a particular field for five or ten years is that they will return to it as a stranger, with so many new people and systems to get used to.

But remember what I said in Chapter 3 about credits. Your time "at home" may have involved you in pursuits that will allow you to polish your résumé, so do not consider it all as lost time. You are a member of a majority because most women take a break from their jobs to raise children. Employers are used to women re-entering the job market, and even though you may be a bit rusty you are probably considered by an employer to be a better risk than a much younger woman, especially if you have finished having children.

So that everything will not be too strange, learn as much as you can about what might have changed in your job field *before* you start making your application, and this will make you less nervous about stepping out. Julie Wilson left her job as supervisor for a telephone answering service in 1968 and, two children later, returned to the job market in 1979:

> *"My old boss said when I left that the job would always be mine if I wanted it back, but of course they often say that just to make you feel good. When I told my family what I wanted to do, they were very encouraging, but I spent more than a couple of days hovering over the telephone. Finally my husband Harold suggested that I go to another company for an interview, just to give me some confidence. He'd been looking at the ads in the Sunday paper."*

So Julie did a very smart thing. She applied for two jobs, and in the course of one interview she was treated to a fifteen-minute "lecture" about how the business had changed since her day. This was invaluable advice, and when she did call her old boss, she knew that she could still handle the job. Another thing Julie did which was smart was to hold a round-table discussion with her family about going back to work. Even when the bank balance makes this an absolute necessity, you should let everyone express their feelings. Some women keep away from their careers for years under the assumption that their husbands would not want them to work without ever having discussed this as a tangible possibility. A lot of men are changing their views, especially with inflation. Everyone should know just how your new job is going to affect their lives and should change their schedules accordingly, so do not try to minimize the changes that will take place.

A lot of women tell their families that it will not make a big difference and try to keep up with all their former responsibilities at the same time as they handle the new job. If your children are old enough to help out more than they already do, then draw up a schedule and assign duties. You will learn now, if you have not before, just how much of an unpaid servant you have been!

Make the family realize that Mom is not leaving home to have fun, but that by sharing the household chores and freeing you to work, everyone is contributing to the family income.

Once you start working, make your job familiar to your family by telling them all about it. Everyone, your husband included, will experience some separation anxiety with the one person away who for so long has represented "home."

Expect a period of adjustment and some problems. Your children may start to get sick more frequently, may have problems with their schoolwork; these are signals for you to come home. Do not be fooled, but continue to be as solicitous as you can. After a few months you will be able to breathe more easily, once everyone realizes that Mom seems to be a lot more fun than she used to.

If possible, show your children where you work and what you do. Both parents should do this if they can. This way your children can imagine what you are doing throughout the day; you have not simply disappeared, been swallowed up by the job.

If you have been out of touch with the working world, make a special effort to get in touch with other groups of working women, or organizations that can help you re-enter the work place; build up a network and offer a support system. Call old friends, even those you have felt guilty about for years since you went your separate ways. You will be surprised just how easy it is to slip back into old relationships. Someone you know may have gone on to a position important enough to be of substantial help to you. Most of all, realize that what you are doing is not unusual. Thousands of women make the decision every day, and few regret it. Just take the time to handle it properly.

Travel

Traveling for business presents some of the same sorts of problems as deciding to go back to work. Often the family is horrified. The idea that Mom should pack a suitcase and fly to Seattle, Washington, for a conference, seminar, or to meet a client is for some reason a totally different matter than if Dad has to do the same thing. Why? Because the mother is *not supposed to leave.* If you travel a lot, your family gets used to it; but if you only travel once in a while, it means that you have your hands full with two big jobs: organizing your family so it will stay afloat while you are gone and organizing your trip.

Try to give yourself as much time as possible. The day *before* the day before you leave is when you should work out who is going to make dinner, feed the cat, and take Sarah to school. Your husband and children will never remember, so make a graphic list, day by day, and pin it where it will be noticed—on the television, for instance, or on the refrigerator door.

Give each family member, not just your husband, your telephone number. Sit them down and tell them where you will be going (this is how my son learned his geography) and what you will be doing. If your schedule is hectic, only make promises that you can keep—about telephoning at certain times, for instance—and never bribe your children with elaborate gifts. Your family has to understand that this is part of your job, not an adventure or, worst of all, something for which you feel you have to offer compensation.

TRAVEL ARRANGEMENTS

I have an excellent travel agent. Your company may also use a reliable travel agent. Nevertheless, do what I do: *double-check everything personally.* I travel constantly, and I have arrived at airports for nonexistent flights, been met by invisible limousines, and shown into "presidential suites" that were broom closets. Do not be fooled by the airline commercials; a Black woman traveling by herself invites undesirable curiosity and envy that is presented as indifference. If you are clearly traveling on business and are reasonably attractive, be prepared to receive a lot of attention from corpulent white businessmen reeking of liquor, and no attention whatsoever from airline employees, taxi drivers, and hotel bell-captains. I exaggerate, of course, but I warn you that unless you personally call and confirm all your reservations in detail (is there a bathtub or just a shower stall?), you will find yourself thrown into a flap by a stupid mistake that could easily have been avoided.

If you are able to make your own arrangements, this is the way to do it:

1. Travel the night before your meeting if at all possible. Delays in flights will not interfere with business, and you will be rested and fresh for your meetings.

2. Choose a large, well-known hotel situated as close to your place of business as possible.

3. When making your hotel reservation, state the time of your arrival (especially if at night), how you will be paying, the name of your company, and your title.

4. Use credit cards and as little cash as possible. Even when traveling domestically, I take traveler's checks. Make sure of your credit card limit, so that the hotel bill will be covered.

5. When you check in, present the front desk with your business card; this is essential if you expect to be treated according to your position and importance. Single women, Black and white, who check into major hotels during conventions are often thought by hotel employees to be prostitutes.

6. Find out how far you are from your business and check the availability of taxis when you check in. If necessary, order a wake-up call, breakfast, *and* a taxi for the next morning.

7. Carry twenty one-dollar bills for tips to doormen, hotel staff, and skycaps.

8. Confirm all return reservations as soon as you arrive.

9. Carry *all* your important documents and business papers in a briefcase or bag that is with you at all times. If your luggage gets lost, at least you can do your business.

10. Reconfirm all your air and hotel reservations the night before you travel.

DESTINATION

Try to get some tips from someone who has lived or visited the place where you are going. Never rely on tourist information; it has nothing to do with business travel. Black women do not travel alone with confidence because we are vulnerable as women and subject to racism as Blacks. In some areas of the country, it is extremely unusual to see a smartly dressed Black woman carrying a briefcase, so be prepared for verbal comment and rude stares. If you have any relatives or Black friends familiar with your destination, ask them about prevailing racial conditions. Never ask a white person. The answer is *always:*

> *"Oh, no, gracious, there isn't any prejudice in* _____ *anymore!"*

which simply means that no one left *them* waiting half an hour for a table when the restaurant was empty.

If you are on a tight schedule, try to keep your axis close to the hotel; do not go charging off into unexplored territory because you were told by a friend that there "used to be" (ten years ago?) a great little restaurant off Route 23. If you have to rent a car, incidentally, check that *everything* works (lights, windshield wipers, even the horn) before you drive off; and if you have only a vague idea of where you are, ask and ask again. Try to centralize your activities around the hotel; this may sound unadventurous, but it is more practical than spreading yourself around a strange city.

DINING

If you are entertaining a business colleague, male or female, at a place chosen by you *or* the colleague, avoid the embarrassment of fighting over the check by calling ahead and arranging for the bill to come to you or, if the restaurant is at your hotel, have it put on your check. Tip fifteen to twenty per cent of the bill (before tax), depending on whether the service has been good or excellent. If it has been poor, do not tip at all.

FREE TIME

Check in with your office, even if you do not have to, and rest as much as possible. Watch the *local* news on television; this will give you something to discuss with your hosts other than business, and visit any point of interest, a museum or natural wonder, but *save your feet.* I travel with a good book, light easy reading that helps me kill time and requires no great effort. Make as much use of the hotel facilities as you can: massage, sauna, swimming pool, or manicure.

ATTITUDE

This is probably as important as anything else. If you have planned properly, you will have enough time to cope with accidents, so expect them. Delays and nonappearances are bound to occur, so be prepared for some discomfort, but always go to the source of the trouble and find out how long you have to wait or where you are being rerouted, or else be prepared to go to another airline or another hotel. Keep the home number and address of one of your business contacts with you so that you can get help after hours.

While traveling, I keep absolutely to myself, yet I have not been on one flight out of thousands where someone has not tried to strike up a conversation. If, like me, you are not particularly interested in talking to strangers (especially when they are looking at your legs), be very firm and polite:

"I'm sorry; I would rather not talk, thank you."

And keep a magazine or book in your hand all the time you travel; plunge into it. One way of ensuring a large degree of privacy is to travel first class—if your company will pay the freight. Your fellow passengers will be less bothersome, more congenial, and polite. They are also likely to be people you might want to do business with, such as company presidents.

CLOTHES AND LUGGAGE

See Chapter 10.

SUMMARY

At first you may find it exciting to travel on business. After a while, it will become a terrible grind. Despite the millions of air miles I log while traveling, I try to stick to a goal of never being away from home more than one night at a time. I will get up at 3 A.M. and arrive home at 1 A.M. if this means not having to spend the night in a hotel!

Self-Management

Expect the unexpected. The woman who tries to solve all her problems by plotting her course and following a schedule religiously soon finds that life is not her accomplice but a capricious enemy. None of us will enjoy a perfect career or be perfect wives and mothers, still less be able to combine the two ambitions with any balance. To think that this can be done leads to utter frustration; you might as well chase rainbows.

If you are young and single and on the threshold of a career, I urge you to think in terms of "either/or." *Either* you will pursue your career singlemindedly and be prepared to sacrifice motherhood, *or* you must be prepared to have your ship thrown off course by marriage and motherhood. It is foolhardy to imagine that by pursuing your career you will be able to afford to be a wife and mother. The question is: can your children afford, emotionally, to have two parents away from home and at least one of them (you) torn between her midcareer crisis and the demands of managing a home?

There is usually a determined time in a man's career when he either does or does not make the jump onto the fast track. This period of intense activity normally occurs between the ages of twenty-five and thirty-five. The same possibility holds true for you, but those are precisely the years during which you are most likely to be sidelined by the demands of marriage and children. Unless you have a specific technical skill that is always marketable for so many dollars an hour, you are bound to lose ground at the precise time that you could be leaping ahead.

I am not suggesting that you have to choose *between* a career and a family, but just that you ought to know the score; the imperfections of our male-oriented society are such that even as we are welcomed into the job market, it is with the implicit understanding that our biological functions will prevent many of us from fulfilling our career goals. Society expects us to give birth and take care of our children. We can work, yes. We can earn a good living, yes. But can we climb the ladder (it is made from a male blueprint) step by step, merit by merit, promotion by promotion, to the very top? Yes, if we remain single, have very understanding househusbands, or dump our children with strangers a lot of the time; no, if we marry ambitious men and treasure the values of family life.

That may be terribly unfair, but those are still the facts. Black women who have made it to the top in their professions have made tremendous sacrifices. They have avoided marriage, have suffered through multiple divorces, and have had to live very lonely lives. You cannot be all things to all people, and the demands of an important career are enormous. They increase, the closer you get to the top. Remember, you are competing with men who do not have to pick up their children from a relative at five-thirty; you are competing with men who feel a different type of responsibility toward their families; you are competing with men who have housewives! Where is yours?

My favorite comment about this problem was made by a dear friend of mine, a fashion designer lucky enough to have her studio in her large Manhattan apartment overlooking Central Park. Her husband works on Wall Street; she has two very lovely children, and after twenty years of designing she is beginning to establish a name for herself. She works from early in the morning until late at night. Some of her clients are in show business and think nothing of coming for a fitting at 2 A.M. One day she turned to me:

"You know, I'm very happy with what I'm doing, but what I really need is a wife; you know, one of the old-fashioned kind who will wash the dishes and cook and put the kids to bed. There's just no one around here to do that sort of thing!"

I told you to put up a chart in your kitchen, to map out the activities for the week, and organize your time. That is half the story. Besides that, you must also learn to *relax*, to have a diversion that is not part of your work or part of your family. This can be simple, like doing crossword puzzles, or healthy, like playing tennis. Try to vary your life with enough light and shade so that you do not feel you are on a treadmill, chained to your job, chained to your family, chained to your guilt.

The goals that we have at twenty are not the ones we have at thirty, forty, or fifty. Our priorities change as we grow older, wiser, sillier. When you were twenty-five, it was very important that you became a supervisor by the time you were thirty. You did, and you have twice the salary but somehow less money to spend than ever before. What happened? Are you working your way to the top to be able to afford a house in the suburbs that you will never be in long enough to enjoy? Are you working your way to the top because you would go crazy if you lived any other way? That may sound ridiculous, but it is the answer I get the most often when I ask young Black women why they are driving themselves so hard.

We are Black; we are women; we want to excel. *We* know that we can do well; give us half a chance, and we will prove to the world that we can do any job as well or better than anyone else. Those are good reasons. We need to prove to ourselves that we can make it. But be careful. On whose terms do we want to make it? Our own terms! This means being able to educate ourselves and train for the credits we need for the jobs that will bring us enough money to raise our children so they will have pride in themselves and us and being able to be an example to our men in such a way that we *all,* all of us together, establish an order that bears witness to our intelligence, capacity for work, leadership, compassion, and family fortitude.

Managing Money

Here is a modern parable: Hard-working Hannah is determined to stand on her own two feet, and she scrimps and saves from early morning until late at night. She has two jobs. She is a stenographer by day and a manicurist in the evenings. At the end of the week, she has $335, which she spends for junk food, movies, clothes, the rent, and a bus trip to the Adirondacks with her boyfriend.

Lazy Lucy is also determined to stand on her own two feet, but she has only one job: she is a secretary with a company that has a health plan, a Christmas Club, employee insurance, and a pension fund. At the end of the week she has only $175 after deductions (some of which are taxes but others of which accrue to her benefit); and after taking out her rent, $7 a day for food, her carfare, and a $10-a-week clothing allowance, she has $50 which she invests in municipal bonds.

In four years Hannah will be broke and laid off with a day's notice.

In four years Lucy will have seniority at work and $10,000.

It is no big secret, but all successful people know how to do it. You do not have to be rich to do it, but if you do it you will get rich. It is called *managing your money.*

The "numerophobia" (fear of numbers) that a lot of us have is a childhood disease that has serious if not fatal side effects if not cured by the time we are wage earners. One of the last vestiges of misplaced so-called "femininity" is the contempt for numbers that leads some of us to proclaim, even with pride:

"I can't even balance my checkbook!"

There are women who deal with complex financial transactions in their jobs but who still despair when it comes to managing their personal finances. Our social environment and educational system inhibit the training of young women in money matters. This occurs despite the fact that women spend more than men on consumer goods. Black women earn almost as much per capita as Black men, but the majority of us manage our finances quite poorly. None of us kid ourselves that we are uninterested in what money can buy, but many of us know nothing about the basic elements of money management.

Example: The economy is structured to favor those who are able to take advantage of legal loopholes in the tax laws, and you do not have to be a millionaire to understand how this can benefit *you*. It is not a simple equation: work hard and earn more money. The value of what you earn can be greatly increased or decreased by how you manage it—that is, by how you spend it and how you save it.

Consider this: In order to equal the *value* of a 1960 annual income of $10,000, a woman today has to earn at least $26,000! Also, money problems account for the greatest source of stress in individuals and are the prime cause of most marital conflict. Most Black women have to work. Even families based on the archaic husband-works/wife-stays-at-home system are now finding that inflation is forcing the former housewife out into the job market. One income is not enough to keep most families in food and clothing.

The woman who keeps working after marriage or who returns to work during marriage and fails to safeguard her income is in for a rude shock if the marriage ends, as almost half of marriages do. If she has pooled her income into a joint account and has used only her married name, she may find herself, after fifteen years of hard work, a nonperson as far as credit records and bank relationships are concerned. If she has allowed her husband to make the major decisions about how their joint incomes were handled, she will also find herself woefully ignorant of rudimentary procedures in finance and unable to distinguish between the relative merits of the options before her.

The younger you are, the more likely your marriage will be affected by financial problems. In most of the cases I examined, I found young Black couples operating in a completely haphazard financial manner. In some instances the husband "gave" part of his income to his wife for her to manage day-to-day expenses, but retained sole authority over major decisions like buying a home. In other cases, the husband and wife deposited their incomes in a joint account, and both ran up bills without consulting each other. Rarely did I find instances of both the husband and wife jointly sharing the responsibility for managing the family's income. Usually the husband did this job and not impressively. Many Black women, though we crave the things that money can buy, are apt to avoid detailed discussions of money itself.

We live in the grip of a society that exercises growing control over our lives. This is done in two principal ways: legal and economic. Legally we are free to live where we want, marry whom we want, work at whatever job we want, and worship in any way we choose. But in fact, we are shackled by economic reality to a continual chain of dilemmas which for many young couples culminates in having to choose between owning their own home *or* having children—such is the absurdity of our economic plight. What many of us forget when we decide to make the sacrifices necessary for having and educating children is that when both parents are working, some of the pleasures that are normally considered to be luxuries, such as eating out or a weekend at the shore, are necessities if the marriage itself is to survive.

If you lack control over your financial life, you will become the unwitting victim of the economy. I reiterate: Success has as much to do with how well you manage your money as with how much money you earn! Women are just as greedy as men. We want our savings to triple overnight. Some of us like to gamble, in different ways. Do we always know the odds? Why is it that the people most likely to get swindled by phony investment schemes are those who can least afford the loss: single women on fixed incomes or living off their savings? Why do we persist in remaining ignorant about the difference between mutual funds and municipal bonds? Why do we let our hard-earned income wither away, simply because we let ourselves be baffled by simple arithmetic? The crux of this problem is not arithmetic, but common sense and a little study.

Even the most down-to-earth of my acquaintances admits that she was so thrilled to get her bank charge card (in other words, to be accepted) that she never figured out what that small piece of plastic would cost her annually. Money that you break your back to earn is tossed away with a signature. Readily available credit encourages us to mortgage our future income; we go into debt on an unprecedented scale and end up working to pay usurious *interest* rates.

Ten years ago a Black couple with a joint income of $30,000 could look forward to raising their children in comfort in a pleasant environment with parks and good schools. Now that is barely enough to enable them to move out of the old neighborhood.

Whether you are single or married, it is of cardinal importance that you control your income and learn to take advantage of the principles that will one day produce a nest-egg. You do not have to have a large income; there is no bottom limit for exercising these principles, even if you feel that your meager salary is spent long before you receive it. There is a way to reverse the decline.

NET WORTH

This is where we start. You may be surprised at just how much you are worth; most people define themselves only in terms of their debts. Your net worth is the difference between what you *own* (your assets) and what you *owe* (your liabilities). On one sheet of paper list your assets on the left, your liabilities on the right. Mark down dollar amounts for the following:

Assets

1. Amount of cash in bank accounts.
2. Market value of any securities that you hold, such as stocks, bonds, or Treasury bills.
3. Value of your home, if you own it. Do not guess; get an appraisal from a real estate firm.
4. The amount of money that is owed *to* you.
5. The value of your personal belongings, as appraised by a professional. These may include furniture, art, antiques, and jewelry.
6. Cash value of your life insurance policies.
7. Value of the vehicles you own, as per a dealer's blue book: cars, bikes, boats.

Liabilities

What do you *owe?*

1. Taxes
2. Mortgages
3. Personal debts
4. Installment loans
5. Insurance policy loans
6. Department store and credit card debts
7. Pledges to charity

Subtract the sum of your liabilities from the sum of your assets, and you have your net worth. Not so bad, is it? The point of determining this is twofold. First of all it inspires financial confidence, and secondly it can pinpoint the weak spots in your financial planning— where is the emphasis in your liabilities, and how can it be reduced?

INCOME

Your next job is to calculate your income. It may not be what it appears from your paycheck. You are not concerned merely with the amount you get paid but with its profitability. In other words, once you have subtracted your job-related expenses, what do you have left? I asked a friend of mine to do this, and she was amazed at how much her job was costing her!

Moira Bird works as an assistant buyer in the sportswear division of a major department store in Detroit. Her salary is $350 a week and her take-home pay is $285, or $14,820 annually.

Moira Bird's Job-Related Expenses

Baby-sitting

Moira pays a neighbor $1 an hour to look after her
three-year-old daughter. $1,920

Transportation

This *should* cost only $2.50 a day, but Moira admits that she
takes a taxi about twice a week.   960

Lunch

At $5 a day Moira is underestimating, since she told me she
sometimes diets but at least once a week goes to a "nice" restaurant
with colleagues.   1,200

Clothes and Cosmetics

Moira's appearance is important for her job, and even though she
gets a discount where she works, she calculates that she spends
$200 a month on these items.   2,400

                                                        TOTAL $6,480

In fact, almost *half* of Moira's salary is spent *on her job* or *because of her job,* which means that her *profit* per year is only $8,340. Of course you can argue that she would still have to eat lunch and buy clothes if she was not working, but my assessment is accurate to within twenty per cent. Making these kinds of calculations can be a chilling experience. One executive I spoke to told me in confidence that it was actually *costing* her money to work, even though her salary was in excess of $40,000! She arrived at this conclusion by subtracting her job-related expenses (like Moira's, these came to slightly more than half her income) *and* the additional tax "bite" that she and her husband endured because her income put them into a higher tax bracket. The difference amounted to $5,000 *less* than if only her husband worked!

Now that you know your net worth and your real income, you can start getting control of your financial life.

PLANNING

Take a good hard look at your situation and decide on the most important goal in your life right now. What will it cost? This might be to own your own home, get a bigger apartment, have a baby, buy a car, be financially independent from your husband (whether or not your marriage is shaky), or perhaps you want to save enough money to go back to college. Make your list and calculate the cost to the nearest penny. Most of us know how much a new car will cost, but a baby? From birth to age five, it is a lot of money. Most of us know how much the house we want costs, but only the "sticker price"; considering rising fuel costs, mortgage rates, and inflation, what will it cost to run over twenty years? Now is the time to get used to using a calculator; if you can work one of those, forget about arithmetic!

When you have your goals in order, compare what you need with what you have. By subtracting your living expenses *and* work-related expenses from your actual income, you will arrive at a figure that represents your potential *savings* or discretionary income.

If you find that you are operating at a loss (going deeper into debt every month), then you have to decide where to apply the brakes. Where are the flaws in your plan? Are you spending too much on your job? At your job? Medical bills? Are you spending more for consumer goods than you can afford? Is your gasoline costing as much as the groceries? Can you plug those leaks yourself or do you need help?

In most municipalities there are professional, nonprofit debt-counseling services. Beware of those which are simply loan companies advertising debt consolidation. Before you *increase* your burden, speak to a professional like an accountant, a lawyer, or a bank officer. If you have your own checking account (and you should), you rate the advice of a bank officer. Some of the smartest advice I have received has been from my local bank manager, who was able to take a wide overview of my situation. Do not go for advice to people who have something to sell (such as investment counselors). Wait until you can afford their product.

Eighty-five per cent of us are going to be on our own for a significant portion of our lives. This means that we are or will be solely responsible for our financial lives, not "looked after" by a parent or spouse. I believe we should *always* look after ourselves, but it is a sobering fact that once we leave our parents' home there will be years before and after marriage when we have to stand alone financially.

Whether this means having to earn our living or manage our savings, we are all going to be in that position, and we must begin to pay our own bills *now*. This is why a personal checking account is a must.

Example: Denise Adams (not her real name) married George West. Denise finished college six months after their wedding and took a job as a market research analyst. Her salary of $325 a week was slightly more than George earned as a postal worker. They lived in Connecticut, not one of the eight states (Arizona, California, Colorado, Idaho, Louisiana, Nevada, Texas, and Washington) that have community-property laws. Denise and George had a joint checking account and a joint savings account, both in the names of Mr. George West and Mrs. Denise West. In the course of ten years they bought a two-bedroom house and a small car as well as a reasonable amount of furniture, all of it on credit. Denise actually did most of the bill paying and kept track of the charge accounts. She was conscientious, and they enjoyed a good credit standing. Then their marriage broke up. George and Denise thought they were being very mature when they simply sold the house, the furniture, and the car, and divided the proceeds. They had no children, and Denise did not want alimony.

So here is Denise Adams, age thirty-two. For ten years she has been earning a decent salary, and she has financed the purchase of a home and a car. She has several thousand dollars and is anxious to buy a small condominium and a Toyota. But she cannot get credit! Why? Denise *Adams* has never had a bank account. Denise *Adams* has never bought a house or a car. Denise *Adams* never borrowed or paid back one penny in her life. Financially, Denise *Adams* has no credit history at all and Denise *West* no longer exists.

Denise can argue that she *was* Denise West, but both the IRS and most credit organizations are very reactionary in their evaluation of the relative contributions made by a husband and a wife. Even though the law forbids discrimination and Denise can argue that for ten years she has been a financial entity, she is automatically regarded as a bad risk because the *men* who run things *assume* that the wife's participation in a joint account and in family affairs is *marginal*. No matter how significant her actual cash contribution to the family income was, it is treated as "extra," and all the major, creditworthy purchases, loans, and debts are deemed to have been undertaken by her husband!

In order to prevent this from happening to you, the least you can do is to insist that any joint accounts include your full name (Denise Adams West), and the best you can do is to have your *own* checking account so that you can establish an unbroken credit record and a personal relationship with the bank. Your own checking account should be in your unmarried name.

Once you have a checking account and are debt-free, consider the best way to finance your goals. Most methods will require a combination of cash and credit. If you do not have the credit, the next section of this chapter will tell you how to get it, and if you do not have the cash, you will have to be patient and save. But remember, savings accounts are among the least profitable methods of earning interest on the money you save. With a twelve per cent annual rate of inflation and savings accounts paying about 5½ per cent, you are losing money every day! Start thinking in terms of a modest investment program, but first accumulate enough in your savings account to cover three months of living expenses. Most financial experts consider this both prudent and *sufficient*. More money than that in a savings account is wasted; it is eroding, not growing. In the event that you lose your job or have an emergency expense, you need enough in your savings account to carry you through without having to interrupt an investment program at what might not be an advantageous time.

ESTABLISHING CREDIT

The Equal Credit Opportunity Act gives equal recognition to the wife's role in all joint credit accounts, whether or not she pays the bills. This means that your name, as well as your husband's, will be forwarded to the appropriate credit bureaus and the consequences of such an account will be applied to your name as well as his. Thus you will have a credit history. If you are recently divorced, for instance, or simply want to start the wise action of creating your own financial identity, you can go to the bank or store where you and your husband have had a charge account and ask for the name of the credit bureau they use. In the Yellow Pages, under "Credit Reporting Agencies," you will find the bureau listed, and for about five dollars you can obtain a copy of your file. If you have been denied credit on the basis of a report from a particular bureau, they are obliged to furnish you with a free copy of all the information they have.

You can only establish good credit by borrowing money. If you never go into debt, you reduce your chances of ever being able to borrow. I suggest that you start to build your credibility in three stages:

The Local Account

This is usually the easiest kind of credit to obtain, with a local merchant. Apply for credit at a nearby department store or specialty shop. You may have to try a few, but do it one at a time. Do not be discouraged if you are turned down, but *write* and request the reason. The creditor must respond within thirty days with a specific statement such as "income too low" or "not at present job long enough." Apply for a low credit limit, two or three hundred dollars at the most. To keep on the rails, ask for a "flexible" or "convenience" account, the type that has to be paid in full within thirty days. This will help you to stop charging beyond your means. After six months apply for a "revolving charge account," which means that if you want you can exercise the option to pay only a fraction of the bill every month, but bear in mind that the remainder is subject to a finance charge that can be the equivalent of a very high interest rate, sometimes as much as *twenty per cent a year*. This means that if you buy an item for $500 and elect to pay for it at the rate of $50 a month for ten months, the finance charges will increase the cost by almost $100! Also, if you default, you will be subject to additional charges, resulting in an even higher rate of interest.

The Bank Card

Programs like MasterCard and Visa are now administered by local banks, but because they can be used nationwide and overseas, the requirements are stiffer than for local charge accounts. If you have a credit history with a local store, a checking account, and an income of at least $7,200, you *should* be eligible for a bank credit card, but you may have to "shop around" for one. Be prepared to take your checking account to the bank that gives you the card. Interest rates on unpaid balances are very high, so you should pay close attention to your monthly statements, analyze them, check the purchases against your own records, and always be aware of what the "borrowed" portion is costing per month in charges. Changes in the banking laws can alter the bank-card financing system, and you may find yourself liable for additional charges; the card itself may cost you twenty dollars or more per year.

The Installment Loan

Your credit is based on two factors: ability and willingness. It is one thing to be *able* to pay back a loan, but if unexpected expenses occur, how *willing* are you to give that loan the attention it deserves? If you want to paint a perfect credit picture for yourself, accumulate $1,500 in your savings account, for the purchase of a household appliance, a home improvement, or a vacation. Then go to your bank and apply for an installment loan for the same amount, to be repaid over a year. Use the loan to pay for your items and use your savings to pay back the loan. Do this for six months; then repay the outstanding balance before it is due. This will cost you a small amount (the difference between the interest your $1,500 earns in savings and the interest charged by the bank for the six-month loan), but it will be worth it to improve your credit history.

CREDIT PROBLEMS

There are over 200 nonprofit credit counseling services around the country. These will assist you to get credit and will tell you what information is legally required by a creditor. For instance, a creditor is prohibited from asking about childbearing or child-rearing plans. These services can also give you specific advice about how to get out of credit difficulties.

Most people have trouble with credit at some point in their lives. Creditors expect this, and if they denied credit to everyone who has ever fallen behind on payments, they would have no customers left! The important thing is to be willing to respond promptly to warning notices. Silence is equated with an unwillingness to pay, whereas your attention to the problem is always in your favor, even if it means sitting down with the creditor and working out a new payment schedule. For the creditor, even if you owe $1,000, $20 a week is better than nothing, so long as you are keeping in touch. If you are being hounded by a particular creditor who is threatening legal action, it pays to know your rights; talk to a lawyer so that you know just how far the creditor can go to collect.

INVESTING

At this point you should have a firm grasp of the following:

a) Your fixed monthly expenses, including the cost of credit.

b) Your net worth.

c) Your actual income.

and you should have at least three months of *a* in savings. You should also have adequate retirement benefits. If you are self-employed, talk to your bank officer about setting up an I.R.A. (Individual Retirement Account) or a Keogh Plan account. You can save a substantial amount every year *tax-free* if you do not use the money until you retire. You should also make a will. This is often overlooked by women who imagine that the law will automatically provide that their assets go to their husband or closest family member. This is not so, and tax considerations could cause your beneficiaries endless trouble unless you make legal provisions. Do it.

Now you have a few hundred dollars to start investing, and you will be able to add to that from time to time. What are your options?

Savings Bonds

Like life insurance and annuities, these are not the best investments during periods of inflation because, like anything that promises a fixed-dollar return, you will have to equal the inflation rate in interest just to stop losing money! Savings bonds return about seven per cent interest, so if you invest $1,000, you will have about $1,700 in ten years, but it may have less than a quarter of the *purchasing power* of your original investment. Savings bond salesmen paint a very rosy picture of your ability to retire in twenty-five years with $50,000, but by then that might just about pay for two months' groceries!

Bank Certificates and
Money-Market Mutual Funds

A *certificate of deposit* ties up your money for a limited period of time (usually six months), with an interest rate pegged at the Treasury-bill rate on the day you buy your "CD." Usually the minimum amount is $10,000, but some banks and savings-and-loan institutions also offer a thirty-month plan for amounts lower than the minimum. The rate may vary considerably but these so-called "small-saver" certificates were recently returning more than ten per cent annually.

A money-market mutual fund is geared to savers in contrast with a straight mutual fund, which is for investors. In the money market, certain high-return securities are accessible only to those who can afford very large investments. Large corporations, banks, and the federal government borrow money for investments from time to time and pay a lot for the privilege. With a minimum deposit of $1,000, you can buy into the money-market mutual fund, which means that your money will be pooled with that of hundreds of others like you and administered by a sophisticated investment fund manager *as if* it were one enormous investment from one source. Money-market funds are *not insured* (bank CD's are), but they are extremely reliable, and you can usually deposit and withdraw whenever you want. The money-market mutual fund return is higher than the CD return.

Stocks

A. Mutual Funds

Unless you have quite a few thousand dollars that you are willing to lose, then the safest stock investment to make is in a mutual fund. Like money-market mutual funds, these consist of the pooled resources of a number of small investors. These are used by professionals who buy and sell the stocks and bonds that are traded on a number of different exchanges every day. The object is to make the mutual fund grow at the fastest possible rate. Mutual funds can be bought through a stockbroker, who will take a commission of about 8¾ per cent, or directly from the fund itself without a commission. If you want a proven strategy for long-term investment that does not require you to know *anything* about specific stock performance, here it is:

Buy mutual funds in a recession and hang onto them for two or three years, until the market recovers (and stocks become more expensive). Then take your money out of mutual funds and put it into high-interest long-term bank certificates or money-market funds. Ignore the stock market completely until there is another recession; then buy into mutual funds again. Only do this if you have extra money; do not use funds that you need for buying a home or for school expenses. It should be disposable income.

B. Common Stocks

If you have $2,000 or more and are determined to take a fling on the market, then purchase common stock. Common stocks are the basic unit of investment, what most mutual funds and money-market mutual funds invest in, shares in any one of the thousands of companies that are owned publicly. You are probably aware of "giants" such as IBM, Xerox, and General Motors, but there are entities "going public" every day that represent an opportunity for you to invest in everything from a chain of department stores to a bubble-gum factory. A common stock entitles you to a piece of the ownership of a corporation. You are buying into the future earnings of the company, and for your investment you may receive a regular dividend as well as a rise in the value of your shares. Most stocks sell at "ten-times" earnings, which means that a company reporting annual earnings of $2 a share will sell each stock for $20.

Unless you are willing to become very knowledgeable about the stock market, read annual reports, and keep your eye on the Dow-Jones Index, you should consider the services of a financial planning company. This will cost about $1,000 a year, but your planner will not take a commission on your transactions. Buying and selling common stock is no occupation for the amateur. Always seek professional advice.

C. Corporate Bonds

Similar to common stocks, these are debt securities issued by corporations in $1,000 denominations. The bond is guaranteed to pay a stated rate of interest until the principal is paid, on the date at which the bond is said to "mature." Your risk is that the company can go bankrupt. The greater the risk, the higher the yield of the bond.

TAX SHELTERS

These are not just for the very rich. Instead of buying corporate bonds (the income from them is taxable), you can buy *municipal bonds*. These are issued to raise money for a variety of local needs, and the income is *not* taxable. Obviously, the higher your tax bracket, the bigger the saving. In addition to municipal bonds, there are areas of investment that are encouraged by congressionally designed tax incentives. These are high-risk areas such as oil and gas exploration, equipment leasing, and housing. The purpose of investing in these areas is to shelter your ordinary income during your peak earning years and at the same time to acquire tangible assets.

Some areas are considered to be "safer" than others, including cattle feeding and equipment leasing. If you are in the fifty per cent tax bracket and you invest $10,000 in an oil-drilling program, you could save about $4,500 over the first two years of your investment, thus reducing your actual investment cost to $5,500 although the *value* remains at $10,000. If your drilling program produces a dry well, you may have to "write off" your investment (at further tax advantages); if the well comes in, you may receive income from your investment for many years, and that income could be from twenty to fifty per cent tax-free because of the oil-depletion allowance.

No tax shelter is foolproof, and if you are contemplating one, you have to be prepared to risk your investment. No matter how attractive such a scheme sounds, talk it over with your bank officer, accountant, or lawyer before participating.

Trust Funds

These can be considered forms of tax shelters because they allow you to put money away now for the future benefit of your children and to avoid having to pay taxes on that particular portion of your income. But because there are administrative expenses involved, the amount of money you are prepared to put into a trust fund should be in the five figures at least in order to be practical. Trust funds are usually administered by lawyers, and lawyers are well paid.

Summary

I cannot overemphasize the importance of controlling your own financial life. It never seems to be that necessary when one is young; the money comes in (not enough) and flows out (too much), and we never find the time to sit down and say to ourselves:

"All right, I know what my career goal is, and if I am dedicated, I will achieve the job I want, but how am I going to handle the income? Will it be enough for the life style I imagine I can afford? Am I doing anything reckless now which could ruin my future credit? I must decide to talk to my fiancé about how we will manage our incomes once we are married!"

This may seem like a crass and premeditated thing to do, to talk about money with your boyfriend, right? But if you avoid this and trust to luck, you will find that after a couple of years of marriage, there is little that you two talk about *except* money.

The All-Round Black Woman

In the following and final chapter, I concentrate on our appearance, the icing on the cake. This is to induce the final notes of confidence as you present yourself to the world, able, ready, and willing to control your destiny and make your mark. We have come a long way since we formulated the Five-Key Plan for success, and we have found that every individual woman must decide for herself exactly what kind of success she wants and, most importantly, must learn to balance all the spinning plates.

There is no point in being a one-dimensional person, even if it seems that one particular dimension outweighs all the others. Nothing lasts forever, and your five, ten, or fifteen years at the peak of your career will be for nought if you mismanage your income or ignore your emotional needs. The great art is in being able to concentrate on the present, with the future always in mind. Imagine that your life has an alarm clock which rings every five years and that every five years you remember to ask yourself:

> *What would happen if I lost my job?*
> *What would happen if I lost my husband?*
> *Am I aiming for the same goal as five years ago?*
> *How fast am I going?*
> *Am I in charge of my life?*

If you cannot answer any of these questions satisfactorily, and especially if the answer to the last one is *no,* then go back to Chapter 1 and reorganize! We are, thank God, not machines. We cannot simply program ourselves at the age of twenty-five and end up, two or three decades later, with our illusions intact. We must be prepared for serious setbacks, and we must be able to alter our plans when circumstances quite beyond our control interfere with our lives: sickness, war, recession, or divorce. We cannot anticipate everything that will happen, but our plans have to be sufficiently flexible so that there is always a strong part of our life able to sustain us when we are undergoing a rough time.

Some of us will find that the advantages of moving into meaningful careers are offset by job-related stress, loneliness, and the problems of integrating our job with our private life, marriage, and raising children. We are all in this together, and we must be prepared and unafraid to seek help when it is needed. It may take a professional to help you sort out the tangles, and I urge all Black women who suffer from fatigue, anxiety, and depression to face the fact that there are many forms of therapy available and that in this day and age we need all the help we can get.

Although very few advertise the fact, I come across many very high-powered businessmen who have received professional counseling at some point in their lives. We have to do the same, when it is needed. Let it out; do not keep it in!

You are an exceptionally brave woman, a pioneer, a *new* Black woman. You have to withstand the combined forces that do not want you to succeed: enemies within our society and enemies from without.

This country provides us with tangible benefits, laws, and programs of which we must take full advantage if we are to succeed and emerge, in the twenty-first century, as leaders in every sector of human endeavor. If we are to create a legacy of which our daughters and sons can be justifiably proud, we have to take care of the *whole* Black woman!

🌴🌴🌴🌴🌴

10

Looks Aren't Everything— But They Count

"The way you put yourself together indicates how you feel about yourself. We as Black women have to get beyond the 'mind set' that we need to look different every day—every time we enter a room, we do NOT need a new outfit."

Susan Taylor, Editor in Chief, Essence

Your appearance should always be of secondary importance in any serious endeavor. With the exception of a very small number of occupations that stress beauty (such as acting and modeling), there are no venues that can be conquered on the strength of the way you look. Unhappily, the converse is not true.

If your appearance is unsuited to the predetermined image of your would-be employer, then it may cost you the job. As Black women we have extremely high visibility, and everything about us is scrutinized, especially if we work in a predominantly white organization. In other words, we are not going to get hired because of our looks alone, but we may get *not* hired because of them! What can we do about this?

Everything! Just as you can control your career, your marriage, and your financial affairs, you can just as easily control the way you look and make it work for your success, not against it. First, get rid of the notion that there is any particular way you *must* look. There is no surefire appearance "mold" into which you can squeeze in order to emerge as the perfect-looking bank employee, research assistant, or marketing analyst. I cannot simply say, put on a green midlength gabardine skirt and a V-neck purple sweater and the world will be your oyster! We all wish it were that simple, but like everything else it takes care and planning.

In previous books I have discussed appearance in great detail, from head to toe; but I have always insisted, as I shall to my dying day, that no one, but no one, can look truly terrific by attention to makeup, hair, and clothes alone. To me these are important details that enhance the basic image. The basic image can only be constructed according to one overriding principle:

Good Health

For me there is no dividing line between health and beauty. Quite regardless of your physical characteristics, a woman who keeps herself in peak condition is more beautiful, more attractive, and much more likely to succeed, even if she has indifferent features, than an ostensibly pretty woman who does not take care of herself.

If you plan to be successful, then you have made up your mind to work hard. If you expect to work hard, you must keep yourself fit. Mind and body engage in a constant dialogue about keeping fit. No matter what you think about the demands of your job, they are physical and mental. A job can be physically exhausting even if it does not demand vigorous behavior, just as a routine service job may not appear to be mentally taxing but can lead to a great deal of mental fatigue. The *first step* is to recognize the demands of your job.

Do you:

1. Remain in the same position for a long time?
2. Perform the same task over and over again?
3. Alternate bouts of strenuous activity with periods of stillness?
4. Drive or ride more than twenty minutes to and from work?
5. Have to "psych" yourself up for important meetings?

If the answer is *yes* to any of these questions, then you will probably also answer *yes* to one or more of these.

Do you:

1. Wake up tired after a long night's sleep?
2. Notice that your weight fluctuates over short periods of time?
3. Experience muscle spasms or muscle aches?
4. Have irregular periods?
5. Have difficulty relaxing unless you are distracted?
6. Become easily irritated?

These are all common symptoms of work itself, not necessarily of overwork. They can be produced by just an average amount of normal labor if that labor is not integrated into your whole being and especially if it is internalized and does not provide any physical outlet in the form of self-expression or physical exercise.

I walk as much as I can. I try to give myself time to walk to and from important meetings. While I am walking, the left side of my brain, which is normally run ragged from calculating and criticizing, has to concentrate on the repetitive function of what I am doing. Thus occupied, it shuts down and relaxes its analytical functions, takes a well-earned rest. Meanwhile, the right side of my brain is given full rein, and that is my creative, intuitive faculty. I see things differently, get imaginative ideas, solve problems that have been stumping me, and generally shift my priorities so that instead of arriving at the meeting tight as a drum, I am ready and willing to entertain new ideas, and I am also in a better position to present my ideas.

As a mechanism, the human body is capable of a variety of efficient tasks, from reproduction to the work that puts a person on the moon. The motivation for these tasks is provided by the brain, but the fuel for all of them enters through the mouth. Unless we monitor what we eat, we cannot function at the top register of our capacities. I know that there are plenty of women and men who boast that they have terrible eating habits and have never been sick, but every human body has a different metabolism, a different threshold for pain, a different "ideal" weight. Unless you care about what you eat, you will *one day* be sick, will *one day* lose or gain weight dramatically, and will *one day* find your ability to function impaired.

The fifty-one-year-old woman who is a senior vice president, who suddenly finds herself acutely disoriented and is forced to take a sudden vacation, may in no way relate this to the fact that she diets one week and gorges the next. Her doctor may tell her that her problems are being caused by menopause, and for the next ten years she may experience one form of discomfort or another, unaware that steady exercise and a reasonable diet could stabilize her whole metabolism and let her complete her crowning years at work with great vigor and energy.

Why gamble with the odds against you? There is much you can do to improve your chances for success, to ensure that you will have the energy, drive, and endurance to survive when the heat is on. Between sessions of very hard work, you must be able to relax properly and avoid stress. If you do this, you can be confident that the physical personality that you present when you walk into a room is one of *vitality!*

It is a great mistake to compare ourselves to men and to conclude that since they can be successful and still be sloppy, overweight, and unattractive, the same goes for us. I know women who are so adamant that they should only be judged on merit that they waste no time at all on extraneous superficialities.

Frankly I abhor men who move as if they hate their bodies, who take no pride in their appearance and want everyone to know it! As Black women, we have to realize that between a total *lack* of regard for our appearance and an overweening concern for *nothing but* our appearance, there lies a wide world of difference that provides us with an incentive to strive for a look which is appropriate to our jobs, which acts as an inspiration to ourselves, and which creates a positive feeling in others. A total disregard for one's appearance is just as distracting and likely to mitigate against our chances for success as an overemphasis on the latest in fashion and wild makeup.

The answer is not some kind of uniformity, as suggested in recent years by a number of fashion writers struggling to answer the question of "what should today's career woman wear?"

First of all, there is no look which would succeed in all jobs in all parts of the country. With all due respect, what might be considered flashy for a stenographer in Idabel, Oklahoma, could be ostentatiously dowdy in New York City.

Before the clothes comes the body. As a career woman you must achieve and maintain an optimum *weight;* this means a permanent diet geared to the demands of your work and your home. This means eating meals that are nutritious, balanced, and *regular.*

DIET

In order to maintain a weight of between 110 and 140 pounds, your caloric intake should not exceed 2,500 calories per day. Unless you are exceptionally short and small-boned or tall with a large frame, your weight should not be less than 100 pounds nor more than 150. If you need to gain or lose weight, there are specific guides in my first book: *All About Health and Beauty for the Black Woman.* I am not going to repeat them here, but will simply give you tips about *weight maintenance,* especially if your job demands infusions of energy throughout the day.

I prefer only one full meal, dinner. I avoid business lunches as much as possible because I like to associate good food with pleasure, not work. Consequently I have a "pick-me-up," energy-crammed breakfast and a very light lunch.

Here is an excellent breakfast for the working woman which comes from the constantly on-the-go television journalist Janet Langhart. Living in Boston and working in New York, she needs plenty of energy, sometimes arising as early as 5 A.M., to conduct an important interview:

"I don't like to cook, but I do need the nutrients. A typical breakfast for me is a high-energy blender drink consisting of orange juice, one egg, wheat germ, and honey."

When I asked Janet how she managed to keep going on days which were so impossible that she had no chance to stop for anything like a normal meal, I found out that she did much the same thing as I do: she keeps an assortment of nuts and dried fruits in her handbag, excellent pickups.

If you must have a "proper" breakfast, keep it light: one boiled egg and a couple of slices of toast. If your winters are bitter, add hot cereal.

My all-time favorite lunch is an egg salad sandwich on whole wheat bread and a glass of milk. This is just enough to satisfy my hunger, but it does not give me the sluggish feeling I get from a hamburger. When I have to eat out at lunchtime, I order a filet of sole almondine and a fresh green vegetable like broccoli or spinach, no appetizer or dessert. My limit is one glass of white wine, which I rarely finish.

I find that being a tiny bit hungry throughout the day acts as an incentive, and I work well in order to "reward" myself with a relaxed family dinner. If I have a large breakfast or a heavy lunch, I find myself slowing down in midmorning or midafternoon and longingly eyeing the office couch.

Here are a few ideas for lunch on the job that you can take to work or get from your local delicatessen:

1. Three slices of plain roast beef
   Green salad
   Apple or orange
   Milk or juice

2. Swiss cheese and ham on *thin* rye bread
   Cole slaw
   One peach
   Apple juice

3. Cottage cheese with saltines
   One banana
   One cup of buttermilk

Number three is a great antistress lunch because it contains a lot of calcium, which nutritionists now say can help women in high-pressure jobs.

Do not keep candy in your desk; if you need to allay your nervousness, chew sugarless gum. It is not always easy to avoid simply going along with what everyone else does at work, especially if you are new on the job and anxious to fit in. For instance, five visits a week to the local fast-food emporium will not only pile on the pounds but will not provide you with the energy and nutrients you need. Steer clear of those places or take a sandwich in your purse, and if you have to go with the crowd, just have tea or a soda.

Office work breeds coffee addicts, and your tolerance may be much higher than mine since I have to admit that even half a cup adds to the pressures of my day. Whatever your limit is, stick to it. If you find that your intermittent treks to the coffee machine are a useful way of pacing your working day or that coffee is served at meetings all day long, take half a cup or learn to say "no, thank you." If your office has the facilities, lay in your own store of fruit juice or relaxing teas.

What nutrition you do not get during the day, you should make every effort to make up for with your evening meal. The problem with many two-career families is that at the end of the day neither spouse feels like cooking, and it is often the strong will of the children that dictates the path of least resistance—to the local pizza parlor or Chinese restaurant. This is not only expensive more than once a week, but it is not at all nutritious. Your evening meal should include meat or fish and two vegetables, at least one of which is leafy and green.

In order to create a constant in your home life, make it a rule (not the exception) to gather at a specific time and make everyone pitch in and help with the preparation, service, and cleanup. This is a good mutual occupation for the family on a daily basis before everyone flies off in different directions for the evening.

Most people think of "dieting" as a weight-loss function. Being aware of your diet is more than that; it is a way to give your body the best fuel it needs to enable you to do your job most effectively and to look your very best.

EXERCISE

A great deal of emphasis is put on exercise as part of a weight-loss program, but it is relatively inefficient in that capacity, whereas the right amount of the proper kind of exercise is the best way to integrate your mental well-being with your physical abilities and to greatly expand your capabilities in both areas. The kind of lives most of us lead put the cardiovascular system into overdrive, and as Black women we are particularly prone to heart problems, stress, and hypertension. So these words can save your life!

Your feeling of fatigue and lassitude at the end of the day is not a simple matter of your body's having been overworked. A normal work-day, even an exceptionally hectic one, does not utilize half of the body's capacity for physical effort. Your fatigue comes from a combination of muscle tension and mental stress; you are like an overwound clock that stops ticking because all the cogs are jammed. What you need is not so much rest as *release*. You still have a great deal of stored, unused energy, but unless you unlock the door, it has nowhere to go. Your mind is racing in circles, and you will have difficulty going to sleep. In order to relax your mind and make your body genuinely tired, you need G.M.A.

This stands for Gross Motor Activity. It covers any type of physical activity that exercises the majority of the muscles and organs of the body. Jogging, tennis, swimming, bicycling, and skiing are just some prime G.M.A. activities, as well as dancing. Fifteen minutes to half an hour a day of any of these after work will do wonders for your head and will greatly strengthen your heart. If you have access to a gym or health club, use a running machine; or better still, take a dance, calisthenics, or yoga class right after work. Use the sauna and steam room, and emerge feeling like new, weary in the right way, relaxed in body but mentally alert.

If you avoid all exercise, your body will become more and more knotted day by day, and this tension will impair your functioning in every possible way. Yoga is one of the best systems for releasing this tension because it incorporates breath control with the gradual, easy flexing of muscles and the stretching of ligaments. Here are a couple of "quickies" you can do right at your desk:

1. Inhale deeply; then exhale very slowly while contracting the stomach muscles. Repeat this three times.

2. Rotate your right shoulder five times backward, five times forward. Repeat this with the left shoulder. Make the action slow and smooth.

3. Reach behind with the right hand and hold the right leg of your chair. Pull slowly and release. Repeat this five times with the right hand, five with the left.

4. Raise both of your legs straight out under your desk. Slowly squeeze and relax them, five times. Lower them *slowly*.

Exercise is not a luxury; it is a necessity for every working woman. Despite how we feel at the end of the day, the move out of the house, from housewife to career woman, has reduced the amount of exercise we get and the number of muscles that are used. From a mental point of view, exercise after work acts as an excellent re-entry device so that when you arrive home, you are perfectly relaxed, not pent up and snappish, full of office problems. It is better to come home half an hour late and be in a pleasant frame of mind than to come home on time and feel like screaming because of the noise of the stereo and the television and the children screaming for attention.

Regular exercise is a tough habit to get into but a very difficult one to break once you make the commitment. Reinforce your determination by doing it with a friend.

DRESS

If *Forbes* business magazine has devoted an entire article to "Tailoring the Corporate Woman," then you know it is not just a question of choosing between a plaid skirt or a pants suit. In fact, an entire industry seems to have sprung up just in *writing* about what women should wear to work, let alone the industry of manufacturing the clothes! First of all, *there are no golden rules.* Women's fashions change more frequently and more drastically than men's fashions, and the fact that we are joining the work force in great numbers undoubtedly has had an influence on what designers emphasize, but it still means that we have to continue to exercise our personal judgment and make our wardrobes sophisticated, suitable, and attractive.

During the seventies it became almost unseemly for women to admit that they wanted to look attractive at work, as if this implied frivolity or a lack of seriousness. Probably many such women confused *attractive* with *alluring.* To me there is a distinction between what I wear during the day and what I wear in the evening. Plunging necklines and slit skirts may be perfect for a night on the town, but in the office they are not *attractive* at all, merely *distractive.* For different reasons I find the opposite extreme just as disturbing. The no-nonsense tailored uniform approach I am sure will endure for a good long time, but I am not one of its greatest fans since to me it seems to suggest a great deal of insecurity, rather than the forthright independent thinking that its wearers would like to project. I do not believe that our chances for success increase in proportion to how manlike our dress code becomes. Menswear manufacturers, facing a slump, discovered a gold mine in the female would-be corporate officer market. What gross lack of confidence! Why should we have to approximate what a man wears? Most of the high-collared, long-skirted executives interviewed by *Forbes* indicated that they dressed in this manner in order to be taken seriously. One woman reported that she heard catcalls when she leaned over in a miniskirt, so she went out immediately and bought four suits with long skirts. Sorry, but she should never have been wearing a miniskirt in the first place, and long-skirted suits are just a cop-out.

Because we have more freedom in the way we can dress than men do, we ought to *use it* to help us get to the top, not to stifle our flair because we are afraid of what *men* might think if we turn up for work in anything but an *ersatz* version of their drab garments. In fact, if you take a careful look at the way men dress, you will find that my arguments can easily apply to them; it is simply a question of *degree*. The middle-management executive who has reached his level of competency proclaims this by his standard three-piece charcoal suit and rep tie. The man who is at the top or clearly on his way there is not afraid of elegance or of the unusual. I am not advocating the outlandishly fashionable or faddish look, but do not restrain your natural flair.

I often wear suits to work, but there are suits and *suits*. I like to wear a dazzling white suit with a silk shirt; I would only wear a tweed suit to a grouse shoot in the Scottish Highlands! On some days I wear simple dresses such as silk or cashmere-knit shirtwaists. Sometimes I will wear flannel pants with a silk shirt. When I talked to Susan Taylor, editor in chief of *Essence,* about grooming the Black businesswoman, she was adamantly opposed to uniformity:

> *"We have to find another way of doing it; we don't want to end up wearing a uniform to work like men do. What we do need is a couple of dynamite pieces that work for an individual body type, that underscore a particular body sense, and that also work in the corporate world."*

Susan's own *power* look is a classic black suit, well cut and softly tailored, that looks very chic and very expensive. By day she wears it with a plain blouse, and by night she makes it sparkle with a rhinestone blouse. Susan also had strong words about our incredible fashion heritage:

> *"We had something very special in the forties. We need to each make a commitment to an individual sense of style. We should use magazines, but only as a jumping-off point. As Black women we need something to reflect our heritage and history. For example, a certain color mix, an earring, a piece of jewelry that speaks of our homeland, or a precious piece passed to us by a grandmother—it might even be the wearing of braids that reflects our heritage; there is a way to find a braid look for the corporate world."*

I agree with Susan. Rule nothing out; simply bring simplicity, taste, and restraint to your choices.

I recommend the classic look for every working woman's wardrobe, even if she has a lot to spend on clothes. My definition of a classic is something of quality that you can live with for a long, long time, the effect of which changes dramatically depending on what you wear it with. A well-cut gabardine blazer is a classic. Wear it with black pants for traveling, with a white pleated skirt for the summer.

Bargains cost a lot of money. A polyester blazer will look awful in three days and will not last six months. Buy the best your budget allows. A silk blouse may cost over a hundred dollars, but it can work for twenty years; it travels well, launders well, and always looks well.

You are a Black woman. You are not going to merge with the scenery; you are going to stand out. And if you are success-oriented, you will want to be noticed. Think of this when you establish your wardrobe and forget what you have read about "sensible" tailored suits (and those awful "ties").

Here are some guidelines.

1. Ease and Comfort

Most women neglect this and suffer all their working lives. It is the one most important thing to consider. By "comfort" I do not simply mean physical comfort, although that is important; I mean what makes *you* feel good. Some clothes give you a spark and others put out your fire. You might buy exactly what the experts tell you has tested out to be the most suitable outfit for a career woman in your position, yet feel lousy in it because it is simply not *you*. You can only operate at maximum capacity if you are not self-conscious about what you are wearing. At home you feel comfortable in a sweater and blue jeans, not at work. What do you find that lifts your spirits but does not distract you, personally? This is a very individual matter. I know some women who never really feel at ease in high heels, and others who are the absolute opposite and live their lives three inches off the ground. Few careers demand that you wear either high heels or flats, so *you have a choice.* If you simply copy a spread in a fashion magazine, you will be wearing an outfit that was suitable for someone else.

2. Local Custom

By "local" I mean everything from the actual place of work to the town or city. Between wearing a uniform and going directly against the grain, there is a middle ground. Geri Dart relocated to Kansas City to work as a legal secretary:

> *"In New York City I thought of myself as conservative compared to what some women wore to the office. I'd call it 'disco'; they even wore designer jeans! When I arrived here the first day at work, I wore a pale lavender blouse and a*

stone-colored dress with a bolero jacket. You would have thought I had stepped out of Vogue, *the way they carried on. In fact, everyone thought I looked terrific, but it caused much too much fuss and I did not want to get into the habit of putting on a fashion show every morning so I toned it down considerably, and now I feel comfortable."*

Sometimes the same company will have, albeit unwritten, different dress codes for different divisions. In the management division of Bell Telephone the men wear dark suits, button-down collars and ties, the women skirts and blouses. In the research division, Bell Labs, the men more often than not have beards and the women wear pants and sweaters. In extreme cases some corporations do have specific dress codes. If you are basically conservative (and never confuse this with dull), it makes choosing your wardrobe easier.

Use your eyes and watch what other women in your business wear. Is it appropriate on them? Would something similar be appropriate on you?

3. Impact

You want to stand out from the crowd. But how? There are many ways of getting attention. A clown gets attention, but also ridicule. What do you want your appearance to say? What makes you different from all the rest, on sight? Not your bright red dress, please!

Quality, imagination, classic elegance. These are the three attributes that your clothes should exemplify. These are the three things you want to say with what you wear. Do not try to use your clothes to say "I am serious" or "I work hard" or "I am very intelligent" because it is not within the vocabulary of clothes to be able to say those things; you have to *do* them. Realize what the limitations are, what your clothes can say and what they cannot say. The quality of a woman and the extent of her creativity are two aspects that are not immediately apparent during a job interview, for instance. But if what she is wearing projects quality and creativity, she will not have to emphasize these things in what she says; she can concentrate on all the very serious aspects of her abilities and let her clothes take care of the general aspects of the sort of person she is.

A. Quality

Old, well-cared-for leather shoes are *always* better than plastic, rubber, or synthetic shoes. If the style is conservative, it does not matter at all if they look old-fashioned, much better than if they are this season's outrage.

Wool, cotton, cashmere, silk, or gabardine and blends are *always* better than totally synthetic fabrics.

Last year's knitted dress that fits is better than this year's polyester that clings.

A well-worn Burberry raincoat is better than a new fake fur.

A single strand of pearls, looped twice, is better than a ton of gold chains and bracelets or diamond rings.

Monochromes proclaim quality, mixed colors only in the palest pastels. Stick to the neutrals: tan, black, white, gray, or navy blue.

Quality is always simple: crew neck sweaters, frill-less blouses, two-piece outfits (no *vests,* please!).

Do not confuse quality with designer clothes carrying ostentatious initials. Quality clothes can be recognized by the way they are made and the fabrics from which they are made; they do not need to be prominently labelled. Status cannot be bought, only achieved. If I had $1,000 to last for five years and I had to buy a work wardrobe, I would not go bargain hunting for mix-and-match jackets and dresses. I would buy *one* Chanel suit and dozens of silk scarves.

B. Imagination

Avoid the outlandish and the bizarre. Concentrate on one item that is unusual: an accessory, perhaps, like an antique brooch or belt buckle. Imagination with *taste* requires restraint. Two small, simple plain gold earrings in one ear is imaginative; a dozen is overkill.

Imagination and quality must go hand in hand; nothing plastic ever works. Avoid the stiff and the new. Your best clothes should be softly tailored, well fitting, but not imperious or tight. They should fit to flatter your figure, not to emphasize it *or* disguise it. Just as many men wear suits designed to give them shoulders, so women wear brassieres designed to give them busts. Simply draw the line at exaggeration.

You can always show your imagination and quality by buying good, expensive shoes. As an investment they are the best; they will take care of your feet. Handmade leather shoes in classic styles and good colors should be a major part of your budget. By good colors I mean bone, oxblood, lemon, cinnamon, grass—nothing bright, nothing orange! Never buy them in a hurry. Walk up and down the store several times to be sure of the size and fit. You would be surprised at just how many people will look at your shoes in the course of a working day, especially in an office. Make sure the heel height is really appropriate, not just part of your wishful thinking. There is no point in making yourself much taller with very high heels if you really are not comfortable in them.

C. *Classic Elegance*

We come in all shapes and sizes and from sixteen to seventy years of age, so it is impossible for me to say "Wear *this* and you can never go wrong." But I have compiled a chart (below) of items that I think are most appropriate for Black women to wear in *office* situations, no matter what your position on the totem pole, high or low. I favor neutral colors like white, black, gray, and tan, which makes it easy to combine your wardrobe in different ways. To decide what goes with what, just use the mirror and practice.

	FABRICS	COLORS	STYLES
Dresses		all neutral, no "hot" colors. tan; beige; navy blue; burgundy; black; white; gray	two-piece princess skirt and blouse, hem just covering knee
Suits		all above, esp. navy blue for investment banking	two-piece alone or w. blouse or sweater, pants for casual mtgs.
Blouses	WOOL COTTON LINEN GABARDINE CASHMERE	subtle prints, color notes but not "hot"; all neutrals	tailored collar; bow-tie; oriental collar; nothing sheer or fussy
Skirts		navy blue, black, white, and tan	A-line or straight; also pleated, hem covering knee
Sweaters		monochromes, esp. oatmeal, dk. green, navy blue	crew, turtle, or demure V-neck
Jackets		navy blue, ivory, gray, black	double-breasted with sleeves to wrist or basic Chanel
Shoes	LEATHER	brown, luggage tan, black, burgundy, gray	medium heel, sling-back pump w. black toe or standard walking

Just as important as what I specifically recommend is this list of *absolute no's:*

> Ridiculously high heels
> Slit skirts
> National costumes
> Tight clothes of *any* fabric
> Thin dresses that wrinkle and ride up
> Low-cut blouses
> See-through *anything*
> Long sharp nails
> Long loose hair
> Any jewelry that makes a *noise*

DESIGNERS

If you want to buy by the label, then here are my current picks for the Black woman who is on her way *up*.

Expensive:	Calvin Klein
	Ralph Lauren
	Anne Klein
Reasonable:	Perry Ellis
	Carol Horne
	Liz Claiborne
Newcomers to Watch:	Harvè Bernard
	Danielle O

My personal favorite for business is Liz Claiborne. I have been wearing two of her wool suits for four years. They are ivory, two-piece outfits. I have been all over the world in them, including to the White House, and they are still going strong, but they did not cost a fortune.

My favorite newcomer is Harvè Bernard. My sister Betty is a very high-powered businesswoman with her own beauty-product export company, and she is frequently to be found on a plane between New York City and the Ivory Coast (in western Africa). When she had to meet with some very high government officials, I helped her choose a simple black straight-skirt, two-piece "Board Room" suit with a mink collar. It looked like two million dollars and cost one quarter the price of a Halston.

JEWELRY

I certainly agree with designer Clovis Ruffin, who thinks women wear too much jewelry and that we should always remove one piece before going to work. We tend to overdo *gold* jewelry. One chain is enough, one bracelet and one ring. Clinking and clanking is distracting in a work atmosphere, so stick to neatly fitting jewelry, not waist-length necklaces or wide-hooped bangles. Like children, jewelry should be seen and not heard. Precious stones, other than a diamond engagement ring, are out of place at work. Real pearls are *in*, and so are fake pearls; you can never go wrong with a single strand. I do not encourage you to wear jewelry that has your name or that of a designer on it, nor do I think the choice of expensive trademark jewelry, like Gucci, shows much *imagination*. A single unusual, modestly sized bracelet, brooch, or pair of earrings can make a great statement about your quality and creativity.

The ideal bracelet is a single bangle of gold, ivory, silver, or even wood—anything *real,* nothing fake. An armful of coiled exotic bangles is very exciting in the evening, but not at work. The same goes for oversized African hoop earrings. Any necklace that reaches beneath about three inches below your collarbone is too low; it will swing backward and forward and knock things off your desk and everyone else's. Clips that represent common objects, rainbows, or funny faces can be very amusing on an evening out, but you do not want a conversation piece in the office. Stick to something traditional.

ACCESSORIES

Unless you are a chronic loser, your belts, watches, pens, and above all your *briefcase* should be of the highest quality you can afford, the most classic styles. These are the gifts to hint that you want for your birthday and Christmas: a Mahler briefcase, an Elsa Peretti pen from Tiffany, and a Cartier watch.

Try to carry only one bag, which can hold your papers *and* your personal items. Most top manufacturers have our market in mind and are making organizational bags and cases that are well compartmentalized. Buy only leather or canvas. Imitations look cheap and do not last. The same goes for your belts. Any fabric will do, so long as it is not plastic.

Your watch is important; it should be accurate and visible. There are times when you will want to look at it unobtrusively, and if you have to snap open the top and press a button to get a digital readout, you are hardly being discreet.

Hair

Naturally I suggest you solve this problem as often as possible by wearing wigs and hairpieces. After all, they are designed for the working woman. I wear them every day, and it saves much time and bother.

When it comes to *hairstyles,* we must be careful to establish our priorities. A talented newscaster was recently fired and then reinstated for wearing a beaded corn-row style. I applaud her cultural determination, but I think it may have been misplaced. To me, a hairstyle which is elaborate, exotic, and quite obviously a *statement* as well as a style— whether it is a cultural, political, or social statement—is out of place at work unless your *business* is making cultural, social, or political statements. I am not arguing anyone's rights to make such statements, but they may be just as distracting at work as a rousing speech or pamphleteering.

By the same token, I think there are much more important things for which we ought to fight than the right to wear a particular hairstyle, whether it is one that expresses our racial heritage or not. In the world of inequality that we face today, a hairstyle is not worth a pitched battle. We should be fighting for tangible benefits like equal pay and equal opportunity, not for symbols. We should save the crusades for the major issues and on the job should wear our hair in ways that are:

1. Appropriate for the job.
2. Suited to our features.

One reason that I wear my wigs and hairpieces all the time at work is because I hate to have to think about it after 8 A.M., and when I see other women fiddling with their hair during the workday, I think of it as a grand waste of time.

As for specific styles, there are none that I would rule out as being always unsuitable but a few I would recommend:

1. Short or medium, well-cut Afro.
2. Short or medium loose curl.
3. Pageboy with bangs.
4. Medium length, processed, pulled to a chignon.

5. Long, unprocessed, in *neat* braids without beads or coins.

6. Any neat medium-length style that is *off* the face.

MAKEUP

Obvious makeup is not appropriate for most working situations. By obvious I mean strong and stagy. Most of the women I deal with are in the beauty business, but the most successful of them, Black and white, *appear* to be wearing very little makeup. In fact, they simply know how to use makeup very well, to enhance their features, to give their skin a glow and a slight sparkle so that they look fresh and keen all day.

If at eleven in the morning I am introduced to a businesswoman who is wearing bright green eye shadow, I will judge her negatively from the start. I am just as capable of prejudice on sight as the next person, and although I do my best not to judge another businesswoman on something as extraneous as her makeup, it will be part of my overall impression. I am always going to be put off by too much rather than by too little. My dictum about makeup at work: *Less is more.*

Most Black women are fortunate to have features and complexions that are naturally *alive.* We should all establish regimens for skin care that are strict and cleansing, and should use just a modicum of cosmetics. There are complete makeup schemes for the working woman in both *All About Health and Beauty for the Black Woman* and my second book *How to Be a Top Model.* Briefly, you should try to achieve a soft, classic look, with no harsh high tones or strong accents. Plum, rose, or coral for your eyes and lips are best, rose or coral for your cheeks. Makeup should be like your clothes, soft, well structured but simple, classic and elegant, above all *understated.*

The best advice I can give you about makeup: Take your time, use a light, feathery stroke, and blot off as much as you can! Put your makeup on in *natural light* if possible and check what you have done in *artificial light.* Also:

1. Invest in *quality* cosmetics; these will keep your skin healthy.

2. Invest in quality skin-care items: cleansers, masques, moisturizers. Your makeup will look better and stay looking good longer on a well-cleansed skin.

3. Keep your cosmetics clean.

4. Keep a duplicate set in your desk so that you are not carrying all your pots and pencils around all day and so that

you are able to do a complete overhaul for a major meeting.

5. Get *one* look down pat, so that you can get it on in five to ten minutes. If you try to follow the latest trend, you will be half an hour late every other morning.

MAKEUP "TRICKS"
FOR THE WORKING WOMAN

I have collected these from my own experience and that of my busy friends; they are designed to *perk you up* during the day and to keep you looking good until dinner time.

* Keep a bottle of your favorite fragrance in your desk drawer and give yourself a light squirt in midmorning and midafternoon.
* *Moisturize!* All day long. For face, neck, and hands this is an absolute must. Most of us work in artificial heat or air conditioning; it dries our skin and saps our energy. Remember to tissue off the excess moisturizer or you will fingerprint everything you touch!
* Always have your nail polish handy to touch up chips.
* Keep a soft eyebrow pencil for touch-ups at your desk.
* A dab of lip gloss, Vaseline or Elizabeth Arden Eight-Hour Cream, should be applied just before a meeting.
* Eye drops may be used. Better to freshen your eyeballs than to cake your lashes.
* A spritz of rosewater should be sprayed all over your face, very lightly.

In addition to your second set of cosmetics, you may also want to keep the following at your place of work, just in case you have to dash to a late afternoon meeting followed by drinks or dinner and do not have time to get home:

1. Change of blouse or sweater.
2. Spare stockings.
3. Extra shoes.
4. Hair equipment, even hot rollers.
5. Toothbrush and paste.

WHEN YOU TRAVEL

For appearance's sake, your luggage should be rugged and of good quality. After a few trips this will have paid for itself in faster, more efficient service. The better the luggage, the bigger the tip, bellmen think. If you are going to be carrying your own, then canvas with leather reinforcements is the best.

No matter how long your trip, only take *two* pieces at the most. It took me years of constant travel to get my basic twelve down to one. If you can squeeze everything into a carryon, you will have plain sailing; you can avoid delays at baggage pick-up terminals and avoid arriving in Detroit while your luggage is in Alaska. Make sure that *all* your business material travels on the plane with you, as well as basic overnight requirements: makeup, toothbrush, and gown.

Avoid cute luggage and heavy luggage. The secret of traveling well is to travel *light*. Make a list of *everything* you need and take *half*. The more you travel, the more you will find out about what you need and what can best be left behind. No two women are the same in this respect, but I will trade four pairs of shoes for one traveling iron on any trip I take!

Make a basic checklist and run off a dozen copies; use it for every trip. I pack like an automaton now, barely thinking. Another trick I have is to keep a case packed with the basics:

* Sewing kit
* Travel iron
* Toothbrush and paste
* Tissues
* Pantyhose

All I pack are the actual clothes I need. For a three-day business trip that involves at least one evening of socializing, I take the following:

1. Two white suits
2. Ivory silk cocktail dress
3. Tissue-thin, short wool cape
4. Cashmere sweater
5. Silk evening pumps
6. Four camisoles

The camisoles, in different colors (all pale, neutral), give my suits a new look every day, sometimes with the jacket open and sometimes closed. I take pearls, two strands, and keep them on! I pack the clothes in their plastic cleaner bags, and as soon as I arrive at the hotel, I hang anything that is wrinkled in the bathroom and turn on a hot shower to steam them smooth.

Always take a complete, plastic-lined (do you want nail polish all over your evening dress?) travel kit of cosmetic and sewing items. Never say:

"I'll get it in the hotel lobby when I arrive"

because that is just what they will be out of. This goes doubly so for shampoo, facial tissues, and tampons.

When traveling there is only one law, Murphy's: if anything can go wrong, it will!

To keep your cool and remain *independent of the system* (that is the name of the game), try to be as self-sufficient as possible, even if it means getting wheels for your suitcase.

On your actual journey, dress as compactly as possible; avoid hats that can fly off or gloves that can get left behind. Keep your hands as free as possible. If you look around any major airport, you will see that the men traveling on business are carrying one item, at the most two, while women are laden down with handbags, business bags, shopping bags, and clutching purses and tickets. It is always easier to carry one large tote bag, even if it is outsized, than five assorted smaller bags.

I put all my liquids into plastic bottles to avoid spillage, and I never forget aspirin. Fold and pack carefully; this way you will save space and time. Fill all the nooks and crannies; you can fit neatly into one medium-sized bag what you tumble into two large ones. Wrinkleable items like stockings and underwear go into the corners. Some clothes can be rolled (skirts) and others folded (sweaters) to take up a minimum amount of space.

All your luggage should be clearly labelled with your *destination* and name, including your carry-on bags. Lock your luggage and tie the keys inside your briefcase or purse.

TEMPO

Proponents of biorhythm speculate that each of us adheres to regular cycles of increasing and diminishing energy and that in each area of our life there is a different cycle. When it comes to Black women at work, we have to recognize that none of us are able to operate all day every day at the same pitch. Some of us work well in the early morning, some in the late afternoon. We need to adjust our tempo to the job and vice versa.

Certain jobs, especially those with large organizations, have an inherent pace that you either fit into or fall from. A ten o'clock bull session (a rowdy, energetic "idea" meeting) may be followed by ninety minutes of concentrated telephone work. A lunch break is used to discuss half work, half gossip with a colleague. In the early afternoon you move about, checking reports and schedules, and return to your desk at three for an hour of telephoning. At four-fifteen you are called to an unexpected meeting with a client who has just dropped in, and you have to appear bright-eyed and bushy-tailed.

That is the kind of schedule to which the body can adapt; it has highs and lows, periods of intense concentration followed by periods that are free-flowing. If your work schedule is *not* like this, but requires a more or less constant application of effort, you have to insert your own tempo changes in order to ensure that your performance remains constant.

If I sit at my desk for more than forty minutes, I get up, walk around, glance out the window, think of something completely off the subject for half a minute, and then get back to work. This is called an energy break, and we all need them. Brief one-minute rest periods lessen tension and combat fatigue. Without them your standard of work gradually lowers toward the end of the day; none of us are machines. Stretch and walk if you have been sitting; sit and put your feet up on a chair if you have been standing. In office situations men are always leaning back with their feet on their desks. It is a common, if not comely, posture. Most of the time it is not to show off but to get a natural break.

How can we do that? Put our feet on our desks? Certainly not! Pull over a chair or pile a stack of telephone books under your desk. Get a small stool or, if you are near a couch, make some of your calls from there, sitting upright against one side with your shoes off and your legs stretched out.

If you build up quickly to a fierce pitch of work fever in the middle of the day, you will probably pay for it with an afternoon of loose ends. Acceleration burns up a lot of energy, energy that you need to keep going in the home stretch. Maintain a steady pace throughout the day, alternating long work periods at medium intensity with brief work periods at high intensity.

There is a very sound biological reason for the need to break your sedentary position every once in a while and move around: the return of blood to your heart is diminished by sitting or standing still. It does not pump as hard to the brain, and this makes your thinking sluggish. You will wake up your mind, as well as your body, by adjusting to a higher tempo for a short period of time.

Tension and fatigue show in our faces. We cannot assume a mask all day long; that in itself creates a lot of stress. Small breaks designed to improve your performance will also improve your appearance. This can also be applied to the calendar: by the week, month, and year.

In order to look your best for your job, from the inside out, you need good nutrition, exercise, appropriate clothes, a neat hairstyle, light makeup, and *recreation.* What you do with your time off can have a positive or a negative effect on your success at work. If you party hard on Sunday night, it may take until Tuesday to really come to grips with your job. But if you lie around doing nothing all weekend, you may come to work on Monday restless and unfulfilled. Like your work week, your weekend should consist of high-activity periods sandwiched between longer rest periods. If you have children to take care of, you must also get some time for yourself; do not feel guilty for stealing it, even though you see little enough of them during the week. Stay in bed as long as you can on Sunday morning, even if it means a few hours of chaos.

You *must* indulge in some physical exercise on the weekend, even if it is only a long brisk walk. You have to get rid of the pent-up tension of the week. Make a firm commitment to jog, swim, or play an organized sport like tennis.

We will not succeed in the working world, or in our personal lives, if we fail to recognize the need for *balance,* yin and yang, hard and soft, fast and slow. If it is all one way and not the other, we are bucking Nature, and sooner or later Nature always wins. We can only keep up appearances for so long; if our beauty does not come from *inside,* there will be a collapse, sooner or later. It *is* important to dress well and speak well and do your job with dedication and intelligence, but in order to be successful, you must project strength and health—and this is impossible if you are not strong and healthy *inside.*

We cannot, nor should we wish to, insulate ourselves from financial worry, marital stress, racial prejudice, and all the tiny issues that come up every day to throw us off balance. What we must do is *cope.*

People do not want to hire a woman who can avoid problematical situations but prefer one who can face them squarely and deal with them through thick and thin without losing her soul. I know that the people who work for me and with me have their share of life's inequities, and I expect that on some days a particular person will be "up" and on other days "down." That is life. What I do not want to see is someone killing herself on the job, suppressing serious problems in the home. Something has to give, and usually the person who is troubled may deny it to their colleagues for weeks on end until suddenly she breaks down at the worst possible time for the office.

We are Black women on the way *up.* We have more than our fair share of problems, and some of these problems are best shared with the family, some with friends, and even some with our colleagues and superiors. It is in knowing what problems to share, when and with whom, that we must learn patiently and must practice. This is what I mean by balance.

Even though I have cautioned against excessive familiarity on the job, many of us are afraid to express ourselves because we are not entirely comfortable with our positions in a white society. Sensitive to the stereotyped image of the happy-go-lucky, forever-smiling Negro of American mythology, we are often at pains to suppress our sense of humor, even with one another. I was astonished at the number of times business owners told me that they regarded a sense of humor as an important qualification for a top position! A good sense of humor, as opposed to defensive clowning, is a sure sign of security, of self-confidence. If you feel good about yourself, you are the solid, dependable person we need to run that division; that is how the thinking goes.

Without *trust,* you will never reach the top. Unless you can inspire trust in others and be trusted, you may be able to carve out a narrow path to within a few feet of the summit, but you will never end up *in charge.* Success is all about being *in charge.* You may be brilliant, you may be able to sell a million dollars worth of merchandise a month, you may be a great beauty, you may have a Ph.D., you may be able to get people to do whatever you want, but unless you are *trusted* you will not be put *in charge* of anything, from a delivery route to a Fortune 500 corporation.

How do you get to be trusted? It is very simple. There are six ingredients. Be patient; this is the last list in the book!

1. *Honesty.* No stupid lies or cover-ups. Say "I didn't do it because I was too tired," *not* "I did it and put it on your desk, but the cleaning man must have tidied it away."

2. *Loyalty.* Every business has its secrets. Keep them.

3. *Understanding.* Your boss and your colleagues are human beings, not robots. They cannot be all things to all people, and cannot be right by you all the time.

4. *Directness.* If you have a problem, speak up. If you disagree with a decision, with a policy, state your points out in the open. No double-talk, no politicking.

5. *Constancy.* It does your work no good if you arrive early and stay late the first five weeks on the job, and then have a succession of "colds, dying relatives, and personal problems" as soon as the weather gets warm. Demonstrate your reliability.

6. *Wit.* That spark, that occasional flash of insight and humor can be inspiring. If you can look people in the eye— whether they are subordinates, colleagues, or the head of the company—and share a joke, then you will be trusted.

Few of you will be able to work always with and for each other, which means that you will be seeking the trust of people that are, in many ways, quite different from yourself. They may have preconceived notions about Black women; some may be benign and some may be hostile, but you must push through that wall of difference and impress upon the circumstances of your job that you are a unique and very special human being; you are an *individual*—Lena, Mrs. Jackson, Ms. Smith. Whoever you are, be *yourself*. In your job your Blackness, your womanhood are obvious. You do not have to be concerned about overemphasizing or de-emphasizing those marvelous attributes. What is obvious is your *character*. Are you trustworthy, honest, direct, understanding, constant, and able to smile once in a while? Of course you are! I know it and you know it, but do *they* know it? If not, why not? Well, they can tell from your smart clothes that you are a woman of quality, and they know from your résumé that you have been educated and have experience. But that is all they know until you *show* them the rest. If you can do that, day by day, step by step, routine by routine, decision by decision, risk by risk, you will rocket to the top, the very top.

So, take a deep breath, relax, and go to work.

Appendix

Chapter One

Recommended Reading:

Abarbanel, Karin and Siegel, Connie M. *Woman's Work Book*. New York: Praeger Publishers, 1975.

Dunlap, Jan. *Personal and Professional Success for Women*. Englewood Cliffs, N.J.: Prentice-Hall, 1972.

Ruth Halcomb. *Women Making It: Patterns and Profiles of Success*. New York: Atheneum, 1979.

Higginson, Margaret V. and Quick, Thomas L. *The Ambitious Woman's Guide to a Successful Career*. New York: American Management Associations, 1980.

Hunter, T. C. *Beginnings: The Patterns of Success*. New York: Crowell, 1978.

Kellogg, Mary A. *Fast Track: The Super Achievers and How They Make It to Early Success*. New York: McGraw-Hill, 1978.

Korda, Michael. *Power: How to Get It, How to Use It*. New York: Random House, 1975.

———. *Success*. New York: Random House, 1977.

Newman, Mildred and Berkowitz, Bernard. *How to Take Charge of Your Life*. New York: Harcourt, Brace, Jovanovich, 1977.

Ringer, Robert J. *Looking Out for No. 1*. New York: Fawcett, 1978.

Staff of Catalyst, Inc. *What to Do With the Rest of Your Life*. New York: Simon and Schuster, 1972.

Trahey, Jane. *Jane Trahey on Women and Power (Who's Got It, How to Get It)*. New York: Rawson Associates, 1977.

Chapter Two

Recommended Reading:

Nutter, C. F. *Résumé Workbook: A Personal Career File for Job Applications*. Cranston, R.I.: Carroll Press, 1978.

Staff of Catalyst, Inc. *Planning Your Career*. New York: Simon and Schuster, 1976.

Learn at Home:

To obtain information about accredited home-study courses in a wide variety of fields, write:

National Home Study Council
1601 Eighteenth Street N.W.
Washington, D.C. 20009

The National University Extension Association
One Dupont Circle ✕360 N.W.
Washington, D.C. 20036

M.B.A.

For information about university M.B.A. programs and the availability of financial assistance, write:

Council for Opportunity in Graduate Management Education
   (COGME)
Central Plaza
675 Massachusetts Avenue
Cambridge, Mass. 02139

Fellowships for Minorities
Consortium for Graduate Study in Management
101 N. Skinker Boulevard
Box 1132
St. Louis, Mo. 63130

Management Courses

Information about management-training programs and workshops geared to Black women is available from:

American Management Associations, Inc.
135 West Fiftieth Street
New York, N.Y. 10020

The Business and Professional Women's Foundation
2012 Massachusetts Avenue N.W.
Washington, D.C. 20036

Engineering

Information about accredited degree programs and financial assistance for women thus enrolled is available from:

Loan Fund in Engineering Studies
The Business and Professional Women's Foundation
2012 Massachusetts Avenue N.W.
Washington, D.C. 20036

Financial Assistance

The following organizations will send you information about financial assistance programs for Black women seeking to complete or further their studies:

Project on the Status and Education of Women
Box R
Association of American Colleges
1818 R Street N.W.
Washington, D.C. 20009

The Foundation Center
888 Seventh Avenue
New York, N.Y. 10019

Publications Office
National Science Foundation
1800 G Street N.W.
Washington, D.C. 20550

Bureau of Higher and Continuing Education
U. S. Office of Education
Room 4913-ROB3
400 Maryland Avenue S.W.
Washington, D.C. 20202

Business and Professional Women's Foundation
2012 Massachusetts Avenue N.W.
Washington, D.C. 20036

Scholarship Search
1775 Broadway
Suite A627
New York, N.Y. 10019

The federal government has published a complete guide to organizations that offer loan, scholarship, and fellowship assistance to Black women. Virtually every career field is mentioned. It is called *Selected List of Postsecondary Education Opportunities for Minorities and Women,* and if it is not in your local library, it can be obtained for a small charge from:

Superintendent of Documents
U. S. Government Printing Office
Washington, D.C. 20402

Chapter Three

Recommended Reading:

Barnett, Rosalind and Baruch, Grace K. *The Competent Woman: Perspectives on Development.* New York: Halstead Printing, 1978.

Cooper, Ken. *Nonverbal Communication for Business Success*. New York: American Management Associations, 1979.

Linver, Sandy. *Speak Easy: How to Talk Your Way to the Top*. New York: Summit Books, 1979.

Madow, Leo. *Anger, How to Recognize and Cope With It*. New York: Charles Scribner's Sons, 1974.

Matthew, Kathy. *On Your Own: Ninety-Nine Alternatives to a 9–5 Job*. New York: Random House, 1977.

Redford, S. R. *Jobmanship*. New York: Macmillan, 1979.

Scheele, Adele M. *Skills for Success: A Guide to the Top*. New York: William Morrow, 1979.

Seaman, Florence and Lorimer, Anne. *Winning at Work! A Book for Women*. Philadelphia: Running Press, 1980.

Tennov, Dorothy. *Super-Self: A Woman's Guide to Self-Management*. New York: Thomas Crowell, 1977.

Career Listings

The *Occupational Outlook Handbook* is an invaluable tool for every Black woman who is trying to decide on a career. It is a 660-page volume containing detailed descriptions of virtually every job in the U. S., with educational requirements and average salaries. It costs approximately $8.00 and is available from:

> The Superintendent of Documents*
> U. S. Government Printing Office
> Washington, D.C. 20402

Professional Job Finders

Your local library should have a copy of the following publications which list reputable firms:

Career Counselors: *Directory of Counseling Services*
                        International Association of Counseling Services
                        5203 Leesburg Pike ✗400
                        Falls Church, Va. 22041

Employment Agencies: *Membership Directory*
                        National Association of Personnel Consultants
                        1012 Fourteenth Street N.W.
                        Washington, D.C. 20005

Executive Recruiters: *Directory of Member Firms*
                        Association of Executive Recruiting Consultants
                        30 Rockefeller Plaza
                        New York, N.Y. 10022

* Also available from this source: *Occupational Outlook for College Graduates*.

Directory of Executive Recruiters
Consultant News
Templeton Road
Fitzwilliam, N.H. 03447

Chapter Four

Recommended Reading—General:

Donaho, M. and Meyer, J. L. *How to Get the Job You Want.* Englewood Cliffs, N.J.: Prentice-Hall, 1976.

Figler, Howard E. *The Complete Job Search Handbook.* New York: Holt, Rinehart, and Winston, 1980.

Gerstl, Joel and Jacobs, G. *Professions for the People: The Politics of Skill.* New York: Halstead Press, 1976.

Gootnick, D. *Getting a Better Job.* New York: McGraw-Hill, 1978.

Jackson, Tom. *Guerrilla Tactics in the Job Market.* New York: Bantam Books, 1978.

Lathrop, Richard. *Who's Hiring Who.* Third edition. Berkeley, Calif.: Ten Speed Press, 1977.

Medley, Anthony. *Sweaty Palms: The Neglected Art of Being Interviewed.* Belmont, Calif.: Lifetime Learning Publications, 1978.

Sprague, N. and Knatz, Hilary F. *Finding a Job: A Resource Guide for the Middle-Aged and Retired.* Garden City, N.Y.: Adelphi University Press, 1978.

Stanat, Kirby and Reardon, Patrick. *Job-Hunting Secrets and Tactics.* Chicago: Westwind Press/Follett, 1977.

Courses

The following organizations and institutions offer programs in specific job finding skills and career orientation for Black women:

Alabama
      Talladega University
      Talladega, Ala. 35160

Illinois
      Northwestern University
      Evanston, Ill. 60200

Iowa
      Project Second Start
      Drake University
      Des Moines, Io. 50311

Massachusetts
      Hampshire College
      Amherst, Mass. 01002

      Harvard University
      Cambridge, Mass. 02138

Radcliffe College
Cambridge, Mass. 02138

Michigan
University of Michigan
Ann Arbor, Mich. 48100

Nebraska
University of Nebraska
Lincoln, Neb. 68500

New York
National Council of Negro Women
198 Broadway
New York, N.Y. 10038

Women Advancing Through Career Help
New York University Midtown Center
11 West Forty-second Street
New York, N.Y. 10036

Women in Self-Help
N.Y. State Department of Labor
2 World Trade Center
New York, N.Y. 10047

Womanschool
108 East Eighty-ninth Street
New York, N.Y. 10017

Brooklyn College
Brooklyn, N.Y. 11210

State University of New York
Stony Brook, N.Y. 11790

Hofstra University
Hempstead, N.Y. 11511

City University of New York
New York, N.Y. 10031

YWCA
610 Lexington Avenue
New York, N.Y. 10021

Michigan
Birmingham Community Women's Center
380 South Bates
Birmingham, Mich. 48009

Oklahoma
University of Oklahoma
Norman, Okla. 73069

Virginia
Brother Virginia Community College
Annandale, Va. 22003

Current Data

Free information about the changing job market for Black women can be obtained from:

National Commission on Working Women
1211 Connecticut Avenue #310
Washington, D.C. 20036

The National Career Development Project
Box 379
Walnut Creek, Calif. 94596

Jobs At A Glance

The following is my analysis of the current job market for Black women, based on information supplied by the United States Department of Labor. I have selected those careers which offer the best chances for entry and advancement, and given the appropriate qualifications. Salary scales are *approximate estimates only* and may vary by as much as 100 per cent up or down, depending upon location, length of service, qualifications, and (in some cases) union affiliation.

Occupation	Annual Openings	Salary
The Professions		
Accountants	61,000	26,000
Bank Managers	28,000	16,000
Chiropractors	1,500	25,000
Dentists	5,500	50,000
Lawyers	37,000	50,000
Optometrists	1,600	40,000
Physicians	19,000	65,000
Podiatrists	600	40,000
Veterinarians	1,700	33,000
Health		
Dental Assistants	11,000	12,000
Dental Hygienists	6,000	15,000
Dental Lab Technicians	2,800	20,000
Dietitians	3,300	22,000
Dispensing Opticians	1,200	25,000
Electrocardiograph Technicians	Not available	16,000
Electroencephalographic Technicians	500	16,000
Emergency Medical Technicians	Not available	18,000
Health Service Administrators	18,000	30,000
Medical Laboratory Workers	14,800	17,500
Medical Records Technicians	4,900	15,000
Nurse's Aides	94,000	10,000
Occupational Therapists	2,500	25,000
Operating Room Technicians	2,600	17,500
Optometric Assistants	1,200	12,000

Occupation	Annual Openings	Salary
Pharmacists	7,800	22,000
Physical Therapists	2,700	25,000
Radiologic (X-Ray) Technicians	9,000	14,000
Registered Nurses	85,000	18,000
Respiratory Therapy Workers	5,000	12,000
Speech Pathologists	2,700	20,000

Science and Technology

Occupation	Annual Openings	Salary
Agricultural Engineers	600	30,000
Biochemists	900	25,000
Biomedical Engineers	175	30,000
Broadcast Technicians	Not available	15,000
Ceramic Engineers	550	30,000
Chemists	6,100	28,000
Computer Programmers	9,200	22,000
Computer Operators	12,500	12,000
Civil Engineers	7,800	30,000
Economists	7,800	35,000
Electrical Engineers	10,500	30,000
Engineers	46,500	30,000
Engineering Technicians	23,000	18,000
Forestry Technicians	700	16,000
Geologists	1,700	30,000
Geophysicists	600	30,000
Industrial Engineers	8,000	30,000
Life Scientists	11,200	25,000
Metallurgical Engineers	750	30,000
Mining Engineers	600	30,000
Ophthalmic Lab Technicians	1,400	16,000
Psychologists	6,700	30,000
Photographic Lab Technicians	2,700	16,000
Petroleum Engineers	600	30,000
Statisticians	1,500	28,000
Systems Analysts	7,900	28,000

Administration

Occupation	Annual Openings	Salary
Bank Clerks	45,000	8,000
General Administration (M.B.A.) Executives	Not available	50,000
Market Research Workers	24,000	25,000
Personnel Workers	17,000	30,000
Purchasing Agents	13,400	30,000
Receptionists	41,000	8,000
Secretaries	305,000	11,000
Statistical Clerks	23,500	11,000
Typists	59,000	11,000

Occupation	Annual Openings	Salary
Insurance		
Claim Representatives	10,250	15,000
Underwriters, Agents, and Brokers	30,000	16,000
Sales		
Automobile Sales Workers	10,400	18,000
Cashiers	119,000	14,000
Real Estate Agents	50,000	25,000
Retail Sales Workers	226,000	15,000
Travel Agents	1,900	15,000
Wholesale Trade Sales Workers	40,000	22,000
Service and Security		
Construction Inspectors (Government)	2,200	17,000
Cooks and Chefs	86,000	15,000
Cosmetologists	28,500	20,000
Correction Officers	13,000	15,000
Health and Regulatory Inspectors (Government)	5,800	17,000
Homemaker and Home Health Aides	36,000	12,000
Pest Controllers	2,500	16,000
Police Officers	16,500	15,000
Social Workers	22,000	16,000
Transportation		
Airplane Pilots	3,800	60,000
Flight Attendants	4,800	16,000
Local Busdrivers	3,100	16,000
Local Truckdrivers	64,000	22,000
Repair and Maintenance		
Air-Conditioning, Refrigeration, and Heating Mechanics	8,200	20,000
Automobile Mechanics	37,000	20,000
Business Machine Repairers	4,200	16,000
Computer Service Technicians	5,400	18,000
Industrial Machinery Repairers	58,000	16,000
Maintenance Electricians	15,500	18,000
Telephone and PBX Installers and Repairers	3,000	20,000
Television and Radio Service Technicians	6,100	16,000
Truck and Bus Mechanics	6,800	17,000
Heavy Industry		
All-Round Machinists	22,500	17,500
Assemblers	77,000	12,500

Occupation	Annual Openings	Salary
Blue-Collar Worker Supervisors	69,000	20,000
Boiler-Making Workers	3,100	20,000
Machine Tool Operators	19,600	18,500
Lithographers	2,300	22,000
Welders	35,000	22,000

Construction

Carpenters	58,000	22,000
Cement Masons	4,400	22,000
Drywall Installers	Not available	22,000
Electricians	12,900	25,000
Floor Installers	3,200	18,000
Glaziers	1,000	22,000
Insulation Workers	2,600	20,000
Ironworkers	4,100	20,000
Operating Engineers	36,000	22,000
Plumbers and Pipefitters	20,000	22,000
Sheet-Metal Workers	3,500	22,000

Communications and Design

Architects	4,000	35,000
Display Workers	3,300	24,000
Floral Designers	4,200	10,000
Interior Designers	3,600	25,000
Photographers	3,800	22,000
Public Relations Workers	7,500	25,000

Career Information

The following organizations provide up to date information about career opportunities.

Accounting
American Woman's Society of Certified Public Accountants
P.O. Box 389
Marysville, Ohio 43040

American Society of Women Accountants
35 East Wacker Drive #1036
Chicago, Ill. 60601

National Association of Accountants
919 Third Avenue
New York, N.Y. 10022

The Institute of Internal Auditors, Inc.
249 Maitland Avenue
Altamonte Springs, Fla. 32701

American Institute of Certified Public Accountants
1211 Avenue of the Americas
New York, N.Y. 10036

Advertising
   Special Committee of Equal Employment Opportunities
   American Association of Advertising Agencies
   200 Park Avenue
   New York, N.Y. 10017

Banking
   National Association of Bank Women Inc.
   111 East Wacker Drive
   Chicago, Ill. 60601

   National Association of Urban Bankers
   P.O. Box 3451
   Grand Central Station
   New York, N.Y. 10017

   American Bankers Association
   1120 Connecticut Avenue N.W.
   Washington, D.C. 20036

City Management
   International City Management Association
   1140 Connecticut Avenue N.W.
   Washington, D.C. 20036

Clerical (Secretarial)
   The Association of Black Executive Secretaries
   3095 Caralee Drive
   Columbus, Ohio 43219

   9 to 5 Organization for Women Office Workers
   140 Clarendon Street
   Boston, Mass. 02116

   National Secretaries Association
   Crown Center
   2440 Pershing Road ⅜C-10
   Kansas City, Mo. 64108

   Women Office Workers
   680 Lexington Avenue
   New York, N.Y. 10022

Conservation
   Office of Personnel
   U. S. Department of Agriculture
   Washington, D.C. 20250

Computer Operating and Data Processing
   Data Processing Management Association
   505 Busse Highway
   Park Ridge, Ill. 60068

   American Federation of Information Processing Societies
   1815 North Lynn Street
   Arlington, Va. 22209

Education
   Teachers Corps
   U. S. Department of Education
   400 Maryland Avenue S.W.
   Washington, D.C. 20202

   American Federation of Teachers
   11 Dupont Circle
   Washington, D.C. 20036

   National Education Association
   1201 Sixteenth Street N.W.
   Washington, D.C. 20036

Engineering
   Society of Women Engineers
   345 East Forty-seventh Street
   New York, N.Y. 10017

Engineering (by category)
   Aerospace
      American Institute of Aeronautics and Astronautics
      1290 Avenue of the Americas
      New York, N.Y. 10019
   Agricultural
      American Society of Agricultural Engineers
      2950 Niles Road
      St. Joseph, Mich. 49085
   Biomedical
      Alliance for Engineering in Medicine and Biology
      4405 East-West Highway #404
      Bethesda, Md. 20014

      Biomedical Engineering Society
      P.O. Box 2399
      Culver City, Calif. 90230
   Chemical
      American Institute of Chemical Engineers
      354 East Forty-seventh Street
      New York, N.Y. 10017

      American Chemical Society
      1155 Sixteenth Street N.W.
      Washington, D.C. 20036
   Civil
      American Society of Civil Engineers
      345 East Forty-seventh Street
      New York, N.Y. 10017
   Electrical
      Institute of Electrical and Electronics Engineers
      United States Activities Board
      1111 Nineteenth Street N.W.
      Washington, D.C. 20036
   Industrial
      American Institute of Industrial Engineers, Inc.
      25 Technology Park/Atlanta
      Norcross, Ga. 30092

Mechanical
  The American Society of Mechanical Engineers
  345 East Forty-seventh Street
  New York, N.Y. 10017
Metallurgical
  The Metallurgical Society of AIME
  P.O. Box 430
  Warrendale, Pa. 15086

  American Society for Metals
  Metals Park, Ohio 44073
Mining
  The Society of Mining Engineers of AIME
  Caller Number D
  Littleton, Colo. 80123
Petroleum
  Society of Petroleum Engineers of AIME
  6200 North Central Expressway
  Dallas, Tex. 75206

Environmental Planning and Protection
  Environmental Protection Agency
  401 M Street S.W.
  Washington, D.C. 20460

  Ecological Society of America
  c/o Dr. Frank McCormick
  University of Tennessee
  Knoxville, Tenn. 37916

  American Planning Association
  1776 Massachusetts Avenue N.W.
  Washington, D.C. 20036

Health
  American Medical Association
  535 North Dearborn Street
  Chicago, Ill. 60610

  Association of American Women Dentists
  435 North Michigan Avenue
  Chicago, Ill. 60611

  American Nurses Association
  2420 Pershing Road
  Kansas City, Mo. 64108

  American College of Nurses-Midwives
  1012 Fourteenth Street N.W. #801
  Washington, D.C. 20005

  National Midwives Association
  Box 163
  Princeton, N.J. 08540

  American Academy of Physicians' Assistants
  2341 Jefferson Davis Highway #700
  Arlington, Va. 22202

American College of Hospital Administrators
840 North Lake Shore Drive
Chicago, Ill. 60611

Association of University Programs of Health Administration
1 Dupont Circle
Washington, D.C. 20006

Insurance
National Association of Insurance Women
1847 East Fifteenth Street
Tulsa, Okla. 74104

Insurance Information Institute
110 William Street
New York, N.Y. 10038

Society of Actuaries
208 South LaSalle Street
Chicago, Ill. 60604

National Association of Life Underwriters
1922 F Street N.W.
Washington, D.C. 20006

Law
National Association of Women Lawyers
1155 East Sixtieth Street
Chicago, Ill. 60637

American Association of Law Schools
1 Dupont Circle ⌗370
Washington, D.C. 20036

National Federation of Paralegal Associations
P.O. Box 14103
Ben Franklin Station
Washington, D.C. 20044

Management
American Management Associations
135 West Fiftieth Street
New York, N.Y. 10020

National Black MBA Association
507 Fifth Avenue
New York, N.Y. 10017

National Association for Female Executives, Inc.
160 East Fifty-sixth Street
New York, N.Y. 10022

Personnel
American Society for Personnel Administration
30 Park Drive
Berea, Ohio 44017

Public Relations
P.R.S.A.
845 Third Avenue
New York, N.Y. 10022

Sales

Careers for Women, Inc.
26 East Eleventh Street
New York, N.Y. 10003

Careers for Women, Inc.
9911 West Pico Boulevard
Los Angeles, Calif. 90035

Sales Marketing Executives International
Career Education Division
380 Lexington Avenue
New York, N.Y. 10017

The National Retail Merchants Association
100 West Thirty-first Street
New York, N.Y. 10001

Science

Association for Women in Science, Inc.
1346 Connecticut Avenue N.W.
Washington, D.C. 20036

Scientific Manpower Commission
1776 Massachusetts Avenue N.W.
Washington, D.C. 20036

American Association for the Advancement of Science
Committee of Opportunities in Science
1515 Massachusetts Avenue N.W. ✕1515
Washington, D.C. 20005

Guide to Programs
National Science Foundation Publication Section
1800 G Street N.W.
Washington, D.C. 20550

Science (by category)
Astronomy
Education Office
American Astronomical Society
University of Delaware
Newark, Del. 19711
Biochemistry
American Society of Biological Chemists
9650 Rockville Pike
Bethesda, Md. 20014
Chemistry
American Chemical Society
1155 Sixteenth Street N.W.
Washington, D.C. 20036
Geology
American Geological Institute
5205 Leesburg Pike
Falls Church, Va. 22041
Geophysics
American Geophysical Union
2000 Florida Avenue N.W.
Washington, D.C. 20009

Society of Exploration Geophysicists
P.O. Box 3098
Tulsa, Okla. 74101
Oceanography
American Society of Limnology and Oceanography
I.S.T. Building/Great Lakes Research Division
University of Michigan
Ann Arbor, Mich. 48109

International Oceanographic Foundation
3979 Rickenbacker Causeway
Miami, Fla. 33149
Physics
American Institute of Physics
335 East Forty-fifth Street
New York, N.Y. 10017

Securities (Sales and Brokerage)
Securities Industry Association
20 Broad Street
New York, N.Y. 10005

Information Services Division
American Stock Exchange
86 Trinity Place
New York, N.Y. 10006

Transportation (Air)
FAA Education Materials
Federal Aviation Administration
800 Independence Avenue S.W.
Washington, D.C. 20581

State Occupational Opportunities

State occupational information coordinating committees have been established by the federal government to provide you with particular information about the job market in your region. These are called SOICC offices,
and the following is a list of where they may be found:

Alabama
Alabama Occupational Information
Coordinating Committee
State Department of Education
First Southern Towers, Suite 402
100 Commerce Street
Montgomery, Ala. 36104

Alaska
Alaska Occupational Information
Coordinating Committee
Pouch F, State Office Bldg.
Juneau, Alaska 99811

Arizona
>   Arizona State Occupational Information
>   Coordinating Committee
>   1535 West Jefferson Avenue, Room 345
>   Phoenix, Ariz. 85007

Arkansas
>   Arkansas State Occupational Information
>   Coordinating Committee
>   P.O. Box 5162
>   Little Rock, Ark. 72205

California
>   California Occupational Information
>   Coordinating Committee
>   535 East Main Street
>   Ventura, Calif. 93009

Colorado
>   Office of Occupational Information
>   Colorado Occupational Information
>   Coordinating Committee
>   770 Grant Street, Room 222
>   Denver, Colo. 80203

Connecticut
>   Connecticut State Occupational Information
>   Coordinating Committee
>   Hartranft Hall
>   55 Elizabeth Street
>   Hartford, Conn. 06053

Delaware
>   State Occupational Information
>   Coordinating Committee of Delaware
>   820 North French Street
>   Sixth Floor
>   Wilmington, Del. 19801

District of Columbia
>   D.C. Occupational Information
>   Coordinating Committee
>   500 C Street N.W., Suite 621
>   Washington, D.C. 20001

Florida
>   Florida Occupational Information
>   Coordinating Committee
>   325 John Knox Road
>   Suite L-500
>   Tallahassee, Fla. 32303

Georgia
>   State Occupational Information
>   Coordinating Committee
>   151 Ellis Street N.E.
>   Suite 504
>   Atlanta, Ga. 30303

Hawaii
    Hawaii State Occupational Information
    Coordinating Committee
    1164 Bishop Street, Suite 502
    Honolulu, Haw. 96813

Idaho
    State Occupational Information
    Coordinating Committee
    Len B. Jordan Bldg.
    650 West State Street
    Boise, Id. 83720

Illinois
    Illinois Occupational Information
    Coordinating Committee
    623 East Adams Street
    P.O. Box 1587
    Springfield, Ill. 62705

Indiana
    Indiana Office of Manpower Development
    State Board of Vocational and Technical Education
    17 West Market Street
    401 Illinois Bldg.
    Indianapolis, Ind. 46204

Iowa
    Iowa State Occupational Information
    Coordinating Committee
    523 East Twelfth Street
    Des Moines, Io. 50319

Kansas
    Kansas Occupational Information
    Coordinating Committee
    Department of Human Resources
    634 South Harrison, Suite C
    Topeka, Kans. 66603

Kentucky
    Kentucky Occupational Information
    Coordinating Committee
    103 Bridge Street
    Frankfort, Kent. 40601

Louisiana
    Louisiana State Occupational Information
    Coordinating Committee
    P.O. Box 44094
    Baton Rouge, La. 70804

Maine
    State Occupational Information
    Coordinating Committee
    State House Station 71
    Augusta, Me. 04330

Maryland
>   Maryland Occupational Information
>   Coordinating Committee
>   Department of Human Resources
>   1100 North Eutaw Street
>   Baltimore, Md. 21201

Massachusetts
>   Massachusetts Occupational Information
>   Coordinating Committee
>   Park Square Bldg., Suite 341
>   31 St. James Avenue
>   Boston, Mass. 02116

Michigan
>   Michigan Occupational Information
>   Coordinating Committee
>   309 North Washington, P.O. Box 30015
>   Lansing, Mich. 48909

Minnesota
>   Department of Economic Security
>   690 American Center Bldg.
>   150 East Kellogg Boulevard
>   St. Paul, Minn. 55101

Mississippi
>   Vocational Technical Education
>   P.O. Box 771
>   Jackson, Miss. 39205

Missouri
>   Missouri Occupational Information
>   Coordinating Committee
>   8300 East High Street
>   Jefferson City, Mo. 65101

Montana
>   Montana State Occupational Information
>   Coordinating Committee
>   P.O. Box 1728
>   Helena, Mont. 59601

Nebraska
>   State Occupational Information
>   Coordinating Committee
>   West 300 Nebraska Hall
>   University of Nebraska
>   Lincoln, Neb. 68588

Nevada
>   State Occupational Information
>   Coordinating Committee
>   Capitol Complex
>   505 East King Street
>   Kinkead Bldg.
>   Room 603
>   Carson City, Nev. 89710

New Hampshire
Department of Employment Security
32 South Main Street
Concord, N.H. 03301

New Jersey
New Jersey Occupational Information
Coordinating Committee
Department of Labor and Industry
Division of Planning and Research
P.O. Box 2765
Trenton, N.J. 08625

New Mexico
New Mexico State Occupational Information
Coordinating Committee
Suite C, Harvey Bldg.
839 Paseo de Peralta
Santa Fe, N.M. 87501

New York
State Department of Labor
Labor Department #12
State Campus
Albany, N.Y. 12240

North Carolina
North Carolina Department of Administration
112 West Lane Street
Raleigh, N.C. 27611

North Dakota
State Occupational Information
Coordinating Committee
1424 West Century Avenue
P.O. Box 1537
Bismarck, N.D. 58501

Ohio
State Department Building
S-65 South Front Street
Room 904
Columbus, Ohio 43215

Oklahoma
State Occupational Information
Coordinating Committee
School of Occupational and Adult Education
Oklahoma State University
1515 West Sixth Street
Stillwater, Okla. 74074

Oregon
Oregon Occupational Information
Coordinating Committee
875 Union Street N.E.
Salem, Ore. 97311

Pennsylvania
Pennsylvania Occupational Information
Coordinating Committee
Labor and Industry Bldg.
Seventh and Forster Streets
Room 1008
Harrisburg, Pa. 17121

Puerto Rico
Puerto Rico Occupational Information
Coordinating Committee
414 Barbosa Avenue
Hato Rey, P.R. 00917

Rhode Island
Rhode Island Occupational Information
Coordinating Committee
22 Hayes Street, Room 315
Providence, R.I. 02908

South Carolina
SOICC Director
1550 Gadsden Street
Columbia, S.C. 29202

South Dakota
South Dakota Occupational Information
Coordinating Committee
108 East Missouri
Pierre, S.D. 57501

Tennessee
Tennessee Occupational Information
Coordinating Committee
512 Cordell Hull Bldg.
Nashville, Tenn. 37219

Texas
State Occupational Information
Coordinating Committee
Texas Employment Commission Bldg.
Fifteenth and Congress Avenue
Room 648
Austin, Tex. 78778

Utah
Occupational Information Coordinating Committee
State Board of Education
250 East Fifth Street South
Salt Lake City, Utah 84111

Vermont
Vermont Occupational Information
Coordinating Committee
P.O. Box 488
Montpelier, Vt. 05602

Virginia
   Vocational and Adult Education
   Department of Education
   P.O. Box 6Q
   Richmond, Va. 23216

Washington
   Commission for Vocational Education
   Bldg. 17
   Airdustrial Park
   Mail Stop LS-10
   Olympia, Wash. 98504

West Virginia
   West Virginia State Occupational Information
   Coordinating Committee
   Capitol Complex
   Bldg. 6
   Room 221
   Charleston, W.Va. 25305

Wisconsin
   Wisconsin Occupational Information
   Coordinating Committee
   Educational Sciences Bldg., Room 952
   1025 West Johnson
   Madison, Wisc. 53706

Wyoming
   Wyoming Occupational Information
   Coordinating Committee
   1520 East Fifth Street
   Cheyenne, Wyo. 82002

Working for the Government

The largest employer in the United States is the federal government.
It employs people in every job category and must adhere rigidly to affirmative action policies. The following is a list of regional information centers
that can help you choose the appropriate career. For your local center, call
this number toll-free: 800-555-1212.

California
   Eastern Columbia Building
   851 South Broadway, Los Angeles 90014

   Federal Building ✕1001
   450 Golden Gate Avenue, San Francisco 94102

District of Columbia
   Metro Area
   1900 E Street N.W. 20415

Georgia
   Federal Building
   275 Peachtree Street N.E., Atlanta 30303

Illinois
    Dirksen Building ⌗1322
    219 South Dearborn Street, Chicago 60604

Massachusetts
    3 Center Plaza
    Boston 01208

Michigan
    477 Michigan Avenue, ⌗155
    Detroit 48226

New Jersey
    Federal Building
    970 Broad Street, Newark 07102

New York
    Federal Building
    26 Federal Plaza, New York 10007

The following publications can be obtained for approximately 75 cents from the Superintendent of Documents, U. S. Government Printing Office, Washington, D.C. 20402

> *Working for the U.S.A.* Stock ⌗ 006-000-00964-6
> *Federal Jobs Overseas.* Stock ⌗ 006-000-01033-4

Black Career Consultants

These firms specialize in placing qualified Black women in management positions:

Karen Johnson Associates
515 Madison Avenue ⌗402
New York, N.Y. 10022

Richard Clark Associates
11 East Forty-fourth Street
New York, N.Y. 10017

Chapter Five

Recommended Reading:

Alihan, Mila. *Corporate Etiquette.* New York: New American Library, 1974.

Bender, Marilyn. *At the Top.* Garden City, N.Y.: Doubleday, 1974.

Buskirk, Richard H. *Handbook of Management Tactics: Aggressive Strategies for Getting Things Done Your Way!* New York: E. P. Dutton, 1978.

Cannie, J. K. *The Woman's Guide to Management Success (How to Win Power in the Real Organizational World).* Englewood Cliffs, N.J.: Prentice-Hall, 1979.

Cohen, Herb. *You Can Negotiate Anything (How to Get What You Want).* Secaucus, N.J.: Lyle Stuart, 1980.

DuBrin, Andrew J. *Survival In The Office: How to Move Ahead or Hang On.* New York: Van Nostrand-Reinhold, 1977.

Haragan, Betty. *Games Mother Never Taught You.* New York: Warner Books, 1978.

Hart, Lois. *Moving Up: Women and Leadership.* New York: American Management Associations, 1980.

Harvard Business Review. *On Management.* New York: Harper and Row, 1976.

Henning, Margaret and Jardin, Anne. *The Managerial Woman.* Garden City, N.Y.: Doubleday, 1977.

Ilich, J. and Schindler-Jones, B. *Successful Negotiating Skills for Women.* Reading, Mass.: Addison-Wesley, 1981.

Jennings, Eugene. *Routes to the Executive Suite.* New York: McGraw-Hill, 1976.

Kantor, Rosabeth. *Men and Women of the Corporation.* New York: Basic Books, 1979.

Kennedy, Marilyn M. *Career Knockouts: How to Battle Back.* Chicago, Ill.: Follett, 1980.

————. *Office Politics.* Chicago, Ill.: Follett, 1980.

Miller, Martin. *Climbing the Corporate Pyramid.* New York: American Management Associations, 1973.

Osborn, Ruth. *Developing New Horizons for Women.* New York: McGraw-Hill, 1977.

Pogrebin, Letty. *Getting Yours: How to Make the System Work for the Working Woman.* New York: David McKay, 1975.

Rogalin and Pell. *Woman's Guide to Management Positions.* New York: Simon and Schuster, 1976.

Shubin, John. *Business Management.* New York: Barnes and Noble, 1957.

Staff of Catalyst, Inc. *Landing Your Career.* New York: Simon and Schuster, 1976.

Uris, Auren. *Techniques of Leadership.* New York: McGraw-Hill, 1957.

Weck, Thomas L. *Moving Up Quickly: How to Use Executive Job-Hunting Techniques to Land a Better Job.* New York: John Wiley, 1979.

Welch, Mary S. *Networking: The Great New Way for Women to Get Ahead.* New York: Harcourt, Brace, Jovanovich, 1980.

I recommend that you subscribe to the following publications:

Essence
The Magazine for Today's Black Woman
Published monthly by Essence Communications, Inc.
1500 Broadway
New York, N.Y. 10036

Forbes
Published biweekly by Forbes, Inc.
60 Fifth Avenue
New York, N.Y. 10011

Black Enterprise
Published monthly by Earl G. Graves Publishing Co., Inc.
295 Madison Avenue
New York, N.Y. 10017

Networks

The following is a list of organizations devoted to the career needs of the professional woman. Their aims and policies vary, and only a few are devoted exclusively to Black women. Membership often involves the payment of annual dues and specific career qualifications.

Black Professional Women's Network
500 East Sixty-second Street
New York, N.Y. 10021

Council of Concerned Black Executives
516 Fifth Avenue
New York, N.Y. 10036

The Nzingha Society*
2569 Adam Clayton Powell, Jr. Boulevard
※25K
New York, N.Y. 10039

Catalyst, Inc.
14 East Sixtieth Street
New York, N.Y. 10022

Women in Management, Inc.
P.O. Box 11268
Chicago, Ill. 60611

Network of Executive Women
Graduate Department of Public Affairs
University of Washington
Seattle, Wash. 98195

Women's Action Alliance, Inc.
370 Lexington Avenue
New York, N.Y. 10017

National Association of Female Executives
c/o NAFE
485 Fifth Avenue
Suite 405
New York, N.Y. 10017

Many professions have network associations of their own, such as:

Women in Communications, Inc.
National Headquarters
P.O. Box 9561
Austin, Tex. 78766

Financial Women's Association
One Banker's Trust Plaza
New York, N.Y. 10006

* This is basically a philanthropic organization; networking is a byproduct, not an objective.

Women in School Administration
2553 Trevilian Way
Louisville, Kent. 40205

For directories with complete listings of all regional network organizations, contact:

National Association of Negro Business and Professional Women's Clubs
2012 Massachusetts Avenue N.W.
Washington, D.C. 20036

The National Alliance of Professional and Executive Women's Networks
8 Grove Street
Wellesley, Mass. 02181

Federation of Business and Professional Women's Clubs
2012 Massachusetts Avenue N.W.
Washington, D.C. 20036

Chapter Six

Recommended Reading:

Lederer, Muriel. Blue-Collar Jobs for Women. New York: E. P. Dutton, 1979.

Training Courses

Programs and Schools: A Supplement to the Directory of Postsecondary Schools With Occupational Programs is a federal government publication that lists all accredited schools that teach a trade or skill. It may be obtained from the U. S. Department of Education's National Center for Education Statistics.

Apprenticeships

Labor unions and school guidance offices can provide information about apprenticeships. Some cities have Apprenticeship Information Offices (AIC's) affiliated with the local U. S. Employment Service. The U. S. Department of Labor's Bureau of Apprenticeships and Training has prepared several pamphlets containing background information about apprenticeships. These can be obtained from:

Office of Information
Inquiries Unit
Employment and Training Administration
U. S. Department of Labor #10225
601 D Street N.W.
Washington, D.C. 20213

Additional material about opportunities for Black women in apprenticeship programs can be obtained from:

Women in Apprenticeship Program
National Urban League
500 East Sixty-second Street
New York, N.Y. 10021

Women in Apprenticeship Project
80 Fifth Avenue #1602
New York, N.Y. 10011

Trade Careers Organizations

General information about job possibilities for Black women in craft and trade jobs can be obtained from:

Women in Non-Traditional Employment
80 Fifth Avenue
New York, N.Y. 10011

Women in the Trades
198 Forsyth Street
New York, N.Y. 10002

The Women's Bureau
Department of Labor #S3317
200 Constitution Avenue N.W.
Washington, D.C. 20210

Trade Career Opportunities

Information about job opportunities and required qualifications for specific jobs are available from the following:

Air-Conditioning and Refrigeration (Maintenance and Repair)
    Air-Conditioning and Refrigeration Institute
    1815 North Fort Meyer Drive
    Arlington, Va. 22209

    Air-Conditioning Contractors of America, Inc.
    1228 Seventeenth Street N.W.
    Washington, D.C. 20036

Apparel Manufacturing
    International Ladies Garment Workers' Union
    1710 Broadway
    New York, N.Y. 10019

    National Outerwear and Sportswear Association
    One Pennsylvania Plaza
    New York, N.Y. 10001

    United Garment Workers of America
    200 Park Avenue South #1614
    New York, N.Y. 10003

    Apparel Manufacturers Association
    1440 Broadway
    New York, N.Y. 10018

Automobile Repair and Service
 Automotive Service Industry Association
 444 North Michigan Avenue
 Chicago, Ill. 60611

 Automotive Service Councils, Inc.
 188 Industrial Drive ⌗112
 Elmhurst, Ill. 60126

Broadcast Equipment Maintenance and Repair
 National Association of Broadcasters
 1771 N Street N.W.
 Washington, D.C. 20036

Cosmetology
 National Beauty Career Center
 3839 White Plains Road
 Bronx, N.Y. 10467

 National Hairdressers, and Cosmetologists Association
 3510 Olive Street
 St. Louis, Mo. 63103

 Barbers, Beauticians, and Allied Industries International Association
 7050 West Washington Street
 Indianapolis, Ind. 46241

 National Association of Cosmetology Schools
 808 Main Street
 Boonton, N.J. 07005

Construction (General)
 Women Working in Construction
 1854 Wyoming Avenue N.W.
 Washington, D.C. 20009

 All Craft Center
 19–23 St. Mark's Place
 New York, N.Y. 10003

 Labor Education Advancement Program
 National Urban League
 500 East Sixty-second Street
 New York, N.Y. 10021

 AFL-CIO Building and Construction Trades Department
 815 Sixteenth Street N.W.
 Washington, D.C. 20006

 Associated General Contractors of America
 1957 E Street N.W.
 Washington, D.C. 20006

Construction (by skill)
 Bricklaying and Stonemasonry
  International Union of Bricklayers and Allied Craftsmen
  International Masonry Apprenticeship Trust
  815 Fifteenth Street N.W.
  Washington, D.C. 20005

Brick Institute of America
1750 Old Meadow Road
McLean, Va. 22101
Carpentry
United Brotherhood of Carpenters and Joiners of America
101 Constitution Avenue N.W. ⌗409
Washington, D.C. 20001

National Association of Home Builders
Manpower Development and Training Department
Fifteenth and M Streets N.W.
Washington, D.C. 20005
Cement and Terrazzo Installation
Operative Plasterers and Cement Masons' International Association
of the U.S. and Canada
1125 Seventeenth Street N.W.
Washington, D.C. 20036

National Terrazzo and Mosaic Association
2-A West Loudon Street
Leesburg, Va. 22075
Drywall Finishing
Association of Wall and Ceiling Industries International
1711 Connecticut Avenue N.W.
Washington, D.C. 20007

National Joint Painting, Decorating, and Drywall Apprenticeship and
Training Committee
1709 New York Avenue N.W.
Washington, D.C. 20006
Electrical (Construction)
International Brotherhood of Electrical Workers
1125 Fifteenth Street N.W.
Washington, D.C. 20005

National Joint Apprenticeship and Training Committee for the
Electrical Industry
9700 East George Palmer Highway
Lanham, Md. 20802
Elevator Constructing
International Union of Elevator Constructors
5565 Sterrett Place, Clark Bldg. ⌗332
Columbia, Md. 21044
Floor Covering Installation
Carpet and Rug Institute
P.O. Box 2048
Dalton, Ga. 30720

Resilient Floor Covering Institute
1030 Fifteenth Street N.W. ⌗350
Washington, D.C. 20005
Glazing
International Brotherhood of Painters and Allied Trades
1750 New York Avenue N.W.
Washington, D.C. 20006

Machine Operating
   International Union of Operating Engineers
   1125 Seventeenth Street N.W.
   Washington, D.C. 20036
Painting and Paperhanging
   International Brotherhood of Painters and Allied Trades
   1750 New York Avenue N.W.
   Washington, D.C. 20036

   National Joint Painting, Decorating, and Drywall Apprenticeship and
      Training Committee
   1709 New York Avenue N.W. ※110
   Washington, D.C. 20006
Plastering
   Operative Plasterers and Cement Masons' International Association
   11275 Seventeenth Street N.W.
   Washington, D.C. 20036
Plumbing and Pipefitting
   National Association of Plumbing-Heating Contractors
   1016 Twentieth Street N.W.
   Washington, D.C. 20036
Roofing
   National Roofing Contractors Association
   1515 North Harlem Avenue
   Oak Park, Ill. 60302
Tilesetting
   Tile Contractors Association of America, Inc.
   112 North Alfred Street
   Alexandria, Va. 22314

Computer Servicing
   Division of Vocational Technical Education
   U. S. Department of Education
   Washington, D.C. 20202

Electrical Engineering
   International Brotherhood of Electrical Workers
   1125 Fifteenth Street N.W.
   Washington, D.C. 20005

   National Electrical Constructors Association
   7315 Wisconsin Avenue N.W.
   Washington, D.C. 20014

   National Joint Apprenticeship and Training Committee for the
      Electrical Industry
   9700 East George Palmer Highway
   Lanham, Md. 20801

Hotel and Restaurant Work
   The American Hotel and Motel Association
   1407 South Harrison Road
   East Lansing, Mich. 48823

   Council on Hotel, Restaurant, and Institutional Education
   Henderson Human Development Building ※12
   Pennsylvania State University
   University Park, Pa. 16802

National Restaurant Association
One IBM Plaza #2600
Chicago, Ill. 60611

National Institute for the Foodservice Industry
20 North Wacker Drive #2620
Chicago, Ill. 60606

American Culinary Federation Educational Institute
920 Long Boulevard #1
Lansing, Mich. 48910

Household Work
Household Employment Program
National Urban League
500 East Sixty-second Street
New York, N.Y. 10021

National Committee on Household Employment
7705 Georgia Avenue N.W. #208
Washington, D.C. 20012

Machining
International Union, United Automobile, Aerospace, and Agricultural
    Workers of America
Skilled Trades Department
8000 East Jefferson Avenue
Detroit, Mich. 48214

National Machine Tool Builders Association
7901 Westpark Drive
McLean, Va. 22102

Medical Technology
American Society for Medical Technology
5555 West Loop South
Bellaire, Tex. 77401

International Society for Clinical Laboratory Technology
818 Olive Street
St. Louis, Mo. 63101

American Medical Technologists
710 Higgins Road
Park Ridge, Ill. 60068

Photography Technology
Photo Marketing Association
603 Lansing Avenue
Jackson, Mich. 49202

Professional Photographers of America, Inc.
1090 Executive Way
Des Plaines, Ill. 60018

Printing
Printing Industries of America, Inc.
1730 North Lynn Street
Arlington, Va. 22209

Graphic Arts Technical Foundation
4615 Forbes Avenue
Pittsburgh, Pa. 15213

Security Police
International Association of Women Police
P.O. Box 1978
Sun City, Ariz. 85372

International Conference of Police Associations
1241 Pennsylvania Avenue S.E.
Washington, D.C. 20003
F.B.I.
Federal Bureau of Investigation
U. S. Department of Justice
Washington, D.C. 20535
Correction
CONtact, Inc.
P.O. Box 81826
Lincoln, Neb. 68501

The American Correctional Association
4321 Hartwick Road
College Park, Md. 20740
Firefighting
National Fire Protection Association
470 Atlantic Avenue
Boston, Mass. 02210

Telephone Technology
Telecommunications International Union
P.O. Box 5462
Hamden, Conn. 16518

United States Independent Telephone Association
1801 K Street N.W. ⚹1201
Washington, D.C. 20006

Television and Radio
National Association of Television and Electronic Servicers of
    America
5908 South Troy Street
Chicago, Ill. 60629

Electronics Industries Association
2001 I Street N.W.
Washington, D.C. 20006

Trucking
American Trucking Associations, Inc.
1616 P Street N.W.
Washington, D.C. 20036

For information about military careers write:

Army Opportunities
P.O. Box 300
North Hollywood, Calif. 91603

Navy Opportunity Information Center
P.O. Box 2000
Pelham Manor, N.Y. 10803

Department of the Air Force
26 Federal Plaza
New York, N.Y. 10001

Marine Corps
207 West Twenty-fourth Street
New York, N.Y. 10011

Chapter Seven

Recommended Reading:

Dible, Donald M. *Up Your Own Organization! A Handbook on How to Start and Finance a New Business.* Fairfield, Calif.: Entrepreneur Press, 1971.

Griffin, Barbara. *A Successful Business of Your Own.* Nashville, Tenn.: Sherbourne Press, 1974.

Financial Assistance and Advice

The Small Business Administration (SBA) has a program of management assistance and sponsors: SCORE (Service Corps of Retired Executives). This association of retired executives consults with new businesses on all facets of business management. The SBA also has a loan assistance program and publishes literature about every conceivable subject of interest to the entrepreneur.

Local S.B.A. Offices

Alaska
    1016 West Sixth Avenue
    Suite 200
    Anchorage, Alaska 99501

Arizona
    3030 North Central Avenue
    Suite 1201
    Phoenix, Ariz. 85012

Arkansas
    320 West Capitol Avenue
    P.O. Box 1401
    Little Rock, Ark. 72201

California
    211 Main Street
    Fourth Floor
    San Francisco, Calif. 94105

Colorado
    1405 Curtis Street
    Twenty-second Floor
    Denver, Colo. 80202

Connecticut
  One Financial Plaza
  Hartford, Conn. 06103

Delaware
  844 King Street
  Room 5207
  Wilmington, Del. 19801

District of Columbia
  1030 Fifteenth Street N.W.
  Suite 250
  Washington, D.C. 20417

Florida
  400 West Bay Street
  Room 261, P.O. Box 35067
  Jacksonville, Fla. 32202

Georgia
  1720 Peachtree Road, N.W.
  Sixth Floor
  Atlanta, Ga. 30309

Hawaii
  300 Ala Mona,
  Room 2213, P.O. Box 50207
  Honolulu, Haw. 96850

Idaho
  1005 Main Street
  Second Floor
  Boise, Id. 83701

Illinois
  219 South Dearborn Street
  Room 437
  Chicago, Ill. 60604

Indiana
  575 North Pennsylvania Street
  Room 552
  Indianapolis, Ind. 46204

Iowa
  210 Walnut Street
  Room 749
  Des Moines, Io. 50309

Kansas
  110 East Waterman Street
  Wichita, Kans. 67202

Kentucky
  600 Federal Plaza
  Room 188, P.O. Box 3517
  Louisville, Kent. 40201

Louisiana
     1001 Howard Avenue
     Seventeenth Floor
     New Orleans, La. 70113

Maine
     40 Western Avenue
     Room 512
     Augusta, Me. 04330

Maryland
     8600 LaSalle Road
     Room 630
     Towson, Md. 21204

Massachusetts
     150 Causeway Street
     Tenth Floor
     Boston, Mass. 02110

Michigan
     477 Michigan Avenue
     Detroit, Mich. 48226

Minnesota
     100 North Sixth Street
     Minneapolis, Minn. 55403

Mississippi
     100 West Capitol Street
     Suite 322
     Jackson, Miss. 30201

Missouri
     1150 Grande Avenue
     Fifth Floor
     Kansas City, Mo. 64106

Montana
     301 South Park Avenue
     Room 528, Drawer 10054
     Helena, Mont. 59601

Nebraska
     Nineteenth and Farnum Street
     Second Floor
     Omaha, Neb. 68102

Nevada
     301 East Stewart
     P.O. Box 7525
     Downtown Station
     Las Vegas, Nev. 89101

New Hampshire
     55 Pleasant Street
     Room 211
     Concord, N.H. 03301

New Jersey
970 Broad Street
Room 1635
Newark, N.J. 07102

New Mexico
5000 Marble, N.E.
Room 320
Albuquerque, N.M. 87100

New York
26 Federal Plaza
Room 3100
New York, N.Y. 10278

North Carolina
230 South Tryon Street
Suite 700
Charlotte, N.C. 28202

North Dakota
657 Second Avenue North
Room 218, P.O. Box 3086
Fargo, N.D. 58108

Ohio
85 Marconi Boulevard
Columbus, Ohio 43215

Oklahoma
200 Northwest Fifth Street
Suite 670
Oklahoma City, Okla. 73102

Oregon
1220 Southwest Third Avenue
Room 676
Portland, Ore. 87204

Pennsylvania
1000 Liberty Avenue
Room 1401
Pittsburgh, Pa. 15222

Puerto Rico
Carlos Chardon Avenue
Federal Bldg., Room 691
Hato Rey, P.R. 00919

Rhode Island
40 Fountain Street
Providence, R.I. 02903

South Carolina
1835 Assembly
Third Floor, P.O. Box 2786
Columbia, S.C. 29202

South Dakota
101 South Main Avenue
Suite 101
Sioux City, S.D. 57102

Tennessee
404 James Robertson Parkway
Suite 1012
Nashville, Tenn. 37219

Texas
1100 Commerce Street
Room 3C36
Dallas, Tex. 75242

Utah
125 South State Street
Room 2237
Salt Lake City, Utah 84138

Vermont
87 State Street
Room 204, P.O. Box 605
Montpelier, Vt. 05602

Virginia
400 North Eighth Street
Room 3015, P.O. Box 10126
Richmond, Va. 23240

Washington
915 Second Avenue
Room 1744
Seattle, Wash. 98174

West Virginia
109 North Third Street
Room 302
Clarksburg, W.Va. 26301

Wisconsin
212 East Washington Avenue
Room 213
Madison, Wisc. 53703

Wyoming
100 East B Street
Room 4001, P.O. Box 2839
Casper, Wyo. 82601

The Office of Minority Business Enterprises (OMBE), c/o U. S. Department of Commerce, Washington, D.C. 20230, has regional offices that provide management, training, and technical services and occasionally hold conferences for Black women in business.

Depending on the state, the OMBE offices can be listed under the federal, state or city branch of government. Consult your local telephone directory for the OMBE office in your area.

Additional Organizations for Business Owners

Association of Women Business Owners
1000 Connecticut Avenue N.W. ✕1101
Washington, D.C. 20036

American Women's Economic Development Corp.
1270 Avenue of the Americas
New York, N.Y. 10020

Advocates for Women
593 Market Street ✕500
San Francisco, Calif. 94105

The Minority Business Information Institute
295 Madison Avenue
New York, N.Y. 10017

Minority Small Business Capital Ownership Division
c/o Small Business Administration
26 Federal Plaza
New York, N.Y. 10001

Career Assistance and Information for the Self-Employed Black Woman

Acting
American Theater Association
1000 Vermont Avenue N.W.
Washington, D.C. 20005

Dancing
American Dance Guild
152 West Forty-second Street ✕828
New York, N.Y. 10036

National Dance Association
1201 Sixteenth Street N.W.
Washington, D.C. 20036

American Dance Therapy Association
2000 Century Plaza
Columbia, Md. 21044

Fashion Modeling
Modeling Association of America
P.O. Box 12163
2400 Merchants Drive N.W.
Knoxville, Tenn. 37912

Interior Design
American Society of Interior Design
730 Fifth Avenue
New York, N.Y. 10019

Music
American Federation of Musicians
1500 Broadway
New York, N.Y. 10036

National Association of Schools of Music
11250 Roger Bacon Drive
Reston, Va. 22090

Photography
Professional Photographers of America, Inc.
1090 Executive Way
Des Plaines, Ill. 60018

Writing
Women in Communications, Inc.
P.O. Box 9561
Austin, Tex. 78766

The Society of Professional Journalists
Sigma Delta Chi
35 East Wacker Drive
Chicago, Ill. 60601

American Council for Education in Journalism
102 Reavis Hall
Northern Illinois University
Dekalb, Ill. 60115

The Newspaper Guild
Research and Information Department
1125 Fifteenth Street N.W.
Washington, D.C. 20005

Chapter Eight

Recommended Reading:

Becker, Gary S. *Economics of Discrimination.* Chicago, Ill.: University of Chicago Press, 1971.

Gelber, Steven M. *Black Men and Businessmen: The Growing Awareness of a Social Responsibility.* Port Washington, N.Y.: Kennikat Press, 1974.

Jongeward, Dorothy and Scott, Dru. *Affirmative Action for Women: A Practical Guide for Women and Management.* Reading, Mass.: Addison-Wesley, 1973.

Sahlein, Stephen. *The Affirmative Action Handbook: Dealing With Day-to-Day Supervisory Problems.* New York: Executive Enterprises, 1978.

Wallace, Michelle. *Black Macho and the Myth of the Superwoman.* New York: Dial Press, 1979.

The following organizations provide information and assistance to Black women subjected to on-the-job sexual harassment or racial and sexual discrimination:

American Civil Liberties Union
1600 Pennsylvania Avenue S.E.
Washington, D.C. 20003

Equal Employment Opportunity Commission
Field Management Division O.F.S. ⊁4232
2401 E Street N.W.
Washington, D.C. 20506

The Working Women's Institute
593 Park Avenue
New York, N.Y. 10021

Chapter Nine

Recommended Reading:

Adams, Jane. *Sex and the Single Parent.* New York: Coward, McCann, and Geoghegan, 1978.

Fraiberg, Selma. *Every Child's Birthright: In Defense of Mothering.* New York: Basic Books, 1977.

Gabriel, Joyce and Baldwin, Bettye. *Having It All: A Practical Guide to Overcoming the Career Woman's Blues.* New York: M. Evans, 1980.

Heller, Robert. *Super Self: The Art and Science of Self-Management: A Practical Guide to Getting the Most Out of Your Life.* New York: Atheneum, 1979.

Hersh, Dr. S. P. *The Executive Parent.* New York: Sovereign Books/Simon and Schuster, 1979.

Langer, Ellen J. and Dweck, Carol S. *Personal Politics: The Psychology of Making It.* Englewood Cliffs, N.J.: Prentice-Hall, 1973.

Levinson, Harry. *Executive Stress.* New York: New American Library, 1975.

Lichtendorf, Susan and Gillis, Phyllis. *The New Pregnancy.* New York: Random House, 1979.

Machlowitz, Marilyn M. *Workaholics.* Reading, Mass.: Addison-Wesley, 1980.

Porter, Sylvia. *Sylvia Porter's New Money Book for the 80's.* Garden City, N.Y.: Doubleday, 1979.

Quinn, Jane Bryant. *Everyone's Money Book.* New York: Delacorte Press, 1979.

Williams, Marcille G. *New Executive Woman: A Guide to Business Success.* New York: New American Library, 1978.

If you are having credit problems or simply want information about the availability of credit for Black women, write to:

National Foundation for Consumer Credit
1819 H Street N.W.
Washington, D.C. 20006

Consumer Information Center
Dept. 538G
Pueblo, Colo. 81009

Division of Credit Practices
Federal Trade Commission
Washington, D.C. 20580

Chapter Ten

Recommended Reading:

Molloy, John. *The Woman's Dress for Success Book*. Chicago: Follett, 1977.

Sims, Naomi. *All About Health and Beauty for the Black Woman*. Garden City, N.Y.: Doubleday, 1978.

————. *All About Hair for the Black Woman*. Garden City, N.Y.: Doubleday, 1982.

Index